# A BARTENDER'S
# GUIDE TO
# ★ POLITICS ★

## WHAT'S WRONG WITH THE SYSTEM
### *and*
## HOW WE WILL FIX IT

### JOHN H. CORRELL

Published by:  John H. Correll
               3290 Elvehjem Road
               McFarland, WI 53558

Visit our website at http://bartendersguidetopolitics.com

ISBN: 978-0-9829528-0-1

Book design by Lee Lewis Walsh, Words Plus Design, www.wordsplusdesign.com

Printed in the United States of America

# Contents

# Preface

This work began with my inability to understand elementary economics in college. It always seemed so removed from the reality of my Midwest life experience. I could not understand how there could be so many forms of money. And while lecturers seemed sophisticated, what they presented never seemed to add up. Finance seemed to be a combination of criminal conspiracy and frauds of many colors. Political science, too, seemed a conspiracy, and nearly as bad. When I asked questions of my professors, I was met with looks of puzzlement, bewilderment and discomfort, even terror. Their answers were evasive, nonresponsive and not satisfying.

It was my wish to write a book that explored the science of political science. To reduce the economic, historical, legal and political ideas that make up political science to the "fundamental particles" and to discover the forces that bind politicos and repel their constituents. It was my wish to write a book that was politically neutral so that no one might say this is a Republican or a Democrat or a socialist or a communist or a balmy utopianist. In remaining strictly neutral I sought to discover the very nature of the laws that govern political science. It was my hope that by looking closely at politics I might discover forces and ideas overlooked by the founding fathers and the thinkers of yesterdays.

Because of my experience in litigation, I found I was on occasion able to communicate with juries with a special clarity that defense attorneys found quite unnerving. It was my hope that this skill would enable me to communicate any discoveries in a clear and compelling manner both to folks of common experience and to justices of our supreme courts and all found in between.

Against editorial advice I have occasionally indulged in stereotyping and name-calling. I have limited my stereotyping and name-calling to only the truly deserving: it wouldn't do to have a book of this nature become too boring to hold the reader's attention. My first apology is to the editors, for I have been impossible to work with. But that is the nature of a litigator.

My sincerest apology for the detail and depth of Chapter Nine, The Executive Branch. It was rewritten 71 times, and still remains a bit detailed and convoluted. Time spent thinking on the tyrannical nature of the administrative process is so critical to any change of government that it is worth a bit of study and reflection.

My apology to readers for the repetition of certain terms and conclusions. Each theme occurs in an historical concept, then should be reviewed from the perspective of the legislature, the executive and the judiciary. It again appears in the conclusion. To omit each perspective is intellectually unfair to the reader.

Finally, there is the paucity of footnotes, which prompts my editors' scorn and causes them to conclude that this book is "not a scholarly treatment" of its subject. This allegation deserves explanation. All of history is based on hearsay. Generally historians were not there to see the events they recorded. On the rare occasions they were present, they viewed only a small bit of the panorama that unfolded. In these cases their perceptions are biased and usually based upon recollection. They often form opinions in areas where they are not experts. Hearsay is inadmissible in courts, why then should it deserve the dignity of a footnote?

Politicians lie, pander, create and sell privileges and spawn monopoly after monopoly, then talk of free markets. Their real goal should be creating justice (equality) and liberty for all. Virtually their every act diminishes our liberty.

Political scientists seem to know little history, less law, no economics at all. Since the ratification of the Constitution they have devoted their efforts to nothing but how to steal elections from the wishes of the majority.

Economists have no commonsense definition of money. Numbers should be absolute, definite, definitive. In the hands of economists they become vague, relative and unreliable, hence worthless and less. Data resembles an avalanche viewed from below. Statistics can be found for opposite sides of virtually any proposition. Economists conspire to lie to us as to the amount of inflation politicians are creating for us, and then seem to suggest somehow that citizens are the cause, all or in part, of inflation.

For these reasons dignifying the words of economists, political scientists and politicians with footnotes is hard for me.

My editors say my generalizations and lack of footnotes will offend the *scholastic critical thinkers.* Modern education has pretty well destroyed critical thought by failure to grant diplomas to those who disagree with the thinking of our eastern educated aristocracy. And those few who make it through the system have little factual predicate on which to base their thinking. In most newspapers the editorials begin on page one, with the headlines. In Madison, Wisconsin, ninety-nine percent by weight of newspaper is high gloss advertising. The only reliable news comes from the Internet and *The Economist* magazine, which should be mandatory reading for all. Sadly these, too, have their frailties.

John Howard Correll, J.D.
July 29, 2010

# Book One:
# Founding the Republic

# The Moment of Enlightened Government

Historically government has been formed by conquest, with all the power being held by the conqueror. Individual rights were occasionally wrestled from the government, as exemplified by the *Magna Carta* in 1215. The exceptions to this general rule were the Greek "city-states" and the Swiss Confederation. Thus monarchy remained the near universal form of national government until the American Revolution.

During the Age of Enlightenment there was a renaissance in political thought. It began with Thomas Hobbes who published the *Leviathan* (1651) proposing that laws were not of divine origin and suggesting a social contract as the basis for government. The unsung giant of political thought, John Locke, wrote *Second Treatise on Government* (1690). This was the fulcrum of modern political science. He gave the first plausible explanation of man creating government by social contract, defined inalienable rights, including the right to revolution, defined the role of government in creating value in property and made rudimentary observations about limitations on the three branches of government.

Tedious old Montesquieu wrote *The Spirit of the Laws* (1748), an exhaustive collection of anecdotes about governments, in great historical detail. But in his mind, the judiciary was still an arm of the executive, the monarch. The court had no power over the executive branch.

It was a mere 38 years from Montesquieu to the ratification of our Constitution in 1787. At that moment the forces of **demos** (voice of the people) and **tyranny** collided and fused into a new form of government that was premeditated and designed by our Founding Fathers, a brilliant and diverse group. Rationally examining **representative government,** their collective spark of genius was to create for the first time in history a government where the judiciary had power over the executive branch.

> For the first time in history, the judiciary had power superior to the executive branch of government. The result was the possibility of a balanced tripartite government.

It is now time for our Supreme Court to impose limitations on our legislative and executive departments to restore balance in tripartite government.

# Chapter 1

# The Evolution of the Republic

L et us trace the evolution of the science of government from pre-historic times. The fundamental organs of a government are:

- A war leader or executive
- An administration; ministers or administrators
- A lawgiver, a legislature
- A judiciary, which usually takes the form of courts
- And religion: none, one or many; state-controlled or independent.

The first stage of government is the **monarchy,** which merges the governmental functions of war leader (executive), law giver, judge and usually some degree of religious function (mystery in a single person claiming divine descent). The monarch usually claimed the right to pass such powers by inheritance. Pure monarchies are the norm for preliterate societies.

The next stage in the evolution of government is **oligarchy.** An aristocratic class of privileged persons usually emerges which offers military support to the monarchy in exchange for privilege. The monarch eventually becomes a figurehead and a council of powerful aristocrats, or perhaps elders, dilutes or splits the powers of the king among themselves. The king must seek their approval for war and for other important decisions. By this stage of societal evolution religious arts, mysteries and functions have usually devolved to a special class of persons, skilled in their use. In some societies economic privileges are granted for military support of the government. Historically, the oligarchy is associated with myths, legends and epics, all oral traditions. Writing and the ability of the common man to read are not encouraged as this level of education usually results in the commoners pressing their primitive governments to allow some unwanted shade of either democracy or republican government. Note that even in modern oligarchies, where there is a high level of literacy, there is an extreme government effort to control all forms of media.

The next stage in the evolution of government may be **tyranny.** Frequently, but not inevitably, power is seized by a single person without claim of hereditary or constitutional right. Some view this as a necessary stage in the development of democracy, for it emulsifies the accrued privileges of the aristocratic class. There is usually immediate strict government control of the media, and, if tyranny persists, the levels of education, literacy and critical thinking quickly degrade, as the intelligentsia is imprisoned, "reprogrammed" or eliminated.

The next stage is some form of **democracy.** In a pure democracy the people have a voice in creating and enforcing the laws and in deciding how laws are to be applied. A practical size limitation to democracy exists, perhaps 10,000 to 50,000 citizens. This means, where there are more than 50,000 citizens, democracy must take the form of a **republic** where representatives are elected and given the power to make binding decisions for the rest. Government of this sort is always associated with written history and literate citizens.

> **Democracy** is government where all citizens have an equal voice.

Government develops in stages and it is interesting to note how the stage of governance correlates with the evolution of writing and literacy in a society. Writing leads to recording events and precedents, reading leads to thinking and is the foundation of a reasoning society.

In prehistoric societies the records were kept orally in the form of legends, myths and epic sagas.

> The king had latitude to be arbitrary. As historical
> events were recorded, populations got wise and
> simply would not stand for arbitrary actions, and
> the king's powers began to be limited.

Athens, Greece is a key example. How could it go from a prehistoric tribal village to a world power and the cultural center of the world in a mere 151 years? The answer lies in the education leading to the prosperity of its citizens.

## Athenian Political History

Because democracy was invented in Athens, a bit of its history is in order. In prehistoric Athens, law took a tribal format. Whether in families, clans or brotherhoods, unwritten laws were based upon self-help, self-defense or communal defense. The members of these groups had the right to avenge wrongs and perpetrators might seek exile abroad or sanctuary within. To prevent feuds lasting generations, primitive trials or hearings were held in public places. Elders were seated in a circle on polished stones and a hearing was held where both sides were restrained by public officers and gold (blood money) was awarded to the prevailing party. Laws, procedures, decisions and precedents were not recorded. They thus were arbitrary, irrational and mysterious.

About 621 BC, Draco (sometimes known as Dracon) wrote a code of criminal laws. It was published and any citizen who could read could now appeal to the Areopagus, a council of city elders, for redress. This knowledge broke the mystery and monopoly held by the aristocracy. Now there were precedents to follow and rights of citizenship developed. Because the penalty for most transgressions was death, the term "draconian" became synonymous with harsh law.

About 594 BC, Solon wrote a codification of existing laws, both criminal and civil, and a constitution. These laws were published on stellae erected around Athens. Business types now had the calculus for various opportunities. Business opportunities soon became "rights." Contracts became meaningful and enforceable. Courts were open to all, including non-citizens. Solon's writings remodeled the economy, especially agriculture and local commerce. Trade and commerce sharpen wits and minds. Desire for material objects proves a powerful motivator. Athens quickly ascended in power and importance leading to its dominance in the lucrative Mediterranean trade. But Solon's constitution was a failure. Bullheaded Athenians armed with logic, rhetoric and oratory and debate skills quickly transformed Athens into a "nation" of lawyers that in fact had no attorneys; every person was his or her own advocate.

The written laws of Solon led to a culture that recognized, allowed and prized personal development. Through conquest and commerce, his codification became the standard of the other Greek city-states. These unprecedented citizen liberties led to **economic opportunities** that allowed Athens to develop a concentration of strong dynamic citizens and to quickly create an economy that was way out of proportion to its small population. And the laws created in Athens endured: Greek law became the international standard until Roman law, which in a real sense followed those Athenian precedents.

The wide availability of economic opportunities led to a cultural explosion never before witnessed in the history of mankind. In 104 years, Athens went from the disarray of tribal illiteracy to being a world power, defeating a Persian army at Marathon. It was 151 years from illiterate tribalism to the golden age of Pericles, where Athenians led the world in the following areas:

- Entertainment: drama, comedy, tragedy
- The humanities: philosophy, logic, ethics, rhetoric, oration, debate, art, sculpture, architecture
- Education: history, science, medicine
- Naval power, shipping, maritime commerce, colonization
- Law and governance

Within 200 years, the Athenians moved from a prehistoric tribe to a cultural center producing the following giants:

**Dracon** and **Solon** (see above).

**Aeschylus** (525–456 BC), father of Greek tragedy, military hero.

**Militiades** (dates unknown), Athenian military commander who engineered the most significant and surprising land battle in ancient history at Marathon.

**Themistocles** (c. 514–499 BC), father of the Athenian navy, brilliant naval commander and architect of the Athenian victory at Salamis, ostracized about 471 BC and then welcomed to live in Persia.

**Sophocles** (495–406 BC), Athenian by residency, wrote over 100 plays.

**Pericles** (c. 490–429 BC), Athenian statesman and naval commander at Mycale, where the Persian naval fleet was finally destroyed.

**Herodotus** (c. 484–425 BC) Father of history, born at Halicarnissus, noncitizen resident of Athens, where he was awarded a large cash stipend for literary talent.

**Euripides** (c. 484–407 BC), great Greek tragedy playwright who wrote about 92 plays.

**Thucydides** (c. 471–404 BC), the world's first objective historian, who wrote history so others might learn from the past.

**Socrates** (c. 470–c. 399 BC), A distinguished warrior and military hero; brilliant, tenacious, philosopher extraordinaire. He devoted his life and energies to the pursuit of purity of his soul and the soul of his associates. He eviscerated the politics and science of the day by questioning the basis for such beliefs and revealing these disciplines to be based merely on unproven assumptions. He was reputedly labeled the world's wisest man by the oracle of Delphi, but was tried by Athenians for "impiety" and "corruption of the youth" and forced to commit suicide simply for asking too many questions.

**Aristophanes** (c. 448–385 BC), great dramatist of Athens, an acerbic satirist, who could flourish only in a very democratic state.

**Plato** (c. 428–348 BC), noted philosopher, founded the Academy.

But most important was the creation of the citizen soldier: a creature empowered by rights of citizenship; a grant of liberty never seen before in the world. The opportunities of this liberty were defined by Athenian law, now in writing. As each citizen soldier had to arm himself with private funds, Athenian prosperity allowed any citizen soldier to purchase a helmet, shield and armor of bronze, a sword of steel and, most importantly, develop an iron will to protect his new rights of citizenship.

How effective was this amateur army of citizens turned warriors? Athens came into conflict with the Persian Empire which included all of Egypt, the Middle East and much of India. When the Greeks of Athens looted and burned the city of Sardis in 493 BC, Darius I, the Persian emperor, mobilized an army of 25,000 professional soldiers and in 490 BC sent his son-in-law to destroy Athens.

On August 12, 490 BC, some 10,000 citizen soldiers, (roughly the adult male population of the city of Athens) met those 25,000 Persian soldiers on the fields of Marathon. At a cost of less than 200 Athenians dead, over 6,400 Persian soldiers were dead or captured.

In 480 BC the Persians returned. Xerxes had succeeded Darius I. After crushing a revolt in Egypt, Xerxes turned to the Greek city-states. According to Herodotus, the Persian army sent against the Greek city-states numbered millions and drank rivers dry as they passed. About 1200 triremes (oared battleships) were sent to crush the Athenian navy consisting of 300 ships. The Persians built a bridge to cross the Hellespont (nearly 1400 yards). They were met by 6,000 Spartans and the Athenian citizen soldiers in a narrow pass in the mountains named Thermopylae. Here 300 Spartans were chosen as a rear guard, while the rest retreated. All of the 300 were killed. The Persians reached Athens; the city was destroyed. But disaster in the form of storms sank about 200 Persian ships. Then on September 20, 480 BC, about 400 Persian triremes were ambushed in the shallows of Salamis by 300 Athenian triremes. The Persians lost 200 more ships and all their crews, clubbed and drowned. The Athenians lost 40 ships with many sailors saved. Observing this from his vantage point on land Xerxes retreated across the Hellespont and burned his bridge behind him.

Over the next six years more land and naval battles established Greek supremacy over the Persians. The small Greek city-states had thwarted the world super power. Clearly the course of history was changed. The Greek city-states were free to develop the foundations of the Western world we know today.

What miraculous engine propelled Athens upward? Pericles, in his funeral speech commemorating the Persian defeats, as recalled by Thucydides, said:

> Our polity does not copy the laws of neighboring states; we are rather a pattern to others, than imitators ourselves. It is called **democracy**, because it is not the few, but the many that govern. If we look to the laws, they afford equal justice to all in their private differences.

In other words, there was no strong man in charge of Athens; it was "the many" that governed. Hence there was no mechanism to deal out and enforce privileges.

The **opportunities offered by citizenship** allowed the development of a strong sense of self-worth springing from democratic government. This empowerment along with strong personal and property rights created unprecedented **prosperity** for Athens; prosperity which allowed it to field a small army of powerful, well equipped and highly motivated warriors, each who had something to lose and everything to fight for. These Athenian citizens, with citizens from its sister city-states, ran Persia off the battlefields in a series of astounding victories.

> **Prosperity** in a society is created when the maximum number of citizens is given the maximum opportunity.

But the Achilles heel of Athenian democracy was instability. Its citizens abhorred professional politicians and public servants and opted for amateurs. Most terms of office and civil service were only one year and citizens were chosen by lottery with one term of service per lifetime, except in the council where two non-concurrent terms were possible. Ten generals (*strategoi*) were chosen by election annually to serve for one-year terms. Here unlimited re-elections were possible. Athens was truly democracy in the extreme: for example, in a war, the council of ten generals each day chose the general who would orchestrate the battle for that day.

A simple majority of the **Assembly** (all citizens) could pass a law. This meant a mere 3001 of the 50,000-odd citizens could pass a law, because the quorum for the assembly was only 6000 citizens. In trials, also held in the Assembly, a simple majority of a jury could result in a guilty verdict, huge fine, ostracism or a death sentence. Since a jury was comprised of 201 to 2001 citizens, depending on the offense, a citizen's fate might rest on 101 to 1001 citizens. There was no judge to admit or deny evidence, nor instruct on irrelevant and inflammatory evidence. Judging from the results (frequent exile and all too frequent ostracism), these trials were probably a "free for all." A simple disparity in rhetorical skill produced frequent disasters in the Assembly.

Based upon the instability of Athenian government, our Founding Fathers feared a pure democracy or even too much democracy (voice where a single strong orator could sway the majority one way or the other.

In the years following their military triumphs, utter disorganization, greed, intrigues, frequent ostracisms, poor policies of inept politicians and incessant wars with other city-states and leagues of city-states weakened Athens. By the time of Alexander the Great's campaigns, Athens could offer little resistance. But, in a sense, Alexander never conquered Athens. His respect for the culture (in his youth his tutor was Aristotle) was so great that Athens remained a free city. The Greek classicists were remembered and revered by our Founding Fathers and are studied by us today. Literacy conquers military might.

**Lesson of Athens:**
No tyrant meant no economic privileges,
which led to maximum opportunities for all,
which led to the maximum prosperity for Athens.

## The Middle Ages

The Roman Empire came and went, contributing to political science a **senate**, the notion of a republic and a rich history of decline for us to ponder. A republic, or *res publica* (public thing) was the notion of a government not by citizens directly, but by special representatives, loosely in charge of the general welfare. It was between the authoritarian monarchs and oligarchs, and the near anarchy of pure Athenian democracy. It was brought about by the physical limitations imposed on government by large numbers of citizens in a huge geographic area, which made it impossible for all citizens to promptly assemble to vote on issues.

The fall of the Roman Empire led to the arrival of the Middle/Dark Ages on the European peninsula. Much of history and culture was destroyed. Highly edited fragments of classic Greek works remained in some monasteries. Some writings survived in the Eastern Roman empire at Constantinople, some remained in Egypt and filtered back into Europe. Unfortunately, much was lost in 1453 when Mehmed II of the Ottomans plundered and looted Constantinople. Islamic culture was not kind to the culture of the West.

What of government for the common man? It was again an age of clans, tyrants, war and unrest. Now the tyrants were the kings, barons, dukes, lords of the manors and the men at arms. Nationalism had not emerged and Christianity was often more influential in daily life than the tyrant of the moment. The impact of religion on governance has always been substantial. Early kings usually traced their heritage to gods. Indeed kings turned to Rome for the right to wear their crowns.

But the price of Christianity was considerable: Significant revenues from the *tithe* on the populace and *investiture,* a monetary charge upon the king of the moment for the privilege of wearing the crown, were collected by the Church. The siphoning off of vast wealth to Rome, in the form of specie, caused severe economic depression in Europe. Building phenomenal cathedrals at this time was also a huge economic drain.

Development of political thought was in remission. The concept of citizenship was quite dead. The norm of government as that of a dictatorial monarch was found in the literature of the period. Indeed, Thomas Aquinas (1225–1274) had concluded that *"it is more expedient that a multitude of men, living together, be ruled by one man rather than by many."* He considered no other ruler than a monarch. He could imagine nothing else.

The Judeo-Christian religions did contribute the notion of *"do unto others as you would have them do unto you."* But this was simply for interpersonal relationships; it was not for government. Religion had an impact on society in other ways. Most of the population was tied to the land in serfdom and economic opportunity was rare. Order and stability came from religion. Indeed religion was pervasive and dominated the intelligentsia, as it existed. The Church was the patron of the arts, the only path to literacy and the sole repository of literature (edited, of course). Education was a monopoly of the church. Subsequently the church became a new tyranny; banned literature, heresies, ex communications, inquisitions and burnings at the stake were cultural norms of the day.

## English Political Heritage

England was a bit different from the rest of Europe. Remote from Rome, it was never entirely conquered by Rome's legions. England was mostly insulated from paying annual papal tributes (for the privilege of the king's investiture), from tithes upon its populace, from religious warfare between rival claims to the papacy and from inquisitions suffered upon freethinking intelligentsia. England was safe from continental warfare, unless it chose to invade and hold colonies in France. As a result, it developed differently than the rest of Europe.

The king, occasionally absent on crusades, left the nobility "home alone" and up to no good. They started to develop independent attitudes, reminiscent of the Athenians. The king, often financially drained by distant wars or by ransoms caused by mismanagement of those wars, pressed the nobility for increased taxes. Armed resistance by barons, earls and various lords caused King John to capitulate and to grant 63 enumerated rights, including free church access, pensions to widows of lords killed in battle, guardianship for heirs of tender age, an end to forced remarriages for widows of nobility, trials by peers in local courts, an end to seizure of lands or assets until after trials, and more. This was the *Magna Carta* of 1215.

Few today know that the *Magna Carta* was renegotiated in 1216, 1217 and 1225. Each time the nobles gained a bit more power. As a result of these concessions, noble families in England occasionally had greater wealth than their king. In each case nobles "got it in **writing**," again showing the importance of literacy.

As aristocrats took rights from the king, they were empowered by more opportunity which generated greater personal and national prosperity. The impetus to the rise of a middle class was the escape of serfs from manors who settled in towns and became landless freemen. They turned to primitive manufacturing, trades and shop keeping. In town they were largely exempt from the census, and hence from most taxation and other arbitrary extractions by the local lords. These freemen could now accrue wealth. They, too, sought greater freedoms and exemption from injustices of local laws and arbitrary decisions in local courts. Businessmen turned to contracts — the purse and quill rather than the sword. They bought **charters** from the king or from local lords for annual fairs.

The practice expanded as, following French tradition, these freemen bought from their English king the rights of **burgage.** This was a body of rights including the right to buy, sell or devise tiny plots of land and other interests in real estate; **the right to codify customs and trade practices;** and the right to limited representation in Parliament. Burgages led to the numerous boroughs of England today. **Opportunity** was creating a prosperous middle class years ahead of the Italian city-states. These powerful Norman lords were blissfully ignorant of Greek history and Athenian democracy when they demanded their *Magna Carta*. Most of the Greek teachings were still lost to Europe in the Dark Ages. Nor did Henry VIII quote any Greek or Roman authority as he steered England away from the Roman Catholic Church.

Now common citizens **bought** rights from the king and a larger class was empowered by economic opportunity, creating much greater national prosperity.

## Enlightened Philosophers on Politics

As enlightenment dawned and the darkness of the Middle Ages faded on the European peninsula, philosophy spawned the inquiry that became **political science**. Book **writing** became popular. It was the Englishman Thomas Hobbes who, in 1651, questioned the authority of the church to grant *investiture*. Hobbes hypothecated a rudimentary "**social contract**" as the basis for laws of mankind. He suggested a monarch had no *divine right* and could lose power over citizens in the event he, the king, could no longer protect them. For his thoughts, he was threatened, fled to France and lived out his life as a mathematician. But it was John Locke who was the true genius of political science, and who should be known as the father of the discipline. Out of that darkness of the Middle Ages he did the following:

- He defined **natural law**, the right of *self-preservation* and the desire for just *punishment or retribution* for wrongs suffered.
- He refined and explained the **social contract**: the right to govern comes only from the governed, and the purpose of government is to serve the governed. Hence *all in government are servants of the public.*
- He conceived and defined the concept of **inalienable rights** and enumerated them, but he did not label them as such.
- He said the **sole purpose of government is to serve the citizens** governed, hence all in government are public servants, subject to replacement by revolution, if necessary.
- He explained why the **right to revolution** was an inalienable right.
- He **defined property** and described how government gives property its value.

- He delineated the **limits of powers** of the **magistrate** (state) and of the church and found the boundaries to be "fixed and immovable," separating church from state.
- He found the powers of the state were limited to **external** manifestations and the powers of the church to be **internal** manifestations, and that the church had no powers to repress or punish, creating the basis of the Fifth Amendment rights and freedom of religious choice.
- He described some of the principles of what is today called **due process of law.**
- Most importantly, he explored limits on government, and each department within it, and how they fit together in a set of dynamic equilibrium. For example, a government gives property its value by enforcing its laws; but the governmental power is limited. It cannot take without paying the citizen, for to do so would diminish or destroy the value of property.

His ability to do all this before 1690 was based on an Oxford University education, where he "sipped rather than drank," a brief teaching career at Oxford, participation in the founding of The Royal Society of London for the Improvement of Natural Knowledge (the Royal Society) and active membership therein for years, and his years as a confidant and advisor to Ashley (Lord Shaftsbury). This led to his drafting the Carolinas constitution and his self-imposed exile to France (1675–1679) and Holland (1683–1689), each time for political reasons; and finally to work as an appellate judge on his return to England.

Because John Locke's thinking was so fundamental, profound and influential, it demands a closer look. It is the basis for the U.S. Constitution, civil rights, due process of law and the key to understanding governmental abuses and excesses of today.

Locke's analysis began with a "**state of nature**" before government and legislated law existed (what Aristotle had called the "nature of the state"). To Hobbes, the *state of nature* was one of war, wherein "*the life* *of man"* was *"solitary, poor, nasty, brutish, short."* Locke's *state of nature* was somewhat more peaceful. Locke opined that in the state of nature men had the right to do what they wished, *"a state of perfect freedom to order their actions and dispose of their possessions and person."* (Locke, *Second Treatise on Government*)

**Natural Law:** Locke opined that *"laws of nature"* existed *"being nowhere written and so nowhere to be found, but in the minds of man."* (*ibid.*) Locke took note of natural laws in the writings of Hugo Groitus (1583–1645): laws that *"if there was no God these laws would still hold."* (*ibid.*) Locke said that Man in the **natural state** had rights, (1) to life, or the power to act for self-preservation, or " *doing whatsoever he thought fit for the preservation of himself, and the rest of mankind,"* (*ibid.*) and (2) *"to punish wrong doers, and taking reparations."* (*ibid.*) These were **natural laws** of mankind, more fundamental than laws conceived and passed by governments. They were then superior to laws created by government.

The fundamental **natural law** according to Locke is:
(1) the right to self-preservation,
(2) the right to punish wrongs and get reparations.

These are fundamental, part of the soul of man, hence cannot be given away or taken away from citizens. Note the first rule (self-preservation) is the basis of the right to keep and bear arms. It arises from natural law. This is more fundamental than the bill of rights, and was conceived by Locke nearly a century before the Bill of Rights.

These two fundamental rights, self-preservation and the right to seek punishment and reparation for crimes, were expanded by Locke into what the Founding Fathers later called **inalienable rights.** His actual words were *"Life, liberty, and health, indolence of body (leisure), and the possession of outward things, such as money, lands, houses, furniture, and the like."* Did he not describe the **pursuit of happiness**? Because these words are found in the little known *A Letter Concerning Toleration* (1670) they are usually overlooked today.

Locke defined the **inalienable rights** in 1670, though he did not so label them.

**Social Contract:** The social contract was not an innovation of John Locke. A primitive form was hypothecated by Hobbes.

Locke's **social contract** was based upon the earlier noted natural laws. Locke first observed that unfortunately, because not all men are physically equal and some have a mean streak, "*enjoyment of property he has in this state is very unsafe, and very insecure.*" (*ibid.*) Also, "*punishment [is] dangerous and frequently destructive to those who attempt it.*" (*ibid.*) He then explained that persons formed government; that people "*unite for the mutual preservation of their lives, liberties and estates.*" (*ibid.*) He then suggested men gave up their liberty to do as they wished and "*resigned it* (control) *into the hands of the community,*" (*ibid.*) Locke next observed the wish of all men for:

(1) "*an established, settled and known law, received and allowed by common consent to be the standard of right and wrong, the common measure to decide all controversies . . . plain and intelligible to all rational creatures.*" (*ibid.*)
(2) "*a known and indifferent judge, with authority to determine all differences according to established law,*" (*ibid.*) and
(3) "*power to back the sentence when right, and to give it due execution, to make good their injustices,*" (*ibid.*)

Locke also noted "*the power of the society or the legislative can never be supposed to extend past the common good . . . And all this is to be directed to no other end than peace, safety, and the **public good** of the people.*" (*ibid.*)

Locke has defined the basis of **due process of law**.

The **social contract** pre-dates, and is *the basis for*, government. The implication is that our Bill of Rights lists **natural rights**, not a gift from government.

In *A Letter Concerning Toleration,* Locke questioned the soundness of the policy of "*Christians killing Christians for the purpose of saving their souls.*" He reasoned that a church was a voluntary society and that proper powers of religion were to "*persuade, exhort, admonish, and advise*" but never to "*punish*" or "*excommunicate,*" that the church had no power to "*violence, rapine or persecution.*"

Locke explained that the magistrate (state) had no power to "*care for the souls*" and "*the magistrate's power extends not to the establishing any article of faith*"; his examination of the Bible did not reveal "*any such authority of one man over another to compel anyone to his religion.*" Magistrates have only "*outward power,*" while the focus of religion is "*inward.*" He had thus established the policy for **freedom of religion, separation of church and state** and limitation or prohibition of state power to invade the **privacy of the inner thoughts of man.** Was this not the basis of our Fifth Amendment? Again, because of the religious tenor of the letter, these thoughts are frequently overlooked by political scientists of today.

> Locke has just drawn the line separating **church** and **state** and has also laid the basis for the fifth amendment: the right against **self-incrimination**.

His **theory of property,** a basis of self-preservation, was quite revolutionary; he proposed that it was the social contract that put all value into property: "*men, therefore in society having property, have such a right to goods, which by law of the community are theirs, that nobody hath a right to take them, or any part of them, from them without their own consent; without this they have no property at all.*" (Locke, *Second Treatise on Government*) Property therefore would derive its value from "*laws of society,*" "*settled, known, and established,*" and which property rights were enforceable by "*indifferent judges.*"

Next he found that the **supreme power** "*is bound to govern by established standing laws, promulgated and known to the people, and not by extemporaneous decrees*" (*ibid.*) "*supreme power cannot take property arbitrarily*" (*ibid.*) or "*without consent of the owner.*" (*ibid.*)

> Locke tells us governments cannot take **property** from citizens or property has no value at all.

Locke continues: supreme power is "*placed in executive by the will of the people*" (*ibid.*) "*the supreme power cannot act arbitrarily, but must follow laws*" (*ibid.*), "*The supreme power cannot reduce rights to fewer than man had in a state of nature*" (*ibid.*) "*for society can never, by fault of another lose the native and original right to preserve itself, which can only be done by a settled legislature and a fair and impartial execution of the laws made by it.*" (*ibid.*)

Here Locke says that the executive cannot act arbitrarily and that inalienable rights cannot be taken from citizens: "*when anyone, or more shall take upon themselves to make laws without authority . . . the people are not therefore bound to obey.*" (*ibid.*)

> Locke has just told us that any government that violates the **natural laws** or the fundamental rights of man need not be obeyed. Indeed such a government is not immortal.

This led to the **right to revolution.** Locke debunked Hobbes' (and established government's) claim that "all men are born under government, and therefore they cannot be at liberty to begin a new one." (*ibid.*) He reasoned that executive abuse of power or "*the use of force without authority always puts him that uses it into a state of war as the aggressor and renders him liable to be treated accordingly.*" (*ibid.*) He postulated that "*fathers do not have the power*" to "*bind their posterity to a perpetual subjugation to a government to which they have not themselves submitted.*" (*ibid.*) The idea of resisting an unjust tyrant is previously found in the Summa Theologica of Aquinas and in the *Magna Carta.* Is not the **right to revolution another inalienable right**? Locke did policy thinking about **separation of powers** stating "*Legislative and executive powers in distinct hands*" (*ibid.*) and the "*executive shall not hinder the legislature.*" (*ibid.*)

> Locke has just stated there is a right to revolution against government that violates the inalienable rights of man; that natural rights of man are supreme over legislated laws that violate or deny those "natural rights of man."

John Locke's thinking and writings laid the foundation for inalienable rights, purpose of government, property rights, due process of law and American tripartite government.

Montesquieu in 1748 explained the equilibrium of human interactions in society thus: "***Liberty*** *is the right to do whatever the law permits, and if a citizen could do what they forbid, he would no longer be possessed of liberty, because all his fellow citizens would have the same power.*" (Montesquieu, *The Spirit of the Laws*)

Jean-Jacques Rousseau in 1761 published *The Social Contract*. It began, "*men are born free, and everywhere they are in chains.*" He mused on "*the right of the strongest,*" and on slavery. Then he reasoned:

> "Finally, each man, in giving himself to all, gives himself to nobody; and there is no associate over whom he does not acquire the same right as he yields to others over himself, he gains the equivalent for everything he loses, (but in addition gains) an increase of force for the preservation of what he has." (Rousseau, *The Social Contract*)

We hear this again in the old axiom, "my right to swing my fist stops somewhere short of your nose." The thrust was that all citizens have the same rights.

Previously individual philosophers had authored essays on political science. For the first time in the history of the world, in 1787, a group, seated to amend the *Articles of Confederation,* attacked the problem of designing a government. Now here were assembled the Founding Fathers; a group of practical businessmen, trial attorneys, political sorts and scientists, men highly enlightened in history and political thought. There had never been such an expenditure of time and effort dedicated to explore government and its proper functions. Unlike solitary philosophers, they brought to bear varied points of view, strenuously and articulately debated. Not until this event were *boundaries* between departments of government so clearly defined.

The time of the Founding Fathers was an age of enlightenment: a time of scientific discovery. Newton found the force of gravity varied as to distance. Boyle's law stated that there was an equilibrium between the pressure and volume of a fixed quantity of gas. Chemists were finding all inorganic chemical reactions followed precise numerical proportions. And scientists were present among the Founding Fathers, notably Benjamin Franklin. Those Founding Fathers now sought to create a stable equilibrium between the three fundamental or elemental parts of government: the legislative, executive and judicial departments. Their collective genius was far beyond the grasp of our misdirected politicians of today.

> The Founding Fathers realized that **to create an equilibrium in government it was essential that the acts of the executive were reviewable by a superior power, that of the judiciary.**

This was an historic first. In another, though lesser, first, politics discovered the newspaper, a relatively new format at that time. Here are some of the Founding Fathers' other teachings, which were first published in three New York newspapers. Collectively they are known today as *The Federalist Papers.*

## Gems from The Federalist Papers

*The Federalist Papers* early notes:

ON THE NATURE OF GOVERNMENT

"If all men were angels, we would not need government"
(F 51 pp 4)

"Enlightened statesmen will not always be at the helm" (F 10 pp 9)

"The aim of every constitution is . . . first to obtain for Rulers men who possess most wisdom to discern, and the most virtue to pursue the *common good of society*" (F 57 pp 3)

"The real welfare of the people is the supreme objective. Attaining this objective is the government's only value" (F 51 pp 10)

## ON EQUILIBRIUM IN TRIPARTITE GOVERNMENT

"The necessary partition of power between the several departments as laid down by the Constitution" (F 51 pp 2)

"The distinct exercise of the different powers of government" (F 51 pp 3)

"The members of each [branch] should have as little agency as possible in the appointment of the members of others" (F 51 pp 2)

"Subordinate distribution of power, where the constant aim is to divide and arrange the several offices in such a manner as that each may be a **check** on the other" (F 51 pp 2)

"Justice is the end" goal "of government. It is the end" goal "of civil society." (F 52 pp 10)

"The great security against the **gradual concentration** of the several powers in the same department, consists in giving those who administer each department the necessary constitutional means and personal motives to resist the encroachment of others." (F 51 pp 4)

"The accumulation of all powers, legislative, executive and judiciary, in the same hands, whether of one, a few, or many and whether hereditary, self-appointed or elected, may justly be pronounced the very definition of tyranny." (F 47 pp 3)

"Representatives . . . will possess proper knowledge of local circumstances of their numerous constituents" (F 55 pp 1)

"A part of this knowledge may be acquired . . . in private as well as public station. Another part can only be obtained . . . by actual experience..." (F 53 pp 4)

## ON THE NATURE OF VIRTUOUS POLITICAL ACTIONS

Caution against "the immediate interest one party may find in disregarding the rights of another, or the good of the whole" (F 10 pp 9)

"To secure the *public good* and private rights against the danger of such a faction" (F 10 pp 16)

"Steady administration of the laws" (F 70 pp 1)

"Protection of property against those irregular and high-handed combinations which sometimes interrupt the ordinary course of justice" (*ibid.*)

"Security of liberty against the enterprise and assaults of ambition, faction [special interest groups] and anarchy" (*ibid.*)

Remaining "virtuous while they continue to hold their public trust [office]" (F 57 pp 3)

"The necessary partition of power among the several departments of government" .... "keeping each in their proper place" (F 51 pp 1)

"Against a gradual concentration of several powers in the same department consists in giving . . . necessary constitutional means . . . to resist encroachment of others" (F 51 pp 4)

## ON BAD ACTS OF GOVERNMENT

"Laws so voluminous they cannot be read" (F 62)
"Laws so incomprehensible they cannot be understood" (*ibid.*)

[Laws passed in] "irregular passion or stimulated by some irregular passion, or some illicit advantage, or misled by the artful misrepresentation of interested men" (F 63 pp 7)

Politicians "who possess more confidence than they deserve" (F 1 pp 2)

Laws passed in the "breeze of passion" (F 71 pp 2)

Laws passed in "very transient impulse" (*ibid.*)

"Laws that undergo incessant changes that no man who knows what the law is today can guess what it will be tomorrow . . . what prudent merchant will hazard his fortune in a branch of commerce when he knows not but what his plans may be rendered unlawful before they can be executed" (F 62 pp 15)

"Immediate interest which one party may find in disregarding the rights of another or the *good of the whole*" (F 10 pp 9)

"Public instability [gives] unreasonable advantage….the sagacious, the enterprising, the moneyed few over industrious and uninformed mass of the people. Every new regulation concerning commerce or revenue, or any manner affecting the value of different species of property presents a new harvest to those who watch change, and can trace its consequences . . . laws made for the few, and not the *many*" (F 62 pp 16)

"What is to restrain the House of Representatives from making legal distinctions in favor of themselves, and a particular class of society? They should . . . make no rule of law that will not have full operation on themselves, their friends, as well as the *great mass of society*" (F 57 pp 12)

"Candidates too little fit to comprehend and pursue great national objects" (F 10 pp 19 )

"Unworthy candidates to practice with success the vicious arts by which elections are too often carried" (F 10 pp 18)

"That a dangerous ambition more often lurks behind the specious mask of zeal for the rights of the people …." (F 1 pp 5)

"No man is allowed to be a judge in his own cause because his interest would certainly bias his judgment . . . yet what are many of the most important acts of legislation but so many judicial determinations..." (F 10 pp 8)

"The apportionment of taxes upon the various descriptions of property is an act which seems to require the most exact impartiality; yet there is, perhaps, no legislative act in which greater opportunity and temptation are given to a predominant party to trample on the rules of justice..." (*ibid.*)

"Gradual preeminence in government finally transforming it into tyrannical aristocracy." (F 63 pp 15)

"Permanent elevation of the few on the depression of the many" (F 55 pp 1)

## ON THE DYNAMICS OF A STABLE GOVERNMENT

"While legitimacy of government comes from the majority" the majority is not always right. The majority may be swayed by "impulse of passion" (F 10 pp 2)

"It is imperative in a republic . . . to guard one part of society against the injustices of the other part." "If a majority be united by common interest the rights of the minority will be insecure." (F 51 pp 10)

[The role of government is] "to protect the weaker as well as the more powerful" (F 51 pp 11.)

"Representatives [shall not be] "so small a number that they are an unsafe depository of the *public interest*" (F 55 pp 1).

"The election of the proper guardians of the *general weal*" (F 10 pp 16)

"States shall define the way its federal representatives are chosen, to allow Congress to regulate it would be improper" (F 52 pp 2)

"History informs us of no long lived republic which has not had a senate" (F 63 pp 9)

ON MECHANISM OF ACCOUNTABILITY FOR POLITICIANS

"I am unable to conceive that there are . . . men capable . . . to betray the solemn trust committed to them" (F 55 pp 6)

"First . . . they have been distinguished by the preference of their fellow citizens . . . which [implies a] promise [of] sincere and scrupulous regard to the nature of their engagement" (F 57 pp 8)

"Second they will enter public service . . . [with] a temporary affection at least to their constituents" (F 57 pp 9).

"Third . . . pride and vanity" in doing good work (F 57 pp 10).

Unfortunately these safeguards have proved to be utterly deficient. This, too, was foreseen by the Founding Fathers:

"Distant prospect of public censure would be feeble restraint on power" (F 50 pp 2)

"All these securities would be found very insufficient without the restraint of frequent elections" (F 57 pp 11)

"The right of suffrage is the fundamental right of republic government" (*ibid.*)

"Where annual elections end, tyranny begins" (F 53 pp 1)

Compare these words to the teachings of modern professors and political pundits:

- "Greed is good" from the movie *Wall Street.*
- A "trickle down" economy works to benefit the common man.
- America, the land of the free, has a free market, but enlightened regulators can improve on the free market, for example, by grants of economic privileges or by fixing prices.
- We have free markets where competition is good, but a business can be too big to let fail: e.g., Goldman Sachs (a massive Presidential campaign contributor), while its arch competitor, Lehman Brothers, is allowed to fail.
- Monopoly helps us compete in the international marketplace, hence is good for society.

- Profits are bad, evil, and serve no social function, hence are not to be allowed.
- The holy grail of regulators has become: we must replace profit motive with a new incentive that we can manage by regulation.
- In bailouts we don't even need to change the management that has indeed caused the problem. The solution is to **create a "jobless recovery,"** achieved by the creation of government "jobs," which produce no goods or services; and this at great expense.
- Our Founding Fathers were lawbreakers, revolutionary zealots and terrorists.

These classroom utterances by college professors of today make the words of the Founding Fathers sound even more profound. One must doubt the financial meltdown of 2007-2009 would have occurred with the Founding Fathers at the helm of the ship of state. It is enough to make one question the source of legitimacy of any law.

## Legitimacy of Laws

Political scientists have long pondered laws and the **legitimacy** of legislation. Where does one law obtain *legitimacy* while other written words do not? Why is it that Congressional legislation, assuming it actually was pondered and drafted in Congress, may have a better claim to legitimacy than code written by some obscure administrator?

Kings and tyrants ruled by whim or decree, often codified, and the sword. There was little legitimacy found there. The Ten Commandments were to have derived their authority directly from God. Neither Congress nor any other government can make such a claim.

The Greeks developed an almost pure **democracy** where citizens had a vote in the creation of laws and their enforcement. Isn't this an essential element to the legitimacy of law and government? But just because a law comes from a democracy does not assure such law is legitimate. The majority is not always right. Democracy can be too unsettled, too swayed by the passions and prejudice of the masses that can be unfair to minority and individual rights. In Athens, too many citizens were unjustly punished or even ostracized by highly eloquent but misdirected orators. The unsettled nature of **Athenian democracy** terrified the Founding Fathers. **In fact, there has never been a pure democracy.** Rousseau told us: *"There has never been a real democracy, and there never will be. It is unimaginable that the people would remain continuously assembled to devote their time to public affairs and it is clear they cannot set up commissions for that purpose."*

> Democracy alone does not produce legitimate law. But some measure of democracy is required for legitimacy.

Aristotle reasoned that laws derived legitimacy as follows: *"The state is properly a society of free persons,"* and *"the object of political rule is the benefit of the subjects,"* then inquired, *"Should not equals be treated equally?"* and concluded, *"what is justice if not a species of equality, the right to be treated equally?"* Hence, a legitimate law treats all equally **(which would make grants of privileges illegitimate).**

In Athens, at the time of Pericles, there were thought to be approximately 300,000 persons. There were approximately 50,000 adult citizens. There were also children. There were numerous foreign merchants and students. The most numerous class was the slaves. Each had their own rights, and not all inhabitants had all the rights of citizens. For example a foreign merchant who felt wronged had to have a citizen plead his case before the assembly.

What Aristotle was trying to say is that each specie of inhabitant was entitled to the same rights and privileges as the other members of the same classification of inhabitant. In his words: *"what is justice if not a specie of equality, the right to be treated equally?"* (Aristotle, *Politics*) He asked, *"Should not equals be treated equally?"* (*ibid.*) He concluded *"Equality consists of the same treatment of similar persons."* (*ibid.*) This is important because no *government can stand which is not founded upon justice.* (*ibid.*)

Aristotle concluded that it is the business of government to treat citizens equally, which must mean no creation, by legislation or administrative act, of economic privilege.

As seen in the Roman Empire, too many citizens and too much territory made representative government essential. The Romans backed away from *Athenian democracy* and created the bicameral legislature. They established a **Senate** to review legitimacy of legislation. This was, of course, picked up by the Founding Fathers:

"History informs us of no long-lived republic which has not had a senate." (F 63 pp 9)

By the time of the Middle Ages, the concept of **legitimacy of law** had broadened to include the notion of community. Thomas Aquinas' definition of law found in *Summa Theologica: Treatises on Law* has four parts: it is (1) a thing of reason, (2) made by an appropriate person, vice-regent for the whole people, (3) for the common good of the community, (4) properly promulgated. The contribution of Aquinas, then, is that legitimacy of law comes in part from the relation of the individual to the community.

If democracy is not the infallible engine of legitimate laws, what then is?

Locke said legitimacy in legislature comes from the grant of power from the people, and it is a conditional grant; that it lasts only so long as government serves the general welfare of its citizens. Rousseau explained the mechanics of the social contract and introduced the general will of the people. He concluded that legitimate government obtains its legitimacy from a **social contract.** He reasoned:

Each person puts his person and all power in common under the supreme direction of the **general will** and in our corporate capacity, we receive each member as an indivisible part of the whole. (Rousseau, *The Social Contract*)

We must distinguish between natural liberty, the strength of the individual . . . from the civil liberty which is limited only by the **general will**. (*ibid.*)

The general will "considers only the common interest" and is "always right, and tends to the public advantage . . . never corrupted often deceived." (*ibid.*)

However, Rousseau is unable to describe the preferred form of government to determine the **general will**. He also seems to have in mind a mythic or ideal legislator for the formulation of the general will. He left the device to formulate the general will to our Founding Fathers.

## The General Will, the General Weal, and the Legitimacy of Law

The Founding Fathers used various terms in their quest for legitimate law. The term **general weal** appears at least three times in the *The Federalist Papers*. The term **general welfare** appears in the Articles of Confederation. It also appears in the preamble to the Constitution:

We, the people of the United States, in order to form a more perfect union, establish justice, insure domestic tranquility, provide for the common defense, **promote the general welfare**, and secure the blessing of liberty to ourselves and our posterity, do ordain and establish this Constitution for the United States of America.

It again appears in Article 1 Section 8 of our Constitution. But it is nowhere defined.

The term *public good* appears in *The Federalist Papers* at least 20 times. Similar terminology is used at least an additional 16 times: "*common public interests*," "*common good of society*," "*true interest of the country*," "*public good*," "*good of the whole*," "*great mass of society*," "*common good*," "*laws for the few, not the many*" (a condemned practice), "*depository of public interest*," and "*public weal.*" But none of these terms is ever defined or even described — not in the Declaration of Independence, not in the Constitution, not in the Bill of Rights, not in any of the 85 Federalist Papers.

Their problem arose because the general welfare is not a fixed concept. That would be too limiting for an enduring government. The general weal is organic; it grows and changes with time and circumstance. Our forefathers knew that the legitimacy of laws and government is simply whether or not the general welfare of the citizens is being served. People's needs change over time. So must the concept of general weal. Governments who fail to promulgate the general welfare are not stable and risk replacement by the populace.

To define the **general welfare** the Founding Fathers found it necessary to devise a new form of government, which was to periodically define the changing general welfare of its citizens. This was the second innovation of the Founding Fathers: the **Congress,** which was to be the crucible of the formulation of the general welfare.

> **Congress** was invented by the Founding Fathers to be **the engine** to formulate the general welfare of the nation.

The basis for the thinking of our Founding Fathers was none other than John Locke. He posited the basis for legitimacy of government in his **social contract**: Recall he said that Man in the **natural state** had rights: (1) to life, or the power to act for self-preservation, *"of doing whatsoever he thought fit for the preservation of himself, and the rest of mankind;* and (2) *to punish wrong doers, and taking reparations"* (making good their injustices); and finally that *"the power of the society or the legislative can never be supposed to extend past the common good . . . And all this is to be directed to no other end."*

Recall that Locke defined the public good in terms of individual citizens. It was to be measured as their ability to pursue *"life, liberty, pursuit of indolence of person,"* (*leisure*) and *accrual of property* (in other words, security of person and property). Liberty is simply freedom from tyranny of government. Hence it is that legitimacy of law springs from government respecting the natural rights of man.

And what is liberty but minimal government?

## Limitations on Democracy for the General Welfare

The Founding Fathers noted that while the legitimacy of government **comes from serving the general weal,** the opinion of the majority (**the general will**) was not in all cases right. Recall the majority could be swayed by *"impulses of passions."* (F 71 pp 2) *"It is imperative in a republic . . . to guard one part of society against the injustices of the other part." "If a majority be united by common interest the rights of the minority will be insecure."* (F 51 pp 10) *"The role of government is to protect the weaker as well as the more powerful."* (F 51 pp 11)

> Just because a law has a democratic origin, it is not necessarily a legitimate law. It must serve the **general welfare** and **minority interests** equally.

The Founding Fathers followed the Roman example with a bicameral legislature. Their solution was a House of Representatives to represent the wishes and needs of the constituents; and a Senate, comprised of elders, age 30 or greater, to provide stability to offset the impulses of the House of Representatives. But the combined body was where the general weal was to be measured, formulated and legislated.

They went further. They established a **tripartite** government, with checks by one branch on the others. Power to impeach the president lay with the Congress. Power to strike legislation lay in the courts. Power of the purse was held in the Congress. Power to appoint judges lay within the hands of the president, but approval of these appointments lay with the Congress.

Terms of office were staggered: two, four and six years. Laws had to be passed by both houses, which takes time — time to ponder consequences. The president had to approve all legislation. These steps provided more time and opportunity for deliberation. Finally judicial review created the chance to strike bad laws, all or in part.

All of this is well and good, but have we yet discovered the definition of legitimate legislation? Do we yet have a basis for deciding if a law is good or bad? Whether or not it is in the general welfare? We have been given the engine to create legislation, but how can we tell if it is working for the general weal?

# Chapter 2

# Laws of Privilege

## The Six Kinds of Laws

Perhaps the legitimacy of law can be discovered by reflecting on the history of all legislation. Looking backwards, since the beginning of time there have been only six types of laws passed by all governments. Those are:

- Laws of prohibition
- Laws of regulation
- Laws of taking
- Laws of civil rights, civil procedure, and property and estates
- Laws of incumbency
- Laws granting economic privilege

*Laws of prohibition* are laws that prohibit certain acts or actions, like murder. They are universally and uniformly applied to all members of society. Generally, these laws are well known to all members of society. Procedures of enforcement and sanctions for violation are quite uniformly applied to all members of society.

*Laws of regulation* are laws that regulate behavior, which is to say they hold it within certain defined and measurable parameters. Automotive speed laws are perhaps the most common example. Again, they are quite universally applied to all members of a society and are uniform as to procedure of enforcement and measure of sanction. They are quite well known to all and may even be taught as social values.

*Laws of taking* include taxation, tariffs, condemnation, military drafts and the like. Again, well known to all and meant to be universally applied and enforced.

*Laws of civil rights and procedures, and property and estates* are the basic due process rights described by John Locke as expanded by our Constitution and Bill of Rights. They arise from the natural laws of mankind. They represent the two fundamental rights: the right of self-preservation and the right to have wrongs punished. They are not granted by governments, for they preexisted government; indeed, they are part of the reason people created government.

These civil rights and civil procedures are the rights to life, liberty, indolence (pursuit of happiness), the right to acquire private property and estate (and its protection), the right to orderly courts, known laws, impartial judges, the right of all citizens to be treated equally in courts, the right to revolt to overthrow dysfunctional governments and probably the right to a free market.

> These are sometimes called inalienable rights, for they cannot be given away nor can they be taken away. They pre-date government and were not created by government. They are not gifts of government in any sense of the term.

*Laws of political behavior and campaigning* are nothing but laws promoting incumbency. They are mostly nonexistent, or so vague and full of loopholes they are unenforceable and without legal consequence or penalty. They cover the way campaign funds are gathered, apportioned, held and used for personal purposes, and spent. Auditing is done by persons appointed by politicians and is meaningless because accounting is done after the candidate is sworn into office, hence trial and judgment rests in the Senate, nothing but a bunch of tainted scoundrels. Impeachment follows party lines, not merit of the case.

Policing of elections has morphed into the executive policy of not to prosecute an elected official, unless he or she is of the opposite political party.

*Laws granting economic privilege* — **a privilege is an opportunity granted to a limited group or a single person.** Privilege is not granted to all citizens or it would become a right. Hence it is that only special citizens or corporations get privileges. *Laws of economic privilege* take many forms. The most usual is probably a tax treatment: a tax exemption, or perhaps an invisible tax credit. Or it could be a *law of economic favor,* a unique set of specifications that greatly favor one manufacturing process or business, like ethanol in gasoline. Or it could be offering a low interest loan. A *law of economic privilege* may be a cash subsidy or immunity from personal liability, (sought by LLPs, LLCs or corporations) or a guarantee of indemnification (think of it as free insurance). Such a guarantee often prompts a business to engage in acts that are financially imprudent, for the risk of loss of money to the privileged business is now impossible. An example would be a bank making imprudent loans that other bankers would avoid, because insurance would cover any losses. Privileges often take the form of monopoly; the most horrible example of privilege is a bailout.

## Why Privileges Are Illegal and Bad by Any Measure

These are some reasons privileges are bad:

- They are illegitimate laws in that they are not equally applied to all citizens.
- They are illegal; the federal government was not given power to spend tax money for the benefit of a faction.
- Bidding for grants of privilege with campaign contributions opens the door to corruption of the political system: the result is we are simply creating economic and political aristocracies.

- They distort the democracy of the free market:
  - Bad public policy: subsidies keep dinosaurs in the market-place.
  - They create economic favors and force us to buy what we don't want.
  - Production is now based on manufacturer's bribery of politicos, not market demand or consumer wishes and wants.
  - Create and build monopolies, destroying diversity of small business.
- They accelerate and leverage market distortions, which create bubbles that pop.
- They create opportunity dislocations, sending valuable economic opportunities abroad.
- They cause environmental considerations to be swept aside. The lure of campaign contributions inevitably overwhelms the idea of general welfare.
- They are expensive to administer and to comply with.
- Economic laws of privilege in the form of immunity encourage irresponsible behavior and create opportunities for the enrichment of the minority, by taking advantage of the populace at large.
- Power to grant privilege is the foundation of the corruption of the tax code.
- Most importantly, each and every grant of privilege diminishes the opportunities for the rest of society, until we reach that point where there is insufficient opportunity for many citizens to support themselves and their families by legal means and they may turn to illegal means.
- The existence of privilege makes court administration of justice impossible.

## The Privilege/Opportunity Equilibrium in a Society

To explain how grants of privilege diminish the opportunity for the rest of the citizens, permit an oversimplification. Let us take a snapshot of society and assume that for that moment opportunities in a society are fixed. Every time a privilege is granted to one person, the opportunities to the rest of society are reduced. It follows that the more privileges granted to the favored few, the fewer opportunities there are left for the general populace. Examples of opportunity loss caused by grants of privilege include sending capital, jobs and technology, even entire manufacturing plants, abroad, sending vast sums of money to offshore bank accounts, sending job opportunities to India, manufacturing jobs to Mexico, China and many other nations. How is this in the general welfare?

Said another way, America was known as the land of opportunity because our Founding Fathers abhorred aristocracy and privileges. We have come to allow our politicians to create and sell economic privileges. This is destructive of the most fundamental values in our Constitution. Whenever government creates a privilege it is violating its most fundamental duty: that of the search for and promotion of the general welfare. The duty of government is always to the citizen, not the faction. Privileges to factions diminish the opportunities for the rest of society.

> America used to be known as the **land of opportunity**.
> Have we not become the land of privilege?

## The Privilege Cycle

Privileges in our form of government generate huge problems. Once a government assumes the right to grant economic privileges a cycle begins. Privilege begets economic enrichment. The usual reason politicos grant the privilege is a cash contribution (a bribe, politely called a campaign contribution). The economic enrichment received from the privilege, for the lucky holder, provides funds for more contributions, which lead to more privileges, which lead to more enrichment. The highest bidder for political largess is occasionally a wealthy family. More often it is a corporation; frequently a foreign corporation. How can that be in the general welfare?

Corporations are the usual winners because of their special attributes. They have a long life in which to establish political connections and can accrue vast capital. They employ many specialized people, such as high-powered attorneys, within the business or on retainer in some private law firm, to create pretexts of invention that might extend the life of patents, or to avoid liability for various corporate misbehaviors. The attorneys create limited liability for the corporation's activities, using layers of corporations, limited liability partnerships and similar devices both domestically and abroad in tax havens. The corporations constantly seek legislation to limit their liability or to secure free government insurance programs.

Those who have economic privileges get the financial rewards to purchase more of them. They have the cash to purchase (through campaign contributions) greater and richer subsidies and tax exemptions. The whole scheme of laws of privilege is highly offensive to the general welfare, because it diminishes the opportunities for the rest of the citizens. It is the welfare of the citizen that is the measure of good government.

## The Avalanche Theory of Privilege

To control grants of privilege, one must understand this dynamic: it is difficult to define a privilege that actually promotes the general welfare. The Founding Fathers thought patents and trademarks, for a limited time, to protect authors and inventors, were in the general welfare. Aside from these, is there any possible compromise or some middle ground, where other privileges might be in the general welfare?

Experience suggests that it is not possible to define a middle ground, no halfway point, no line of demarcation between permissible (within the general welfare) privileges and those that are not. It is the nature of grants of privilege to proceed without limit. There is no internal limit, no check, no balance within our government. Such a device of limitation cannot be defined or built. Where has it ever been shown that grants of privilege are necessary to govern or shape society? Privileges upon privileges will invariably have unintended consequences that are contrary the original effect of a law. Pundits may call grants of privilege a slippery slope, but they are more than that. Grants of economic privilege have become an unstoppable avalanche.

> So long as politicians think they have the right to sell privileges, politics will be thoroughly corrupted.

The public is accepting of this practice. They have been talked into thinking it is somehow beneficial to society. Lobbying for and with cash is so blatant in America that people openly admit to being lobbyists. Politicos even license them.

Eventually privileges would demand that there be **two sets of laws**, one for the privileged, one for the *undermenche*, the citizens. To maintain the disparity, there would evolve **two sets of civil procedures**: one for citizens, one for the privileged factions. The courts of privilege would develop their own arcane jargon and their own legal procedures. A separate court system would evolve with its own judiciary or judges so that the privileges could be maintained. There would be **no appeal process**. Not because their judges would be infallible, but because privilege is not bound by precedent, just campaign contributions. This second system would wish secrecy. There would be no need for juries. Indeed inherent in a jury system is transparency, and there would be no wish for transparency in this court system. Is this not exactly what we now have in administrative law courts, run by administrative law judges, with no meaningful appeal?

**Grants of privilege** diminish the **opportunities** for the rest of society, until they can no longer support themselves by legal means. Hence grants of privilege lead to crime and the decline of society. This is bad law by any measure.

> Grants of privilege inevitably diminish our national prosperity.

## Examples of Economic Privileges

What then are grants of economic privilege? Here are some examples:

- Copyright*
- Patents and extensions thereof*
- Trademarks*
- Corporations
- Limited Liability Partnerships
- Licenses
- Tariffs
- Monopoly not prosecuted
- Agenda driven legislation, administration, enforcement and court decisions
- Price fixing: "legal," tolerated or simply not prosecuted
- Price fixing: illegal
- The entire federal tax code
- Tax credits
- Depreciation
- Deductions
- Depletion allowances
- Tax exemptions and tax deferral programs
- Dual citizenship (tax revenue exporting)
- Subsidies
- Direct cash payments
- Price supports
- Grants
- Low interest loans
- Loans with interest deferral
- Loan forgiveness
- Cost sharing programs
- Grants
- Fellowships
- Stipends

- TIFs and free building sites for manufacturers
- Sale of mineral rights from public lands or Native American lands

*The first three were thought by the Founding Fathers to be beneficial to society.*

How are laws of privilege granted and maintained? All are granted by government. Some are passed through Congress. Many arise through administrative rulings. All are administered, hence blessed, by the executive branch. Regardless of origin, all privileges are contrary to the general welfare.

## Absolute Prohibition of Privilege?

The question now becomes: Should government exist to create and maintain opportunities for the privileged few or is the proper function of government to distribute opportunity broadly among its citizens, to empower the greatest number of them to seek personal enrichment, hence elevating their society as a whole to greater prosperity and fulfillment? If all are to be equal before the law, how can there be laws of privilege? This class of laws grants rights to the privileged few, which inevitably generates inequality among citizens. As justice is a "species of equality," how can there ever be justice when one class demands privilege?

Why does government need the power to grant favors and privileges to govern in the general welfare? How can it be argued that the government's assumed power to grant economic privileges has created a better, stronger, more equitable society? Has their illegal license to do so created a more prosperous society? Have economic benefits been delivered in an equal or an equitable manner among its citizens? Have economic benefits been delivered to the hardest workers or the most inventive and innovative members of society? Is the whole of society better off each day than the previous day? Have these powers to conceive and grant privileges created a more secure, stable, and equitable society in any sense?

Absolutes in law always beg exceptions and grants of economic privileges are, of course, no exception. The Founding Fathers carved an exception for laws protecting intellectual property: copyrights, patents and trademarks. Modern politicians have been unwilling to create a black letter law prohibiting grants of economic privileges. Instead they permit themselves to sell privileges to any bidder. But this has simply led to the ridiculous extension of intellectual property laws to 95 years.

What about incorporation of business? Limitations of liability always spawn abuses, especially in corporate law. Perhaps in the area of incorporation of a business enterprise it might be possible to craft a highly limited exception to the economic privilege prohibition, and allow them to exist, with minimal harm to the general welfare. Most corporations derive their existence from the states, not the federal government. Hence the states would have the power to police corporate business practices. The specter of facing lawsuits from 50 attorneys general from the 50 states, each aggressively pursuing monopolistic trade practices and using antitrust damages as a means for balancing their states' budgets, might offer sufficient protection from corporate abuse.

Allowing the federal government exclusive power to police corporations is foolishness. They have already displayed their incompetence to do so. Note that the Department of Justice has excused themselves from meaningful activity in this area as shown in the joint DOJ FTC Report entitled *Antitrust Guidelines For Collaborators Among Competitors.*

> In order to compete in modern markets, competitors sometimes need to collaborate. Competitive forces are driving firms towards complex collaborations to achieve goals such as expanding into foreign markets, funding expensive innovation efforts, and lowering production costs. . . . Such collaborations often are not only benign, but pro-competitive.

Politicians may argue that it is impossible to govern without the power to grant economic privilege to "shape" society and the economy. They have become addicted to the sale of economic privileges. They overlook the idea that every economic privilege is destructive to the free market and the principle that people should have a voice in government and that the sale of economic privileges has destroyed all representative principles upon which republican government is based.

> Laws of economic privilege are always the very definition of bad government. They are always illegitimate laws.

The converse is that a good law must be for the general welfare and hence it contains no grant of economic privilege: no subsidy, no preferential tax treatment, no law favoring one industry or sector of the economy over another sector. The same principle, no economic grant of privilege, extends to the administration and execution of laws. All should be equal in the legislature and in administration as well as before the courts. This economic "neutrality" will maximize the freedom of the marketplace and will give the maximum opportunity to the maximum number of citizens. This is the essence of prosperity.

## Legitimacy of Legislation

We now have a working definition of legitimate law. A law is now understood to be legitimate or enforceable only when:

- It is within the limited grants of power to Congress
- It is drafted in Congress
- It is deliberated upon in Congress
- It is passed upon by both houses of Congress
- It is drafted in the language of the common citizen
- "*an established, settled and known law, received and allowed by common consent to be the standard of right and wrong, the common measure to decide all controversies . . . plain and intelligible to all rational creatures.*"
- It does not infringe upon the natural or inalienable rights of citizens

- It is in harmony with prior legislation and does not conflict with prior laws
- It contains no grant of economic privilege

Any law that does not pass each such test should be stricken from the books by our court system. This is the duty of a functional court.

As we begin the study of our government we will discover most of our laws are nothing but grants of privilege. This is the failure of our government. We will trace how grants of privilege destroy our free market and corrupt our political process. We will see how the executive has taken away our rights to jury trial and due process of law by creating special administrative "laws" and "courts" with special administrative law "judges." It will be shown that none of this has any legitimacy.

# Chapter 3

# Econopolitics

The proper integration of history, economics, and law gives us a new perspective on which to judge politics. The realms of economics and politics have become so intertwined they cannot be separated or easily understood. Hence the need for a new term to describe this new entity. I have taken the liberty of coining the concept of econopolitics. The advantage of integrating economics and politics is that politicians can no longer say something is "an economic problem, not a political problem. Since that is not my department, I am not accountable for it."

## Fundamental Elements of Econopolitics

Integrating economics and politics gives us an environment to judge politicians, and their actions, by decreasing their room to avoid accountability. Within this combined realm of econopolitics there exist the following four entities: the **individual,** the **marketplace, business enterprise,** and **government.**

The characteristics of the **individual** (citizen) are that a citizen is the sole source of life, the only entity that can enjoy liberty, the only entity capable of happiness. No goods, intellectual property or services can be created without the effort of the individual. Within the soul of the individual rest ideas, ideals and principles such as work ethic and fair play. With the individual rests the concept of personal property, the concept of thrift or savings (deferred gratification), the concept of capital or surplus funds working for economic gain, the ideals of arts and culture and the concept of justice and fair government. It is the desire of citizens that creates a market for goods and services. The citizen is the only reason governments exist. A government's failure to meet the needs of the citizens will mean that citizens will take whatever steps necessary to change their government.

> **The effort of the individual** is the sole source of all objects of value.

The natural state of the **marketplace** is a **free market**: one free of governmental influences or regulation. Economic forces in the free market are more fundamental and powerful than acts of governance. The proof that free market is a fundamental or an inalienable right is that a government's attempts to impose its will on the marketplace promptly result in a **black market.** The free market over time overwhelms any attempt to regulate it. The free marketplace is the ultimate democracy. The free market is not defaced by periodic elections, campaigning or ballot counting. Instead the polls are always open and the ballots are dollars. It is not perverted by "representative" or republican functionary machinery. It is explored in depth in Chapter 8.

> **The free market is the ultimate democracy.**
> Forces here are more powerful than acts of government fiat.

Competition in price, quality and style rewards those who produce excellence. Competition moderates prices and is the only economic device that can do so with stability over time. Monopoly is competitive failure, and is always brought about by governmental grants of privileges.

**Business enterprise** is the organization of the pursuit of opportunity. It results from the organization of an individual's efforts to create and sell goods, services and intellectual properties. It exists in various forms: sole proprietorships, partnerships and various associations, usually corporate in form. Business generates goods and service. Business alone can generate surplus wealth, capital and profits. Business alone generates jobs and salaries, based upon gainful employment. Businesses exist for **profits** from the sale of the goods, services and intellectual properties they produce. Businesses profit only if they receive more money than was expended to create and sell these items. Profit is good, for it motivates and directs the marketplace. Profit is the surplus which government may, in part, confiscate (tax) to run its various activities without destroying the capital necessary for businesses to continue. Also, the jobs business creates lead to salaries for government to confiscate.

> Without profits there would be nothing for the government to confiscate (tax), nor would there be any motivation for citizens to work.

All excesses are bad and excess profits indicate a failure of the marketplace. This failure is invariably created by direct government action (grants of economic privileges) or by government inaction (allowing a monopoly it previously licensed to continue to act). **Monopoly** simply cannot exist in a free market. The free market is the only effective limitation on prices. The search for profit is the source of all gainful employment, surplus wealth, all capital (use of some surplus wealth to increase business), and all luxury, all products. Without the incentive of profits there would be no food, no fuel, none of the essentials for life or any of the extravagances that make life fun.

> Competition in the free market is the only mechanism that can regulate (lower) prices and increase the quality of goods and services with long-term stability.

**Government** invariably produces taxation, laws, inflation, fiscal illusion or the appearance it is doing a good job; and, unfortunately, it produces economic privileges. Government is incapable of producing any reasonably priced goods or services or intellectual property. The profound enigma is that the few services that *proper* government does provide are critical to the prosperity of the nation: law, order, justice, stable money, education, a democratic marketplace and physical infrastructure, such as roads, highways and expressways. While government does create jobs, they are merely government jobs that, aside from the few vital services, produce no goods, but plenty of waste and inefficiency. They never produce surplus wealth. That originates in the private sector alone.

Government dictates that property may have value; without good law and fair enforcement of the law, property has little or no value. Governments, when functional, can produce the following: justice, liberty, opportunity and the groundwork for prosperity. Government can skew the democracy of the free market by grants of privilege, especially those of monopoly or unequal taxation. Government regulation is never up to the task of regulating complex behaviors and the integrity of the regulatory process is always under siege of politicos granting privileges to the vested interests.Government was created by citizens for the benefit of citizens. Government was created to serve the citizens, not the other way round. Persons in government quickly get the idea that citizens are there for the amusement of governmental employees; that they, the governmental employees, are somehow vital or desirable. Most government employees are not. Because government is a monopoly, the citizen has no option to take his or her business elsewhere. So we must create a way for governmental employees to be accountable and easily removed from their desks. Without term and career limits and mechanisms to counter governmental arrogance a petty tyranny quickly develops, especially among civil servants.

> A few governmental employees and their actions are vital, indeed critical; most are nothing but expensive surplus and waste.

## Overview of American Tripartite Government

Since middle school we have been taught that our government is a tripartite government with checks and balances between the three branches, as described in the Constitution. The three branches are the executive branch, the legislative branch and the judicial branch. Generally, the blueprint is the same for all the states. (Pennsylvania has only one house in its legislative branch.)

Some authors suggest there is a difficulty separating subject matter jurisdiction between the three branches. I suggest that any ambiguity is simply the result of executive overreaching, judicial weakness and fuzzy thinking.

Over time a fourth department of government, the *administrative branch,* has evolved. In reality it has become the largest "branch" of our government. It is the one with the most employees. Oddly, nowhere in the Constitution is there described or defined an administrative branch. To search for the pedigree of administration let us look at the three branches or "*departments*" more closely.

## THE LEGISLATURE

To **legislate** means to create laws. In the legislature rests the sole power to create all written laws regarding the conduct of a nation's citizens and businesses whether individuals, associations, partnerships or corporations. Legislators are selected on the basis of unique qualifications defined in the Constitution and, once sworn into office, have a non-delegable duty: to determine and legislate for the general welfare. Legislative powers can not be passed on to others, as no one else has these qualifications, for no one else has won election or been sworn to office and cloaked with the authority of the people to so act. Delegation simply cannot be done by Congress. Here and here alone is the sole power to write laws, to remove laws from the books, (courts may strike a law, but not remove it from the books) and to rewrite laws. Herein rests the power to rewrite executive code and judicial code. The power of the Legislature is limited by the powers granted it by the Constitution. In addition, it cannot pass laws in defiance of the natural laws of man nor legislate morality. It is powerless to simply decree prosperity. It cannot grant economic privileges without incrementally destroying prosperity.

## THE EXECUTIVE BRANCH

In short, the president is "the Boss." He can appoint a Cabinet and other positions and they report to him. The duty of the executive branch is to implement and enforce the laws made by Congress. Like-mindedness, not diversity of opinion, is now introduced. Diversity of political philosophy would simply impede execution. Positions are filled by appointment not election. Cause need not be shown for dismissals. Ratification by Congress is the only check upon the appointees for this branch of government. This branch is streamlined, clearly defined, directed from the top. The president is the Commander in Chief of all military personnel. Military officers answer directly to him. The Executive is always ready for immediate action. There are no "sessions;" the executive branch is always "convened."

There is no two-house structure to the executive office; hence there is no need to build a consensus; no need for a vote, as is needed in Congress. The president needs no vote of approval, and need not even consult his cabinet. There is none of the adversarial system found in the courts. There is little of attorneys briefing and arguing merits of cases. There is no extensive deliberation among many justices; there is no backlog of cases. In contrast, the executive branch acts now, and consequences flow with immediacy, perhaps life or death. The gamut can run from clemency to nuclear war.

It is the president and his appointees who spend the money, diddle budget allocations, exceed the budget and run the government on a day to day basis. He decides which laws should be enforced. He decides who should be prosecuted. The executive branch has the unique power to *indict* citizens for criminal acts, but the president has no power to decide guilt of citizens or to set sentences or fines. The office does have the power of forgiveness, the power to pardon convicted citizens, with the *presidential pardon*. (Clinton "sold" more of them in his last moments of office than any president.) The executive branch has the power to create agendas, set policy and to **suggest** legislation. But the power to create written laws, even administrative code, was not granted by the Constitution. The executive branch has the power to veto legislation. It has no power to tax. The president's decisions and actions are subject to review by the Supreme Court, but that takes time. His actions are subject to review by Congress, but only after the fact. As no peers exist to judge a president, it is the Congress that has the exclusive power to impeach a president.

The ideal executive is quick, decisive, firm, persuasive, authoritative, dignified, a touch reserved, revered, popular, and an excellent delegator of responsibilities. He must be highly organized. A handsome appearance helps.

> Contained within the executive branch is enforcement. And herein rests administration.

## THE JUDICIARY

The purpose of the Judiciary is threefold: to dispense justice, a species of equality; to strike laws that are inconsistent with each other, or are beyond the grant of power of the Constitution; and **most importantly,** to keep each branch of government within the defined limits of the Constitution. This means to maintain the equilibrium of a balanced tripartite government.

The federal judiciary is comprised of a Supreme Court and such other courts as Congress creates. The judiciary decides how written laws fit together; how they are prioritized (constitution, statutes, code), and how apparent ambiguities are to be resolved, if they can be resolved. Where two laws appear to conflict, the court may decide to apply one law over the other. The **separation of powers doctrine** means the court has no power to rewrite bad legislation. Courts can simply strike a law, thereby sending it back to the legislature. Courts can decide the executive or the legislature have exceeded a constitutional grant of power and, on that basis, strike a law from the books.

Courts decide how human behavior, generally past acts, is to be affected by written laws. They also have powers to decide how a citizen or citizens must act in the future. But they only do this in a specific instance, and only in a case-by-case basis. They are not philosophers speculating on the future. They have no duty to answer hypothetical questions on future relationships. They rarely can be induced to issue advisory decisions. Courts can be assisted in deciding factual issues by juries of citizens that may be called to issue **verdicts**. Courts may decide there is insufficient evidence to convene a jury and throw a case out of court. If the court finds that sufficient evidence exists, it will rule the case to be tried before a jury or possibly to be tried to the court (without a jury). After a jury trial the court may *overrule* the verdict with its **decisions**, which gives the aggrieved party a right to retry the case before another jury; or the court may affirm the jury verdict with a *final judgment* of that court. Reasons for retrial might be misconduct of attorneys resulting in a mistrial, or simply a rogue jury, one that disregarded the court's instructions. Each step depends upon the evidence presented to the court, according to specific rules. In appellate superior courts there is no jury and these courts are bound to the record of the trial court. If there is not found to be sufficient evidence of sufficient quality in the trial record, the appellate court will probably overturn a judgment of a lesser court and likely send it back for retrial.

Courts decide the punishments, fines, forfeitures or special declarations that are appropriate for the cases that are brought before them. Courts may decide civil damages where the right to a jury trial has been waived. In such (non-jury) cases the courts publish written decisions, which in major cases include a description of the factual history of the case, the *finding of fact*, and also contain a *conclusion of laws*, or what the court found as the laws applicable to the case. Finally, the court will order a *judgment*, based upon findings and conclusions. Courts also have the power to review decisions of lesser courts and tribunals.

A court has no duty to correct every wrong. The federal Supreme Court need not hear every case petitioned to it. Cases of substance, with issues of national importance may be accepted and decided or "tactically overlooked" as perhaps "not yet ripe" for decision. The Supreme Court acts with great deliberation. Acceptance to its calendar takes years. Briefing usually adds about a year. The Supreme Court is the most deliberate in its decision-making; decisions after arguments usually take at least a year. But the court can act with expediency by one of several *special writs*.

Judges are quite different from other public servants. Judges are supposed to have special education, training, experience and mental abilities to perceive and distinguish relationships and alternatives, and the critical mental faculty of discernment, especially in regard to the practical affairs of life. In fact, most judges and justices do have these qualities. The ideal judge is usually very serious, highly intelligent, deliberate, very considerate, reserved, somewhat aloof and highly educated. Customarily, judges at all levels possess a doctorate in law. Generally they elect to sequester themselves somewhat from society in order to retain impartiality. Supreme Court justices are appointed for life or until they alone decide they have lost the capacity to serve. Hence they are insulated from most political pressures.

Supreme Court justices realize that their word on an issue of law is final unless they, at a later time, in another case, choose to change their minds. Stability of law is necessary for predictability. Predictability is necessary for order. Citizens need predictability to guide their personal activities and business decisions.

But change is sometimes necessary. It is usually desirable that change is gradual so as not to create disorder. Hence changes of law are usually done by making a distinction in a later similar case, to preserve continuity.

Justices realize that they are the last safeguard before chaos, disorder and citizens' revolt, which could be peaceful or otherwise. Overreaction and the resulting chaos could be far more disruptive in our highly integrated and interdependent society than revolutions of the past.

Limitations on judicial power do exist. The doctrine of *separation of powers* means that the Supreme Court is extremely reluctant to review the acts of legislators. The posture the court takes is this: if you are displeased with the actions of a legislator, your remedy is at the polls. Vote the person out of office. Unfortunately the power of incumbency, fueled by campaign contributions and the huge *war chests* of unused funds we see today, was not foreseen by the Founding Fathers. They could not have imagined that these things make the "remedy" of voting out of office virtually unavailable to today's voters.

Courts do not pass judgment on most election activities. In every election there is something to challenge. It simply would not do to have every election followed by a year or two of trials to see if each candidate won his or her seat "fair and square." Courts are reluctant to empower a jury to undo an election result, and they are reluctant to substitute a court judgment for an election result. Once you are sworn into office, you are in. At this point politicians are entitled to a trial by their new peers. The Constitution is clear that the jury judging legislators should be of peers (Article I, Sec. 3). The power of impeachment lies in the Senate alone.

But some court review of the election process is necessary and inevitable. This was brought to the Supreme Court's attention in its review of the McCain-Feingold Act. It caused a **dramatic change in standards of review** in the federal election process, implicitly admitting that *free speech is a relative right*, not an absolute one, and that a showing of *quid pro quo* bribery is no longer necessary.

The McCain-Feingold review by the U.S. Supreme Court was a most dramatic decision that did not consider the traditional freedom of speech and freedom of assembly arguments, as demonstrated in *McConnell v. Federal Election Commission* (2003).

The courts have no power to write laws. The underlying policy is that if they had power to write a law, there would be no branch of government to make an impartial review of that law. Courts might have such pride of authorship that meaningful review of the law would be lost.

Courts don't decide who should be a party to court action, but may decide who should not be a party. Courts cannot bring a party into an action. However, they have the power to dismiss someone from an action. They can't join a party to a proceeding (make them a defendant) but they can summon someone to testify in a proceeding. Except for contempt proceedings, they have no power to decide why someone must appear in court. Courts may recommend prosecution to the executive branch, but they cannot initiate prosecution. They may decide factual issues, where the right to a jury trial has not been preserved. The judiciary is empowered to make decisions that determine the issues in a dispute; which are relevant, what facts or factors are not. In *civil* proceedings courts have the power to make judgments (based upon a jury verdict) and enforce them, and to award monetary damages in civil suits. In *criminal* proceedings a court may fine parties, or impose a jail sentence, or both.

**Judicial review** presumes a *tabula rasa* or clean slate. A third party, not the legislator, not the defendant, but a judge must decide: Did the law say what the scrivener meant to say? Is it written in such a way that a third party would understand it? Is the intended meaning given primacy or hidden in complex verbiage? Is the law written in a clear and unambiguous manner? Courts do not pass on whether or not the wording of the law is appropriate for the intent stated in a preamble. Choice of statutory wording is exclusively a legislative function.

Courts do not pass judgments on public policy. They feel that is exclusively a function of the legislature. They carefully avoid political questions: such as, is this a "just war?" Courts don't pass judgment on spending or budget. Nor do they pass on whether a policy is sound policy. That is an exclusive legislative function.

Courts seem extremely reluctant to pass judgment as to whether or not a bit of legislation is a power actually granted by the Constitution. Examples are subsidies and exemptions for privileged parties from taxation. Courts are reluctant to invade the province of the legislature. Theirs is the power of the *pen,* as a final judgment is indelible. Unfortunately justices show undue deference to findings of administrative law judges. Clearly none whatsoever should be shown, as any such act is *ultra vires,* or beyond the power granted to the executive branch in the Constitution. The failure to limit the expansion of powers of the executive branch has led to the failure of meaningful checks and balances, so carefully crafted by our Founding Fathers.

## THE ADMINISTRATION

A tripartite government was the wish of the Founding Fathers. The present reality is quite different. Our government is not tripartite. We have four branches. The executive branch, primarily in the person of Franklin Delano Roosevelt, spawned innumerable agencies to administer various projects. Currently administrative agencies have far more employees than the other three branches of government. And, curiously, they have assumed many powers of the legislative and judicial branches.

The history of modern administration begins in China, where the foundations of meritocracy-based civil service are found. The Latin roots of the word *administer* are, *ad*, meaning motion towards, and *ministare*, meaning to be an aid to, or to serve, a servant. The meaning of *ministerial* is more helpful: it designates a mandatory act or duty on the part of the government agent that requires no personal discretion or judgment in its performance. Thus administrators are agents of the executive, without decision-making capacity or the need to make discretionary choices. Their universe is a simple one: receive the money, collect the toll, issue the license, permit entry to the museum or allow boarding the train. Just do the job. There is no screening to see if the applicant is properly suited. Before them, all are equal. The goal should be efficiency. Service should be expedited, helpful, non political, and without agendas. They are the servants of the citizen. This area of government should be "user friendly."

Modern government has perverted the meaning of *ministerial.* Discretionary decision-making does not go with administration. When administrators start interpreting rules, troubles begin. This guy looks suspicious. This guy may be a terrorist. This guy is acting strange, should I detain him? When thinking is required, we have passed from administration to regulation, enforcement, prosecution or adjudication. Administration is none of these. The worst governmental abuses arise when administrators assume the right and power to draft laws or administrative code, or adjudicate such laws.

We are led to ask: why do we need so much administration? Is this in the general welfare or simply machinery to create privileges for politicians to sell?

# Chapter 4

# The Purpose of Government

The purpose of government is to create justice and national prosperity. Is our present government a sustainable one?

Recall the purpose for government, according to John Locke, was to create personal and national prosperity for the citizens by creating life, liberty, pursuit of indolence and the definition and protection of personal property. He then spelled out citizen's expectations for the performance in courts of law.

Justice was simply defined by Aristotle as *"a species of equality."* Here in American courts of law, none are slaves, and all are citizens, and we have adopted that principle universally. In most courts, on a wall directly behind the judge can be found a dramatic drawing of the lady of justice: balance scale in one hand, the sword, pointing down in the other hand, and a blindfold covering her eyes.

The formula for national prosperity was discovered in Athenian history: the maximum opportunity for the maximum number of citizens.

## Prosperity Theory

Prosperity has a different meaning for persons than for a society. A prosperous society is *flourishing, thriving, successful or has good fortune* (*Random House Unabridged Dictionary*). It has good future prospects. For a person, prosperity means those attributes and more, such as liberty to choose lifestyle and religion. Personal prosperity could be the luck to have good health or business success.

National prosperity depends upon national wealth. It is in part defined by property. The value of property is societal. Two examples: A chest of gold, held by an individual stranded on a deserted island, has no value unless it is taken to a society. The value of the gold depends upon the attitude of social members, that is, what they are willing to do for a bit of gold. The stranded man has no society with whom to interact. The gold might just as well be lead. Or, a large and valuable landholding in the middle of social disorder, for example the Reign of Terror in the French Revolution, would be worth little. There would be no one to work your land and your holdings would soon be confiscated. Indeed, it would be worth less than nothing, as that land might well cost you your life.

### Sound government gives property value.

If possessions are not defended by strong laws, and, more importantly, supported by strong social values that respect the value of persons and property, their value is diminished. Property value is in part related to the values and culture of a society. Work ethic is not created by legislation, nor is respect for property rights. Too many inequities of wealth caused by granted privileges inevitably result in gross disparities that can degrade or destroy the stability of the economy or the nation as a whole.

Poor financial policies generally are the cause of loss of future prosperity. They are usually masked by **fiscal illusions** until abrupt economic changes throw the economy into a deflationary spiral, causing property deflation, exaggerated loss of public confidence, an overreaction in savings, a slowing in the velocity of transactions, a vortex of job losses, economic contraction, further asset deflation, hoarding of specie, further layoffs, and so on. Usually political devices meant to check irresponsible business policies aggravate the decline.

Prosperity is a relative state. It is judged by the relative wealth of other nations. It is also relative with respect to time. The poorest economies of today would have looked prosperous to Egyptian peasants at the time of the building of the pyramids.

Some nations encourage prosperity; others seem to assume prosperity to be indestructible, a constant or perpetual state — once achieved, it will persist. History clearly teaches us the opposite. History is the story of nations rising, then declining. Prosperity is, for any given economy, quite ephemeral, even fickle.

Economists are at a loss to agree on a definition for prosperity. They seem to want mathematical formulas for prosperity. Clearly there are too many subjective variables for that to happen.

> The formula for prosperity is the maximum economic opportunity for the most citizens in any nation.

## Examples of Prosperity

Examples of prosperity for the common citizen are rare. It seems to be a phenomenon of the European peninsula. Before the Dark Ages, aside from the Greek city-states and Rome, there was no recorded prosperity for the common man. There were rich empires perhaps, but there was hardship for all but the upper classes. The golden age of Athens was noted earlier. There were periods of prosperity for Roman citizens from time to time. In the Dark Ages there was brief prosperity for some French, in the Carolingian Renaissance, 775–900 AD. There was usually prosperity for the Vatican. There was some prosperity for the Hanseatic League (1159 to the late 1400s), an allied string of "free" cities along the shores of the Baltic Sea, until it was eclipsed by the development of nationalistic states.

The Renaissance brought some individuals prosperity at the time of the city-states of Italy, as evidenced by Giovanni de Medici's introduction of double-entry bookkeeping into the Medici bank in the 1200s. When Luca Pacioli (1445–1515) wrote his book on mathematics, he spent time explaining the benefits of double-entry bookkeeping. This was strong evidence of the sophistication and wealth of the Italian city-states, especially Venice and Florence. Indeed, as the Dark Ages ended, south and central Italy enjoyed prosperity. In the late 1400s, the Fugger banking family was lending substantial sums to kings and popes and moving papal revenue to the Vatican, a booming and prosperous business. In 1519, Jacob Fugger lent over 4,000 pounds of gold to Charles V to secure his election as Holy Roman Emperor of Germany. But most of Europe, trapped in feudalism, was not blessed with prosperity.

England, Switzerland, the United States and the tiger economies of Asia have had moments of prosperity. But most of history does not show prosperity for the common man throughout most of the world. We do know that prosperity cannot be simply legislated into existence. We know when it comes, it appears rather slowly, over generations, as surplus wealth accrues. We have seen that prosperity comes from extending opportunities to the greatest portion of society. We have seen it with the Greek city-states, with England and with the United States of America. We have seen governments and empires quickly fade, usually as a result of financial mismanagement: grants of economic privileges. When prosperity fades it usually goes very quickly and often disappears dramatically, with many personal catastrophic consequences. We know economists are poor at distinguishing between real prosperity and the fiscal illusion of prosperity. They are better at measuring the depth of a depression, than forecasting one. We know that prosperity is cultural. We know it takes time to develop prosperity.

## Prosperity for England, Yet Not for France

**Politicians** seem the worst persons for understanding and promoting prosperity. Modern liberal thinking espouses the idea that grants of privilege and regulation are appropriate to grow prosperity. How does that square with historical examples of prosperity? **Economists** have no satisfactory explanation as to why England had prosperity and France, 23 miles away, did not. Clearly the French citizens obtained land and property and opportunity abruptly as a result of the French Revolution and the reign of Terror. They received a *tabula rasa* (completely blank slate) for new government, for the prior monarchy and all the politically compromised had been swept away.

This was like no time in French history, for this was not done by a tyrant who seized the reigns of government. The French had before them the American example. They also had the English example closer to home. Why, then, did they turn to Napoleon Bonaparte, a dictator, just 23 years after their revolution?

The major reasons for the difference in the evolution of prosperity in France and Britain were **historical, cultural** and **ideological.** Originally in both countries the source of wealth was farming. The income of nobility was leveraged by large estates worked by serfs (virtual slaves) tied to landholdings. This is to say the serfs came with the land. Manufacture was limited and primordial, and trades were virtually nonexistent on feudal manors. In Europe there was chronic economic depression. There was insufficient demand for specialization and mass production to evolve.

In both countries, serfs eventually escaped from the land and settled in villages. Income was derived from day labor and land or building rents, manufacture and from primitive business organization. Sales, marketing and advertising had not yet been contrived. Specialized trades began to evolve. Mobile populations were exempt from census and taxation. There was now opportunity to accrue wealth.

British history was markedly different from that of France. The fierce Anglo-Saxon independent spirit was never subjugated. The new king in 1066, William the Conqueror (French though he was), never conquered his English nobility. Only 150 years later, in 1215, the English nobility got the king to acknowledge their rights and powers. Their tenacity was evidenced by the fact that the *Magna Carta* was renegotiated in 1216, 1217, and 1225, with the powers of the nobility expanding each time, never allowing the gains to slip through their fingers.

> There is a strong correlation between liberty and prosperity.

Revenue from corporate charters caused the English Crown to grant many international trade corporations, beginning as early as 1390 (as described in Chapter 8). These corporations rapidly proliferated. And Henry the VIII took England from under the Roman Catholic Church, financially and otherwise. The strong English spirit led to rapid growth of villages into cities. There was opportunity for specialization of labor and manufacture for blacksmiths, gunsmiths, tinsmiths, silversmiths, wheelwrights and so on; often sons followed fathers in specialized trades. Stubborn independence and a bit of wealth led merchants to buy more extensive burgages from the English crown; northeast England became a land of boroughs, a land of special trade zones. (Recall that *burgage* is a French term and innovation, yet it seemed no longer to be practiced in France.)

With the scarcity of money, English trade fairs were run largely on the basis of barter or mobile banking. The lack of surplus wealth (or capital) had been a heavy impediment to growth of manufacture and had severely limited trade possibilities. Surplus cash needed to be held safely, as the purse and dagger afforded only so much security. Banks were needed for security of savings. Rare surpluses of money were hoarded in those banks as long-term savings accounts. Fractional reserve banking evolved. A banking industry began to flourish. In 1545 Henry allowed **usury**, or interest charged for the use of money, a practice prohibited by the Catholic Church.

Charging interest meant that now money could be earned without labor. This led to accumulation of capital that in turn led to a dramatic growth of banking houses. This made more capital available for small businesses. The earning power of entrepreneurs could be leveraged by employee labor, as serfs had done for land barons. This led to more surplus wealth which led to bigger banking houses, better capitalization of manufacture, export businesses and profits. This spurred the development of new British businesses, such as insurance (Lloyds of London) and finance. English businessmen were on the way to amassing personal surplus wealth. With wealth some could afford more risky and often profitable foreign trade ventures. This is the time in which the East India Company was born. Although the supply of money and methods of taxation of visible assets remained an acute problem for the government, England had a deeply entrenched culture of business independence.

> There were now new ways to gain wealth, independent of personal labor.

All this had been done before in the Greek and Italian city-states, but England made it a big and lasting business. In England accumulation of surplus wealth allowed refined business practices. Permanent shops for manufacture and sale of goods leading to rudimentary mass production emerged. Manufacturing technology and secret techniques of production evolved. There was little such activity in France. The French were still 200 years behind.

Another reason for the difference in the evolution of prosperity between Britain and France was clearly cultural. Continental Europe was still a group of feudalistic nations. French society was comprised of the monarch, the aristocracy, a small, rudimentary "middle estate" and the rest — the peasantry and riff-raff living hand to mouth. French laws of property rights were primordial. The leaders of the future had been exterminated or neutered by their monarchs for centuries. There was no Protestant work ethic. France was still under the shadow of the powerful Catholic Church, with laws prohibiting usury. Instead vast sums of money went to the tithe, investiture and the building of fabulous cathedrals, often taking generations to complete. This made the French acquisition of capital more difficult. For the French, wealth could only be accumulated from personal labors.

The French had no clearly written code of laws nor access to courts until the Code Civil, now known as the Napoleonic Code (1804). Indeed, Napoleon was reported to have said, *"What will live forever is my civil code."* The French had no history of democracy; they had no bourgeoisie (strong-minded middle class). The French had no experience with capitalism or the free market. The concepts were completely foreign.

Given the choice of work and savings or consumption, the French tended towards elegant consumption. Even today excellent food and stylish clothes seem more important than savings or hard work to the French. Contrast that with the British tolerance for terrible food and unawareness of taste or style in clothing, but legendary frugality and near reverence for savings. While the French kings were absolute and their courts were the height of splendor and opulence, the English kings often had less wealth than some of their nobility. The difference was captured in the literature of the period.

The most important reason was one of philosophy. Remember the British concept of inalienable rights was that of John Locke: life, liberty, pursuit of indolence, and right to acquire estate, while the French inalienable rights were liberty, equality and fraternity. Note carefully where these small differences led. **Adam Smith** captured the British business ethic with his concepts of surplus wealth, surplus stock invested to earn interest, stock (business shares) participating in gain or loss of a business venture, and the notion that accumulation of wealth is a virtue. He also espoused capital, not gold, as the measure of wealth of a nation. The "nation of shopkeepers" later so despised by Adolph Hitler was flourishing.

Smith wrote about property rights, the rights that encouraged individuals to become property owners, to develop their property, to care for it, to use it to generate private wealth; to allocate resources and manufacturing machines for efficient mass production; to strive for market efficiency, for the creation of an equilibrium of all market forces, (by the famous "invisible hand"). The British knew from personal experience of what he was speaking; when he wrote that these forces would elevate the collective standard of living of a society, the British were experiencing just that. The French were distracted by their revolution, by the reign of terror and by Napoleon's coming and going until 1848. Another 75 years had elapsed, and they had yet to start off on the path to prosperity; when they did, they would do it "on the wrong foot."

**Pierre Proudhon** thought and taught that land cannot be held as private property, and that mankind is simply a steward thereof. Therefore title to land is theft and the controlling steward has *no moral right* to charge any citizen for the use of natural resources from that land. He taught that wealth held without personal toil was stolen from the laborer who created the wealth. The biggest class of French economic assets at the time was the land. How do you generate private capital from those teachings? Hence there was little industry. French law did not permit real estate to be easily sold or to be capitalized or used and managed efficiently. Nor did the French allow the accumulation of capital by other means, especially charging interest. So the French went the way of **Karl Marx:** labor was the source of all value, capital was state property and had no private value. Private business interests were held in a certain disfavor. In America we followed English property law with strong personal rights as espoused by John Locke. The French ideal led the French, Russians, and others down the path of socialism and communism.

> The principle cause for the delay in French prosperity was the ideological difference between life, liberty and indolence/property, which led to prosperity, and **liberty, equality, fraternity,** which led to socialism.

The key to prosperity is how a government handles opportunity. Grants of privilege to the favored few diminish the opportunities left for the citizens at large. Maximizing prosperity means involving the greatest number of citizens in gainful employment. The first corollary is that **as privileges diminish the opportunities available to the common man, prosperity fades.** Such is the teaching of history.

## Characteristics of Prosperity

Prosperity has not been found without the following:
- Codified laws
- Access to courts

- Fair administration of the laws
- Strong property rights of citizens

**Case study:** Before the case of *Kelso v. City of New London* (2005), the United States had the strongest property laws in the world. In the Kelso case, the city of New London, Connecticut decided to use its powers of eminent domain to condemn a large tract of private properties within its city limits to allow Pfizer Drugs to establish a large research center. Kelso challenged the right of the city to condemn land for private development. The Supreme Court expanded government's power to condemn property and allowed condemnation to proceed. After the condemnation and demolition, and spending some 78 million dollars of city funds, Pfizer decided to develop elsewhere, across the river, in a different tax district. The case was a strong blow diminishing property rights of citizens. Putting so much power in the hands of a few politicians is not a good idea.

Characteristics of prosperity are:

- Sound currency: money as a stable store of value
- Adequate money supply
- Surplus wealth
- Right to invest surplus wealth for interest
- Free market: diverse and competitive and free from government interference
- Entrepreneur risk takers
- Financial rewards to entrepreneurs and workers
- Maximum citizen involvement in farming, industry and business
- Moderate tax schemes
- Strong work ethic
- Industrious population: high per capita productivity
- Marked differences in wealth of persons within a society
- Many players in each market: no monopoly
- Opportunity widely extended to the citizens (few privileges)

## Causes of Prosperity

Economists are at a loss to explain how prosperity is caused or even to identify the important factors that lead to prosperity. The key to causing prosperity is how a government handles opportunity. Grants of privilege to the favored few diminish the opportunities left for the citizens at large. Maximizing prosperity means involving the greatest number of citizens in gainful employment.

**GENERAL RULE ONE:** A SOCIETY IS PROSPEROUS WHEN THE GREATEST NUMBER OF ITS CITIZENS IS EMPOWERED BY MEANINGFUL ECONOMIC OPPORTUNITY.

Nothing motivates like the opportunity to do something meaningful. Providing opportunity to the citizenry does not include letting big business dominate the shelf space in stores or letting monopolistic companies crush small brands with extravagant advertising campaigns; does not allow agribusiness to dominate the agricultural marketplace with economies of scale, or to destroy small farmers by dictating low prices for agricultural commodities; does not let them destroy the free market by dictating what will constitute an organic food or by promoting starchy, sugary or oily fast foods as healthy and nutritious foods, simply for the benefit of agribusiness and big food producers.

Opportunity does not permit manipulating stock markets by misrepresenting values of corporate assets and liabilities; does not ignore professionals subtly acting in concert to create "bubbles" of apparent prosperity in sectors of the economy which then burst leaving investors penniless; it does not allow appointing dim witted, clueless regulators in charge of security markets who allow Ponzi schemes to go on for decades; does not allow industries to "self-regulate" or permit them to sell toxic contaminated peanut butters or otherwise tainted food stock; and does not stifle new product development through frivolous claims of extension of patents. Opportunity for the common man is not found in grants of exemption from taxation for certain factions, which leave the smaller competitors to pay all the taxes that somehow become cash subsidies to the larger businesses.

Prosperity comes from spreading opportunity, thus empowering the greatest number of the citizens of a society. **Prosperity is a key ingredient in an enduring government**. The grain riots of the Roman Empire signaled its end. Government does not last long when citizens are hungry.

**GENERAL RULE TWO:** PROSPERITY CANNOT BE SIMPLY LEGISLATED INTO EXISTENCE.

No government has that power. The most a government can do is set the stage for prosperity to flourish. Prosperity is cultural. It takes generations to grow. It must be taught. It must be nurtured. Strong values such as hard work, thrift, delayed gratification, savings, investment, education and professional training are all taught to one generation by prior generations. The foundation of prosperity is substance over beauty, construction of enduring projects and economic stability instead of fast financial gains. Elegant consumers squandering vast sums of money for momentary gratification does not lead to national prosperity.

The key to prosperity is that a large percentage of the citizens "buy into" these core values and spend their time and energy building the bedrock of prosperity. To get this personal commitment there must be the lure of opportunity. This hope of opportunity is necessary at all levels of society. There will never be absolute equality of opportunity, but there must be the hope of a chance for success. What lures people to spend hard-earned dollars at gaming casinos or on lottery tickets? They know the odds of winning the games are rigged against them. They know over time they will lose vast sums of money. It is the hope of winning the big pot.

Again, there will never be equality of opportunity. But hope for opportunity can meet the need. The more realistic the hope, the better for the individual and society.

**GENERAL RULE THREE:** EVERY GRANT OF ECONOMIC PRIVILEGE DIMINISHES THE OPPORTUNITIES FOR THE REST OF SOCIETY.

## What Causes Prosperity to Fade?

Doubtless the most studied decline of prosperity was that of Rome. The decline of Rome coincided with changes in the personality of Roman citizens. Originally a strong sense of civic duty prevailed. Politics and military endeavors were considered desirable occupations. Display of wealth in public was discouraged. One's home could be opulent, so long as the exterior walls appeared plain. Business could be conducted by proxy. It was considered an honor to be asked to contribute a public building or a ship for the navy. These strong civic values deteriorated and laws of privilege became the norm. Periodic land reforms provided momentary stability, but senatorial depravity and debasement of classic virtues won out over time. In the words of Machiavelli, the decline of Rome was due to *"ambition in idleness,"* *"meanness mixed with pride,"* *"desire or riches without industry,"* *"aversion to truth"* and *"contempt of civic duties."* Today, in America we have laws of favoritism and privilege, selective enforcement of laws, tax exemptions for privileged persons, fiscal irresponsibility in government and business, and constantly debased currency. Are we Rome yet?

Historians have long pondered the decline of the Roman Empire. Here are some of their conclusions:

- *Moral decay; loss of civic virtue.* (Gibbons) Privileges do that. Why work for something when you can bribe for it? It is far easier than hard work.
- *Tax abuses.* Bartlett found that requisitioning of assets and onerous taxation caused many farmers to associate with wealthy and tax exempt persons, which he hypothecates led to feudalism (a society of class based on privilege).
- *Surge in decadence.* (Vegetius and Ferrill) Why work and risk hazards of the marketplace when you can bribe politicos and create your market and simply add the price of bribery onto the price you charge? Is this not an example of privileges?
- *Disparities of wealth.* (Richta) Privileges inevitably create such inequalities.

- *Revolution and civil unrest.* (multiple authors)
- *Debasement of currency.* (von Mises) Was this caused by grants of privileges that went beyond the ability of the government to support by taxation?
- *Inflation caused by high taxes.* (multiple authors) Are these not words describing the support of a noncontributing privileged class?
- *Over-governance, or governmental arterial sclerosis; more government than needed; diminished returns on societal* [governmental] *complexity.* (Tainter) He has described the engine required to create and enforce privileges.
- *Stupendous fabric [government]* [of Roman Empire or its society] *yielded to the pressure of its own weight.* (Gibbons) Is this the administrative cost of supporting privileges?
- *Price controls.* (von Mises) Merchants being forced to sell goods below costs of production after the third century led to economic failure. Is this not another disguise of economic privilege pressed by government upon the free market? And was the collapse of Rome not due in part to the realities of market forces overpowering the political wishes and will of government?
- *Arbitrary taxation.* (von Mises) Destroyed the trade, innovation and prosperity of the empire. What part of this is not caused by laws of economic privilege?
- *Huge military spending* (waste of capital). (AHM Jones)
- *Decline in, or of technology.* (Richta) Is this not the same as the concept that privilege drives technology away?
- *Internal warfare depletes economic resources.* (Goldsworthy) Isn't this simply seeking power for the purpose of granting privileges?
- *Economic decline.* (Bury) This is the inevitable consequence of grants of privilege.

The decline of the Roman Empire has been blamed upon everything from lead poisoning from plumbing, to weather and climate change, to conquest by superior or more numerous forces, and to population expanding past the carrying capacity of their environment. In fact, most historians have pointed to what we can now recognize as the grants of privilege as the real fundamental cause of the decline of Roman prosperity.

> One of the most significant lessons of history is that grants of privilege inevitably lead directly to creation of aristocracies, progressive domestic unemployment, declining prosperity and finally social disintegration.

It is possible to grant so many privileges that there is little opportunity left for the masses to support themselves by legal means. Privileges granted in the U.S. have resulted in middle management and technical support going to India; menial jobs to Bangladesh, China, Mexico, Taiwan, and the Philippines; technical manufacture to Japan, Korea and China; and menial labor, indeed the trades, coming into the United States from Mexico. Our citizens are left to support themselves by illegal means.

> Our government's assumption that it has the right to create and sell privileges can never be in the general welfare.

Such is the most fundamental lesson of history. In the words of *The Federalist Papers*, *"beware of politicians* [or policy makers] ***who have more confidence than they deserve."***

This raises the question of whether our government is sustainable, for grants of privilege are shown to be the cause of decline. It is pointless to ask our politicians this question, for they are certainly imbued with more confidence than they deserve. They are the last to know the reality the citizens face. Make a trip to Washington and judge for yourself.

# Chapter 5

# Tools of Governance

I n this chapter we consider the following "tools" of the branches of government:

## Congress: Laws passed through the legislature
Laws of civil rights, procedure, property and estate
Laws of prohibitions (misdemeanors and crimes)
Laws of regulation (misdemeanors and crimes)
Laws of confiscation (taxation)
Laws of promotion of privileges as meritorious causes
Laws of campaigning and elections (toothless)

## Executive: Policy
Monetary policy: our government policy is inflation
Policy of credit
Policy of investment
Policy of finance
Policy that administration can be fair or effective
Policy that administration of subjective is in general welfare
Policy of incumbency (congruent with laws of campaigning)
Policy of denial of reality (denial, spin, distraction)
Policy of prosecutorial merit (discretion not to prosecute)

Policy of plea bargaining
Policy of paroles
Policy of pardons
Policy of diplomacy: the UBS story

**Judiciary: Doctrines or quasi-doctrines**
Doctrine that legislative functions are delegable
Doctrines of *res judicata* and *stare decisis*
Doctrine of corporate citizenship
Doctrine of corporate sovereignty
Doctrine that money is free speech; freedom of expression
Doctrine that spending is not reviewable in court
Doctrine of administrative sovereignty
Doctrine of caveat emptor
Doctrine of sentencing and restitution

## Legislative Tools: Laws

As previously stated, **laws** can be classified as six types:

- laws of *prohibition* (crimes and misdemeanors)
- laws of *regulation* (crimes and misdemeanors)
- laws of *taking* (taxation)
- laws *granting privilege*, which are usually economic in nature
- laws of *incumbency*
- laws of *civil rights, civil procedure, and property and estates*

The six classes of laws were defined and commented upon in Chapter 2. **Laws of incumbency** or "laws of campaigning" are currently either nonexistent or vague, full of loopholes and/or without legal consequences. Such laws cover methods by which campaign funds are collected, transferred, sequestered and spent, without control or legal limitation or requirements for accounting. We need another class of laws for meaningful regulation of elections, funding and career limits.

As a result of this deficiency in our laws, most elected officials feel no responsibility to account for the huge sums of money given to them. Any accounting and auditing is done by persons employed by them. There is no definition of how campaign funds may be spent or when they are to be subject to income tax upon the politician who receives them. Campaign war chests are allowed to accumulate until forgotten, then used as personal property. How is that different from a bribe?

As a whole, campaign laws are so deficient, they are hardly meaningful laws at all. Policing elections has morphed into executive policy. Rarely indeed is an elected official indicted. Laws regarding elections are nothing but laws of assuring incumbency. We need changes, as proposed in Chapter 6.

Laws of **civil rights, civil procedure, and property and estates** deserve special mention. Property and estates are the means of life, and the pursuit of indolence and leisure. Property laws in America used to be the strongest in the world, but by grants of privilege government has diluted or weakened citizens' rights by expanding the law of eminent domain and by irresponsible government spending that creates present and future tax burdens that will make property, especially your home, difficult to own. This is also true with laws of money. These laws are destroying the ability of our money to act as a store of value.

Laws give money its value, because it no longer has inherent value like gold and silver. Today its value is based on the force of law (legal tender: must be accepted for debt). Much of the blame for the loss of value of money can be laid at the feet of Congress, for it allocates without regard to its ability to tax; it simply prints money. But most of the responsibility for the loss in value of money must be laid at the feet of the president in office at the time. The executive branch does the spending. And it is policy, for the president controls by enforcement of laws what will occur; that is, what is permitted, and what behavior is prohibited in the business world. Thus it is that the president has defined what we mean by the word **money.** This book reveals a policy of privileges.

## The Definition of Money and Where Economists Go Wrong

**Money:** once its value was obvious. The value of pure gold, once its luster is seen, is obvious to any holder. By contrast, ask a modern economist to define money and you get a series of lectures. Economists have invented at least four kinds of money supply: M0, M1, M2, and M3. Shades of Copernicus! Money should be like pregnancy: it is, or it is not. Economists are simply conspiring with politicians to undermine the concept of money (a store of value) and property value. Instead of basing their advice upon real money (adjusted for inflation), they pander to politicians and deceive us about the nature and amount of inflation in our economy. We should base our income tax code upon real income — that which is adjusted for inflation.

When economists talk together about the **money supply,** they seem to bob their heads in agreement. The rest of us are left scratching our heads. The multiple definitions of money call into question the economist's understanding of reality. There is only one reality. Why do economists need four of them? Clearly philosophy, psychology and politics have affected the economists' notion of the money supply. It seems that economists have no realistic understanding about money, economics and prosperity.

Let us adopt a practical, working definition of money. **Money is simply defined as something a person will take to settle a debt or to perform a service or to deliver a good. It is fundamental to day-to-day motivation. It is the basis for one's future planning and budgeting. It is the essence of prosperity.**

## The Five Stages in the Development of Modern Money

There have been **five stages in the evolution of money**. We will ignore seashells, grain, livestock and the like and begin with specie and **coin**— the *first* stage of money. Next came **fiat** money, that stuff printed by governments. The *third* stage of money was the evolution of **personal bank checks**. The *fourth* stage of money was **plastic or digital**

**money**. The *fifth* stage of monetary development was **"other sorts"** created by businessmen, to be discussed.

### Why has money become complicated and how does this complexity relate to grants of privilege?

Problems with coinage were quantification, denomination, fractionalization, transportation and storage. But the earliest problem with coin was that the amount of money available was too small for commerce to develop. In the Dark Ages, nobility constantly complained that rents were paid in livestock or grain, not coins. Commodities and livestock were perishable and expensive to maintain on a daily basis and costly to transport. Food commodities were a poor store of value, always subject to deterioration. Hence it was that taxes to landlords could not be paid in livestock or commodities. Payment of the debts to landlords demanded coins. The "rub" was that for the peasantry, livestock was comparatively plentiful and coin was extremely rare. Too much bullion was shipped off to Rome in payment of "the tenth" or tithe. Economic development was strangled. Europe was mired in economic depression.

With the *second* stage of money, **fiat money,** governments struck coins of baser metals. They were workable in the local economy, which might have confidence in the local government or empire of the time, but such coin was less acceptable in international trade. There, what mattered most was the quantity of bullion in the coin, rather than the face that appeared on the coin. Money-changers supplied the important function of keeping track of relative values of various coins, but at great expense. Variables included the amount of gold or silver, and the amount of metal removed by wear and tear or even maliciously filed away by unscrupulous traders.

In time fiat money came to be printed by governments on paper or fabric. Eventually laws evolved making such money *legal tender*. This means it must be accepted in satisfaction of debt. So long as government retained its monopoly on the issue of money, it had a valuable tool to control our fate: **monetary policy**. On one hand a government might choose "tight" money for a stable currency to support property values, especially mortgages, against ruinous, destabilizing and destructive inflation. On the other hand it might wish a "freer" monetary policy or to inflate its currency in hopes of creating more transactions and more prosperous levels of trade.

> With **fiat** money came the ability of government to defraud its citizens with **monetary policy**, supposedly for the common good of its citizens.

Conservative or moneyed classes (the minority) preferred "scarce" money in hopes of preserving the value of their accrued assets, especially long-term debts, such as mortgages, and other intangible advantages inordinate wealth might bring. The majority preferred to pay off their debts with cheaper (inflated) money. But, so long as government held a monopoly on the issuance of money, it had a fiscal tool.

A practice developed where many a commercial transaction was finalized in person, before a trusted banker, who kept books of account. Money never changed hands. Often both parties initialed each transaction in the ledger. Occasionally coins would settle account balances. At medieval trade fairs, bankers with their books of account simply went to the fair: they were **mobile bankers**. Accounts were settled at the fair's end or held on account until the next fair. The third stage of money was evolving.

As towns grew and the newly emerging middle class developed, there was a need to store wealth or money in safety. Bankers happily accepted deposits. Specie deposits might sit dormant in a bank vault. Bankers quickly realized money on account was saved for a rainy day and a rather large portion of it could be lent out at interest, with minimal risk to their bank. So long as there was no simultaneous demand for those deposits (a "run" on the bank) all was well. This was the birth of **fractional reserve banking.** This led to laws regulating the fraction of deposits that must be held as safe assets (now thought to be Treasury Bills) that a bank had to keep in reserve.

The concept of fractional reserve banking led to a second impact on the amount of currency in circulation. Money was transformed from stagnant deposits to fast moving commercial transactions. This became known as the "**velocity**" of transactions. It was not that bankers actually printed money, but they could increase the number of transactions in which the money was used in any time period.

Both of these concepts, fractional reserve banking and velocity, increased the money supply. No new dollars, but there was the appearance of more money, because it was used frequently. This was observed to have wonderful effects on economies, for looser money increased trade, business and apparent prosperity.

## The Leverage of Fractional Reserve

Now was the time when bankers had an important role in determining the amount of money in an economy. Bankers were the humorless types who wore their three piece suits all the time, even into the shower, and would only lend money to those who could prove that they did not need it. At that time the Federal Reserve requirement of ten percent of deposits in T-bills, and limitations on loans (not to exceed ten times savings account deposits) had a somewhat effective role in controlling the money supply. The issuance of money was also rather controlled; finance and financial shenanigans were unsophisticated and infrequently encountered. Overenthusiastic or crooked bankers and dips in the business cycles did cause occasional bank failures, but the classical theory of money supply and transactions worked rather well.

The stingy bankers were reluctant to expand the money supply, for to inflate the supply of money would depreciate the notes and mortgages they held in their banks.

Again, the conservatives (the haves) prefer tight money. The business types and the great masses of humanity would prefer to have their debts paid off in cheaper money.

Let us see what the privileges granted to bankers have turned into today. Suppose a bank with fractional reserve banking rights induces citizens to make deposits in savings accounts or certificates of deposit of one million dollars. These deposits can lead to reserves. A fractional reserve requirement of ten percent means the bank must hold 10 percent or $100,000 of these deposits in "ultra safe" United States T-bills. The bank is then free to make $9 million in loans. (This is ten times the remaining $900,000 of deposits.) Assume it pays two percent interest on savings and charges six percent interest on its loans. What is its gross return on the one million dollars? Its potential earnings are not four percent (the spread) but 36 percent, because of the leverage of nine times; from 1 million to 9 million.

But why be satisfied with a mere 36 percent annual gross return? A bank can securitize these mortgages, that is, make mortgage-backed securities to sell on the stock markets. Spend $400,000 of your $9 million on securitization fees to the lawyers, and pay ten percent to your in-house sales team ($860,000), and you can make $7,740,000 profit and still have the $100,000 in T-bills. You should be able to turn this in less than one year. With profits like this, how can banks get in trouble? Why on earth do they ever need bailouts? How much are they paying officers and directors (and our politicians)? Just how big are those salaries and bonuses anyhow?

> With fractional reserve banking, the government still had loose control over the money supply.

An increase in money supply came about with the widespread acceptance of the **personal or corporate check** issued by private parties against money held on deposit in banks. The banker no longer need be present to witness each transaction. Parties to a transaction need not make simultaneous trips to the bank. There has now been an unnoticed change; the money supply has directly and dramatically increased, for checks are used as money. Not legal tender, for a merchant can say "no thanks," but certainly something that is used to settle many, indeed most transactions. There were limitations, for personal checks have less acceptance the farther from home one gets. Merchants tend to accept only local checks. (Today the evolution of electronic check validation gives high levels of protection to merchants near and far.) But the system worked in its own clumsy fashion.

To address geographic limitations and the risk of bad checks, businessmen created the *fourth* stage of money: **plastic/digital currency**. This development changes all the classic rules about money and money supply. First, it is not created by government; it is created by businessmen. Government has not imposed a limitation on the amount of credit a company can extend. Banks have strictly defined reserves. Credit card companies need only estimate their future losses. They are free to expand the supply of plastic/digital money as they wish. With this development our government's control of the money supply is entirely gone. That control is now in the hands of business. How will that ever be in the general welfare?

> Digital/plastic money has no reserve requirement. At this moment in time, the federal government lost control of the money supply and the integrity of currency was no longer in government hands, but in the hands of businessmen, to their advantage. This was not in the common good.

This has become important because there are more credit transactions than there are transactions using currency or checks.

> With electronic transfer of funds, the **velocity theory** is basically irrelevant. Transfer of funds can be nearly instantaneous.

Money is now encrypted in digital form. This destroys or degrades **transparency** and **accountability** for *many* transactions. The paradox is that on the personal side of things transactions appear on monthly statements arranged by subject in great detail. Merchant transactions seem more transparent, yet, at the highest levels, transparency is there only for those privy to arcane codes. Who but the insiders know what these codes mean and what transactions those are? Hence government and private audits become far more problematical. For example, commonplace computer glitches or software glitches can make a transaction or a series of transactions disappear. Audit trails are known only to a few. Where is the paper trail? Indeed the paper trail becomes secondary evidence, dependent on digital records.

> Digital money makes audits problematical and places tracing of transactions with the enlightened few.

If a trial involves financial records, proof of financial irregularities has become very difficult for the attorney. Convincing a jury without the "smoking gun" is nearly impossible. Financial proofs are now less likely to be followed by a jury. They like to see a copy of a check before they are satisfied and convict. Prosecution of financial irregularities becomes almost impossible or unenforceable. White collar crimes always seem to be prosecuted with minimal jail time and token restitution. Will this trend not accelerate?

> Businessmen are now able to run the supply and distribution of currency according to their private wishes, which are not consistent with the general welfare.

Currency policy and **monetary policies** of governments are now entirely out the window. Before, one country might choose to inflate its way out of a problem. Another might prefer stable currency to keep fostering long-term prosperity within its borders. Electronic money now crosses borders invisibly. Currency limitations at the customs office or national borders no longer work. They have become meaningless. One can simply transfer money electronically, across any border. Individuals, businesses and currency speculators are quite free to undermine government monetary policies.

> With the loss of control of the money supply, monetary policy has gone out the window.

The fifth stage in the development of money is **"other"** forms created by businessmen. The modern business types invented more legal ways to make "more money." Not counterfeit, but legal substitutes for legal tender. They started modestly with Green Stamps and the like. Next came the *monetization* of hard assets, like your home. Homes are the most valuable single asset of most people. They have great value and add stability to the economy in downturns or as retirement nears. The MBA types designed **home equity loans**, which mean that the equity portion of the $25 billion in residential value in the U.S. can be easily accessed by credit cards. That makes home equity very much like cash. Now home equity (or savings) can be wasted on consumer goods, which drop 40 to 50 percent in value just leaving the store and soon become rummage or landfill. The stabilizing effect of home equity is lost. And when the downturns occur, loss in the value of homes becomes greatly magnified (reverse leverage) as many other homes are dumped on the market and the pool of equity that used to be in homes is found to be gone.

Financiers have even learned how to monetize the spending habits of our citizens: with frequent-flier miles. When discussing the money supply, economists do not count any of the $800 billion in frequent-flier miles, as of the year 2005, reported in 2009 to be as high as $17-20 trillion, some of which is now redeemable for cash. Why is this not counted as money? Nor have economists picked up on the huge recent deflation that has occurred when the redeemable value of frequent-flier miles was cut by half. Customers felt they were getting something for nothing, even tax free; when they suddenly started getting only half as much for nothing, nothing much was said.

> We now have more frequent-flier miles than there are U.S. dollars in circulation.

## The Sixth Stage of Money: Carbon Credits

We are on the cusp of the development of a sixth stage of money: **the carbon credit.** There are two ways this new form of currency might develop. Periodically the credits, rather like rationing coupons, might be distributed evenly among the citizens or they might be allocated to both *citizens and corporations* based upon existing usage of carbon or earned by some scheme devised by politicians inspired by policy wonks.

Because the environment is in the public domain, certainly not owned by anyone and to be enjoyed by all equally, it would seem obvious that credits that allow the degradation of air quality should be allocated in a strictly democratic fashion. But this book shows this is hardly the way the political mind works; it thinks of selling privileges and of campaign contributions. Thus, politicians want only to allocate credits for carbon use to corporations, not to citizens. Carbon credits should be allocated only among the tax paying citizens of our nation. Foreign corporations are not citizens. Domestic corporations at best are quasi citizens (to be discussed later) and do not behave in a citizen-like manner.

With a democratic carbon credit scheme, the less well off will have the ability to raise personal revenue by sale of energy credits they cannot afford to use. The more wealthy will have to purchase energy credits to squander on energy consuming pursuits. The businesses and pastimes that are the most profligate in energy consumption (cruise ships and airlines) will have to rethink business models. Conservation of energy will then begin in earnest.

In the democratic carbon credit scheme, all goods would have a cash price and in addition a carbon credit price. Unused credits owned by citizens could be sold for cash. A new car price might be $25,000 plus 25,000 carbon credits. A can of beans might be 99¢ and one carbon credit. The refrigerator might be $1,500 plus 1,500 carbon credits, depending upon the energy expenditures of the manufacturing process.

In a second carbon credit method, allocation is made only to corporations and will result in a hodgepodge of privileges, exceptions, exemptions and unfathomable schemes similar to our present federal tax code. It would reward big users, thus penalizing competing industries that have paid money to make themselves "green." The big energy wasters would be handsomely rewarded with millions of dollars in carbon credits, and the forward thinking energy conservers of today would be penalized. For example, the few remaining blast furnace operators waste vast amounts of energy and will, under current proposals, receive the bulk of carbon credits for that sector, while the modern steel micro mills perform their work using a fraction of the energy and will receive very few carbon credits.

This would create a new bureaucracy. It would handicap our industries in the international competitive race for prosperity. New terms would be defined and redefined with insidious loopholes and exceptions. There would be government-like bookkeeping: unbalanced budgets and accounting periods that fit political agendas, and the present government approved bookkeeping: back dating and post-dating of allocations based upon bribery, sums of numbers that can't be verified, audits done by political appointees. There would be differential and preferential enforcement, all run by administrative persons overseen by administrative law "judges" with unrecorded and unpublished decisions, which are generally appeal-proof, and include light fines and silly sentencing for transgressions that encourage breaking the law. With our politicians feeling they have the right to grant economic privileges there would be endless exceptions, adjustments, general tinkering and loopholes we cannot imagine. "Emergencies" of all sorts would appear for politicos to solve. Administration would generate endless new costs in time and money: licenses, fees, paperwork and irrelevant compliance demands. Why reward the corporate wastrels? Why create more jobs for politicos which are simply more chances for them to solicit bribes? Why further diminish our liberties by more empowerment of these politicians?

### Why should carbon credits not be divided equally among tax-paying citizens?

Cap and trade (international apportionment of carbon credits) would quickly be the end of the free market. Historically, planned economies were based upon production. Now we would create a planned economy based on the privilege of using energy, as doled out by politicians. We would introduce another layer of administrative expense, delay and political chicanery to each everyday transaction and business decision. Businessmen would have to kowtow to politicians for their every significant business move. Although politicos would be delighted, what good could possibly come of that? Remember that politicians have proven they are not able to comprehend the concept of budget, the reality of living within a budget or the general welfare of our nation. We have only to read our present tax code for proof beyond a reasonable doubt.

If there comes a time that other nations of the world would shackle their economies with some meaningful carbon rationing scheme, then and only then should we employ one here. At that time carbon rationing should be in the democratic style, not some political abomination of economic privilege based upon campaign contributions.

## Conclusion About Money

Returning to money, there are many things that behave like money or that people treat as money that economists simply do not count as money. As the financial types go to work we see the boundaries between assets and money become blurred. The cumulative effect of these various forms of wealth is substantial. These oversights of economists are significant. The consequence is that the advice an economist gives government is worthless. For reality is quite a different animal than what the economist thinks he is viewing. Hence the politician may think he or she is in charge, but, in fact, he or she is not.

Remember that in the introduction to money, economists have invented at least four stages of money supply: M0, M1, M2, and M3. How can you have at least four different kinds of money and have each discussed in the same unit of denomination, the dollar? Why so many kinds of money?

The evolution of money is nothing but a progression of sophistication in grants of privilege. Each new stage of money has created privileges for certain members of society, at the expense of other citizens. Politicos play upon the public assumption that the value of money is constant. As we understand that good government is government without grants of economic privilege, we begin to recognize that all these types of money are simply evidence of bad government.

Note the ***progression of privilege*** and the enrichment of the privileged classes all created by our government. Notice how government, by grants of privilege, has destroyed the heritage of equality that made America. See how these privileges have become more complex and less recognizable. In the following pages we will see how corporate raiders morph into investment banks and then into FDIC-insured banks. We will see politicos create aristocracies of money, politics and education. We will trace the birth of derivatives and how investment banks have modified the simple derivative into more complex forms, and how this has led to the incalculable destruction of the money supply: the life blood of prosperity. Business and bankers have taken over control of the money supply. It is not being used for the general weal. Instead, untold wealth is being siphoned into private accounts, free from taxation and accountability.

The newest form of money, the insidious carbon credit, as government proposes it, will certainly be the undoing of the free market and prosperity as we know it. Liberty has always been understood to be less government intrusion. With the carbon credit as a political tool, the government will control every movement of society that requires using any energy. The government will make Amish of us all.

The U.S. currency is basically a fraud by government on its citizens. Citizens get less for each dollar over time. This is because of inflation. The biggest problem is that politicos let bankers in on the business of coining money. The worst example is the investment banks. We are simply seeing economic privileges granted to big campaign contributors. How are these acts of our politicians serving the general welfare? All grants of economic privilege are simply bad governance.

## Executive Tools: Policy

Now let us turn to **policy**. It is not law, not legislation passed by Congress. It is the prerogative of the executive branch. Policies do not arise from the representative sampling of public needs described by the

Constitution in the definition of the "House of Representation" but are inherent with the executive. Policies spring from the ideas, imagination, visions and perceptions of the president. They have other names such as agendas, programs, missions, mandates, initiatives and the like. Policies include **monetary policy**, policy of **credit,** policy of **investment**, policies of **finance,** policy of the **pretense that there is due process in regulation** (the preposterous notion that subjective behaviour can be regulated for the general welfare), **policies of prosecutorial merit, plea bargains, pardons, policy of incumbency** and the policy of **diplomatic solution** of problems. Finally there is the policy of **denial of reality.**

## Monetary Policy of Our Government Is Inflation

The first tool of the executive is commonly called **monetary policy.** Inflation is said to occur in an economy when the money supply increases faster than the value of the goods, services, intellectual property, personal property and real estate that is created in the same time period. *"In nearly all countries, the control over money supply [paper money and bank deposits] is under the direct or indirect control of the government. Thus important inflation can occur only with the acquiescence or active support of the government."* (EB 1956 Vol. 12 p. 347) This statement is as valid today as it was in 1956. The central issue is: how can money retain its function as a **store of value,** when the government's official policy is one of inflation, or erosion of the value of its fiat currency? When politicos say they are fighting inflation, ask, "Are they?" Are they limiting government spending to revenues they receive in any given year?

> It is a general rule that governments universally rely on some degree of inflation for either economic growth or the appearance of economic growth.

Inflation gives the appearance of healthy growth or prosperity. This appearance usually keeps the populace happy, so long as it does not understand that its income has not increased in **real** (inflation adjusted) terms. This works for the short term, for inflation has simply postponed the day of reckoning. The failure of people to recognize they are not indeed prospering with higher paychecks and apparently higher asset values is *fiscal illusion.*

Government denies inflation exists and also denies the real rate of inflation. They encourage the illusion of delusion about the true extent of inflation. Politicians pretend they have no fault or blame in the cause of inflation. They insinuate that people don't work as hard as they used to, unions demand more for their efforts, business management is greedy and so on. The reality is they are creating more and more money and the supply of money is outstripping the goods and services in the economy.

> Inflation "is under the direct or indirect control of the government." (*ibid.*)


## Inflation Is Misunderstood By Citizens

The **psychology of inflation:** the average citizen is usually pleasantly surprised when some forgotten trinket is, in some chance transaction, found to have a value far greater than when Grandma bought it. The economist would remind them to adjust the price for loss of purchasing power. For example, a 1956 Chevrolet that cost $2,500, stored for 60 years and in pristine condition, sells now for $25,000. The tax basis is $2,500. Most people view the "gain" of $22,500 as "profit" on a shrewd investment. But this is *fiscal illusion.* Did you "profit" in the amount of $22,500? Not in inflation-adjusted dollars. The car may sell for $25,000 in today's dollars, but they are worth only about $2,500 of the 1956 dollars, so, in "real" terms (inflation-adjusted dollars), this is pretty close to the same amount you used to purchase the car originally, yet the government taxes you on $22,500.

People usually don't take this into account. They routinely think the value of the dollar is constant. But dollars do not have constant value. An economist would take some price index into account for evaluation of assets held over a period of years and point out that there is no "real" gain. The Chevrolet is probably worth about what you paid for it in inflation-adjusted dollars, yet the taxman will still want a big piece of the pie for taxation of a "capital gain." In reality, after taxation, you are going "financially backwards," as the money you receive has lost value in real terms.

With recent fluctuations in our depressed economy, we are seeing another dynamic of inflation. Inflation used to be quite even across the board. All sectors, generally speaking, were affected about the same. Now inflation affects the economy unevenly. One sector can inflate, as speculators puff up "value" in that area, while other sectors can be in decline, as various bubbles pop. For example, food prices rise steadily and commercial real estate is in steep decline. Real estate taxes are increasing and residential real estate prices have fallen two thirds or more in some parts of Arizona and Florida. Health insurance prices dramatically climb, while wages fall. Oilmen try to push gasoline prices higher, as speculators push up oil prices, but at the pump the prices fall back. What is the explanation or cause for these inconsistencies?

We are seeing bubbles created by grants of economic privilege that pop as market forces overwhelm their puny political power. We are seeing the momentary loss of free market stability and government attempts to regulate the market with its *thick and clumsy fingers.* We ask ourselves: is the proper role of government to regulate and control the quality and quantity of goods and services and to set the prices? Politicians, enamored of and misdirected by the bribery of campaign finance cannot be counted on to govern in the general welfare, so long as they have the assumed right to grant economic favors and privileges. Their actions are the cause of speculation-based inflation. Their failure to meaningfully prosecute those who flog the marketplace with these illegal grants of privilege must be recognized and blamed for these goings-on.

Some ask: how long can gold continue to climb in value? We have inflation in our domestic economy because we are printing too much money. The value of gold bullion is not really going up; the value of the dollar is going down. This makes the value of gold appear to go up.

The real question becomes: how long will politicians inflate dollars to cause the apparent rise in gold prices? The value of gold will appear to continue to rise until the politicians change their ways. Do you see that happening soon?

> Count on politicians to deny and misrepresent the extent of inflation in every way they can imagine.

Psychology dramatically affects our perception of inflation. The human animal usually undercalculates the effect of inflation on every aspect of the economy and on his or her transacting therein. The active brain uses about 25 percent of the body's energy, even when doing no physical labor, so it takes lots of real energy to keep track of constantly changing prices. In the minds of the people, who are usually on rather fixed or predictable incomes, there is a strong tendency to assume that prices are fixed or constant. It is far easier and takes less mental energy than trying to keep track of constantly changing prices.

> Confronting the actual rate of inflation in our economy is too scary to do. It is probably 25 percent per year.

This is to say, it is difficult to calculate the consumer price index before you shop for a can of beans. It takes enough energy to remember eggs are $1.50 per dozen, that coffee is about $3.00 per pound and that $2.50 is a good price for regular gasoline. But the one-pound cereal box now contains a mere 14 ounces, so add 12.5 percent to the price of the box. And there is a recent trend to shrink the size of packaged goods boxes. The front may be the same size, but the box is not so wide. With too many numbers to keep track of and math skills on the decline, people usually "go numb" trying to remember old prices and calculate new prices. Distracted by "brands" and fancy advertising, coupons and price breaks, they simply pay too much for what is usually a commodity. No longer putting prices on cans or boxes further insulates us from the price increases. We are not reminded that the last can of beans was only 79¢ and now it is 89¢, when we put it on the shelf at home. There is a science to marketing. From this we must conclude that the public attitude towards understanding inflation is either ignorance or denial.

> The amount of inflation in the American economy is difficult to measure or to comprehend or to remember.

## Inflation As Taxation And How It Affects Taxation

Inflation can be viewed as a tax. Let us take the example of those who hoard cash. It is difficult to apply personal property tax or income tax to them. Those who keep money in or under the mattress, under floorboards, in the hollows of walls, or in the freezer (insulated in event of fire) are quite successful at avoiding taxation and explanation of their source of income. But, if inflation washes away ten or twenty percent of the value of such hoards, it is in effect a taxation. There is no administration expense, there are no returns to prepare. It just works automatically. Agents need not investigate or intrude into the castle of citizens. There is no resentment from citizens, for most are completely unaware. A few are slightly aware of the effect and usually underestimate it. Some may challenge the ten to twenty five percent assumptions above, but consider we have roughly $800 billion in currency and, as of December 7, 2009, the Treasury bought approximately $700 billion in nonperforming mortgages (bailout) from lenders and holders not identified, and then made loans of $1.2 trillion to banks. This means the money supply was at least doubled with no corresponding increase in goods or services. How is that not inflation, perhaps the biggest inflation America has seen?

Inflation has other effects on taxation. **Bracket creep** is widely discussed and understood. Although the standard of living has not changed in the last fifty years, the government takes a greater percentage of your earnings because inflation pushes you into higher tax brackets.

**The most important reason politicians love inflation:** it *washes away* national debt. For example, if there is a $12 trillion debt at a fixed rate of interest for a number of years, at an average of about two percent (T-bills) and if the real inflation is seven percent, the government is "making" five percent or $600 billion without effort, administration, expense or people even being aware. At ten percent inflation, the government is making about $960 billion. At 12 percent inflation the gain is $1 trillion, all pretty much unrecognized by the public.

Now consider the impact of inflation on your annual real-estate tax, the primary taxation that supports local government. Taxation rises because your home is supposed to increase in value. But your home value is probably not rising in real terms; it is probably drifting down in real value due to the wear and tear of living there, ultraviolet degradation of roof and siding or paint, and obsolescence of appliances, mechanicals and technological improvements. Local governments count heavily upon inflation to push real estate values, and hence tax revenues, up. They also use devices such as zoning to keep real estate in tight supply to ratchet up property taxation. Many municipalities have attempted to fund pension liabilities, all or in part, by buying derivatives, on advice of fund managers. At present nothing is being said about the worth of these investments. As these $700 trillion in derivatives or "investment products" are revealed to be worth little to nothing, you can expect governments to increase real estate taxes to make up for losses from these derivative investments. Such increases will force many to leave family homesteads.

What limitation is there upon local governments taxing citizens out of their homes to pay their generous salaries and pensions? Generally courts will not review government spending or taxation: they say they are political issues and not subject to court review. They say your remedy is at the election polls.

**Inflation limitation:** Success at using inflation as a solution for shortfalls in government revenues depends upon doing it so slowly that the bulk of the population does not notice and thus does not care. Inflation is a taxation, and, in their extreme, taxations are universally conceded to be the power to destroy. When the government lost control of the money supply, it lost the ability to control inflation. When this is generally recognized by the public, it will destroy much of the psychology necessary for prosperity. Thus it is that abuse of the government's power to inflate its currency directly impacts or challenges the integrity of its entire economy.

## Dangers of Inflation As Government Policy

Most politicians are dimly aware they have lost control of the money supply. Bailouts are the proof of this assertion. They have more than doubled the supply of money with no corresponding increase in goods or services. On top of that they say they will now back Fannie Mae and Freddy Mac without limitation.

With economists advising politicians based on an unrealistic view of the nature and quantity of money, is it any wonder that we have our present financial nightmare? Visualize the Federal Reserve, a collection of aged dodderers sitting around a table. On the table is a large black box labeled *money supply*. On the front of the box is a large knob for one of them to twist. They think or pretend they are affecting the supply of money. They don't realize the box is empty — that the knob spins freely because it is attached to nothing inside the box. Why are their acts so secret? Why are they still on the payroll? Runaway inflation is just around the corner; it will wash away prosperity.

The next concept is a toughie: with money printed, who gets the benefit of the newly created funds? The concept is **seigniorage,** defined as the difference between the value of money and the cost to produce it (*dictionary.com*). The benefit used to go to the Treasury, to be spent presumably on the general welfare. Now the benefit goes to the bankers and financiers that either create the money or are given the funds. In any case it does not go for the general welfare.

The false perception of the value of the dollar and the strength of our economy leads our politicians and our military leaders to unrealistic notions of their powers and abilities. Our military is preparing for a possible war with China. This rests upon the assumption that China will still keep selling us nuts and bolts to keep our military going in the event of war. It also assumes that China will buy our T-bills, in effect lending us money to pay our military leaders' salaries during a war against them. But perhaps the real worry in our country is not a military threat, but hyperinflation à la Germany in 1923.

## Credit Policy

The **presidential policy of credit** is to facilitate spending in excess of earnings and savings. Interest is deductible from your income tax. Business assets are deductible from the moment of purchase, not as they are paid for. Interest earned on savings accounts is taxable, hence saving money is discouraged. Gone is the ethic of careful shopping, of frugality. Conspicuous consumption is the order of the day. Feel bad? Go shopping to cure the blues. Gone are small pockets of savings citizens can fall back on in downturns of the economy. This is destabilizing. As a result small downturns have more severe implications. Persons on the brink of the abyss make irrational decisions. Speculators and financiers flourish, for the problem of one is opportunity for the other. How is this in the general welfare?

Today extension of **credit** is handled differently than in the days of yore when banks suffered the consequences of any bad loan they made. A flood of unsolicited **credit card** applications appears in the mail weekly. Unsurprisingly, *"debt counselors,"* with brash advertisements on how to get out of debt, fill the media. The attitude of youth towards money is changed. Instead of deferred gratification and responsible spending, the emphasis has become instant gratification and elegant consumerism. Mortgages of today are frequently originated by mortgage brokers in strip mall storefronts! There is none of the responsible credit analysis of the traditional retail banker. Today most loans are promptly bundled and resold as "securities" on the stock exchange. This practice fueled the securitization of worthless paper.

How popular is modern "**credit**"? Robert Peston, editor of the business section at British Broadcasting Corporation, points out that in England for the year 2008, the total personal, business and government borrowing was 400 percent of the English GDP. The USA was comparatively frugal, borrowing only 300 percent of its GDP. He asks how long this can continue. In 2009, for the second time in history,

U.S. consumer credit exceeded our gross domestic product. The last time this happened was 1929. Is hyperinflation next? **Credit** depends upon people's habits and willingness to repay debt. ***But it also depends upon their ability to repay.*** In hard economic times they may have no ability to repay regardless of their integrity or intentions.

This is the legacy of J.M. Keynes. Politicians had discovered the idea of deficit spending before Keynes, but he added legitimacy to the process. After 1929, the country was in the great depression, caused by the grants of privileges that set up the excesses of the "Roaring Twenties." Due to Keynes, the thought in the 1930s was that deficit spending, or spending money the country did not yet have, was the only way out. Money was printed up, to buy our way out of the depressed economy.

Distribution of the "new money" was one problem; just handing it out to the citizens in a democratic fashion smacked of socialism. Far better was to put it in the hands of the conservatives and keep the masses a bit hungry and hard at work. On the one hand the conservatives did not want inflation to diminish the value of their mortgages, notes, stocks, bonds and other financial instruments. But on the other hand, the depression was doing just that. The stock market had tanked and bankruptcies were wiping out notes and mortgages, for people and companies had no ability to pay.

In the end, the distribution of the proceeds, the newly created money, was solved partly by socialism and partly by giving it to conservatives. The socialism was Social Security, which FDR had to force through Congress and the courts. Then the make-work programs such as the Civil Conservation Corps, the Tennessee Valley Authority, and the Rural Electrification Act (REA) came into being.

The tight-money crowd adamantly opposed the new socialism, but FDR was able to push Social Security through Congress and get the Supreme Court to approve it as a valid expenditure of tax revenues. Administration was promptly adopted as the tool for spending and distributing the newly printed money. Any money that found its way into the hands of farmers or businessmen had many administrative "strings" attached. Hundreds of new agencies were created to administer funds, and new programs were created to achieve meritorious goals, completely bypassing the businessmen. The net effect was to destroy our free market. It now exists in name and remembrance alone. It was replaced with a legislated or, more properly, an executive-mandated (agency-driven) market fully institutionalized with World War II.

The jury is still out as to whether the governmental approach to the Great Depression cured it or aggravated it. Many argue relief came not from deficit spending but that the "problem" of the depression was "solved" by the market caused by the massive destruction of material and property in World War II and the deferred consumption from 1929 to 1945 that resumed after the war.

The problems of today are the legacy of J.M. Keynes. He prescribed the powerful medicine of deficit spending. He did not advise any limitations, either temporal (time) or of purpose (emergency use only) or amount. He did not say use only in time of depression or in time of war. So it has remained in full force. Administration quickly became massive and institutionalized; it destroyed the free market in fact and in the minds of "the entitled." Deficit spending became the cocaine of government. In the minds of politicians, "emergency" became not simply fighting economic depression or world wars. Politicians feel that getting reelected is enough of an emergency to justify the use of deficit spending.

The long-term problem is that deficit spending is solving the problems of today by mortgaging the future of our children. There is a limit to how far government financing will go. By putting off addressing the problem today, we are making it bigger for tomorrow. How is this policy in the general welfare?

## Policy of Finance

The next device in the president's tool box is the policy of **finance**. There are two kinds: **public finance** and **private finance**. The magic of what has become finance began in the private sector. It is based on the belief that money, for example a gold coin, can be it two places at the same time. Money that is on deposit in a bank can be out earning the banker interest in an investment, perhaps a car loan or a mortgage. The whole thing depends on people believing in words on paper; bank statements, certificates of deposits, treasury bills, notes and the like. All is well so long as there is confidence in the system or the "magic." Once confidence is lost, a run on the bank ensues and a re-evaluation of currency begins. The air is out of the balloon and a depression is on.

Finance is defined at school as the relationships between:

- Time
- Money
- Interest or other variable return
- Risk (a percent or chance of a bad result)
- Hazard (each type of bad result)

And, indirectly, at least some of the following:

- Representation or disclosure by seller
- Fraudulent representations or negligent misrepresentation by seller
- Transparency
- Perception by investor
- Valuation or evaluation by investor
- Miscalculation by seller or buyer
- Difference in experience between buyer and seller
- Fraudulent behavior by seller
- Gross negligent behavior by seller
- Failure by fiduciary
- Negligence by employee (which will not support a legal action)
- Various limitations on the liability of the seller of financial instruments

Advanced private finance is embellished by leverage. Why should the gold coin support only its face value in a single transaction? Why not ten times its face value? This is the notion of fractional reserve banking. Or take the modern fashionable gold funds. Here a single gold coin may "support" 100 certificates of deposit! Leverage or fraud?

In private finance, certificates, notes, bills and the like are guaranteed by corporations that insulate the officers and directors from personal responsibility. Any time there is no personal responsibility, you have a recipe for disaster.

**Public finance** is a bit different. Now it is the government that issues the pretty paper. The problem is that politicians make many promises to gain their thrones, far more than the ability of the government to pay for with taxation. To make up the shortfall between tax revenues and spending, governments print as much money (inflates its currency) as the public will stand for (inflation), then begin to issue promises to pay those who buy the paper, some time in the future. Only so long as the economy appears prosperous will people continue to buy these things called Treasury bills. Governments dread not being able to sell their T-bills at every auction, knowing that if sales fail, their house of cards will quickly tumble.

A key to understanding the difference between public finance and private finance lies in understanding the term *seigniorage*. When money evolved from stage 1 (specie) to stage 2 (ersatz money), governments no longer needed to put any expensive bullion into coinage. Today a quarter might cost a nickel to coin. Distribution and sale is free. The profit to the government is 20¢, a margin of 80 percent.

A second example might be the $100 bill. The "profits" are even greater. If it costs 25¢ to print, the profit is $99.75, or nearly 100 percent. With public finance, the "profit" goes to our treasury and is presumably used for the general welfare or public good.

It is because the government and financiers both sell their frauds in the private sector that they have become partners in collusion, each selling their own kind of frauds. This is to say that if the economy gets wobbly in the private sector, it can spread to the public sector. This is why the government is so easily recruited to the notion of **bailouts.** Cash bribery helps too.

In reality, private finance has come to take one of two forms: either the science of spending tomorrow's money today, or the highest refinement of the conspiracy to commit *larceny* (taking and holding the property of others with intent to keep it), hybridized with *fraud* (deception deliberately practiced in order to secure illegal gain). There are also clever combinations of the elements of the above. Private finance frequently involves grants of political privilege or favoritism secured by bribery. The second form usually employs the sale of a financial product, a package so beautifully wrapped that the buyer is tempted not to open it and look inside to find it is empty; this is also known as the sale of a financial "product." The "product" is said to include any number of abstract concepts and promises in a fancy and official appearing document. The concepts and promises are either simply not there, or there are fewer than the purchaser was told the product contained, or it contains wording to achieve the gradual extraction of value from that document.

Finance is a blend of bad laws (laws of privilege), bad executive policies and bad doctrines of court utilized either in public finance or private finance, considered in detail here. Some of the executive policies are enforcement of laws of privilege, permitting instances of abuse of laws and allowing criminal acts to go uncharged, unindicted or under prosecuted. Bad legal doctrines recognize privilege over the equality of justice: especially with the doctrine of corporations as sovereign entities.

The mechanics that drive finance are the inability of the average person to understand the time value of money and to comprehend the strength of inflation in an economy, and privileges sold by politicians to the financial types, soon to be studied.

A concept that propels finance is the belief that all persons are good and fair inside. Unfortunately this notion of fair play is not found in the world of finance. In the words of Aristotle in *Politics*, "*Some think that a very modest amount of virtue is enough.*" Honesty is viewed as a weakness, a vulnerability. Financiers are not honorable. They carefully calculate what they can get away with while not going to jail. They look to amass enough wealth to have power to avoid prosecution. Look no further than the 52,000 UBS accounts that were swept under the carpet in 2009 when the USA lost an estimated $100 billion in tax revenues, and the public didn't even get to find how many senators, representatives and other government sorts were account holders.

## Evolution of Financial Institutions

Big finance probably started with Jacob Fugger (aka Fugger the Rich, 1459–1525), who knew the value of political connections and personally financed the election of Charles V (by bribery of the electors) as the Holy Roman Emperor. In return he was made a major banker who collected and forwarded papal revenues, increasing his wealth many fold.

Modern financial institutions and products take various forms:

- Retail banks
- Installment sales contracts (1840s)
- Investment banks (1890s)
- Venture capital, early (1900s)
- The quasis: part government, part private (1935)
  - Quasis gone private — SLM, CCC
  - Government Sponsored Enterprises (GSEs)
- Hedge funds (1949)
- Holding companies
- Modern investment banks (1980s)
- Private equity funds (1982), the barbarians at the gate
- Wealth management firms

**Retail banks:** Finance once had legitimate purposes: to finance a war for national defense; to finance the lives of cash-crop farmers and families who might otherwise get by on a single annual harvest-day paycheck, or to allow a wage-earner to make big purchases like a car or a home. With financing available, persons need not save the entire purchase price before receiving the goods. In that sense, it helped accelerate the development of a middle economic class.

Traditionally, bank financing was done "in-house." This financing was based on **credit**. Judging a person's credit-worthiness was the realm of the banks. Since a banker was lending his bank's capital, he was very careful with loans; both the amount and the characteristics of the person who got the money were important. Careful and conservative assessment of the ability to repay was made, incorporating a history of that person's payments of previous loans and their habits with regard to use of money. Because these loans were kept in-house, the hazards of bad judgments came back to the bank.

The FDIC was established to provide protection from bank failure. With the FDIC came regulation and mandatory protection insurance. Retail banks are highly regulated by the FDIC. It sets the reserves banks must carry for lending money. It can specify the quality of the investment those reserves must take and the quality of loans made by the bank. Regulatory supervision and oversight as to the judgments the bankers make in extending credit are quite shaky and subjective and, indeed, done after the fact.

But retail banking is "regulated" and has "sort of" worked. Failures, when they occur, are usually contained within single banks, and definitely within the banking sector, save for 1929, which was, of course, prior to the establishment of the FDIC (1933). This establishes the *outer limit* of reasonable banking practices or banking in the common good of society. Going beyond this limit is the high-power finance that has proven to be a polite term for fraud and larceny.

The beauty of classic retail banking was that each bank was small enough that the loss of one would not damage the entire financial industry. In the past, no bank was "too big to fail." Hazards were manageable.

Too big to fail is a working definition of monopoly.

The modern-day lust of bankers and financiers to form megabanks in various forms destroys the valuable stabilizing effect of numerous diverse banks. Loss of numbers and diversity is not in the common good. Monopoly never is.

Now let us consider **installment sales contracts**. Modern finance began with Cyrus McCormick. His McCormick Harvest Machine Company pioneered in financing the sale of its grain harvesting equipment to the American farmer in about 1850, inventing the installment sales contract. McCormick recognized what the bankers of the time did not: that the machine would pay for itself in two or three years, and that farmers were good **credit risks**. His recognition of this opportunity vaulted his company to early success. (P. Drucker, *Innovation*) This form of finance caused our economy to explode, pushing it forward and upward as never dreamed by our founders. Regulation of installment sales devices did not come until the establishment of Uniform Commercial Codes (UCC), which were adopted on a state-by-state basis, circa 1952. Installment sales contracts were often abusive and unjust, but they were small in dollar amount and, though numerous, they never led to any economic crisis.

The roots of **investment banks** go back to the 1800s. Goldman Sachs was founded in 1869, and claims to have pioneered the sale of commercial paper to entrepreneurs for capitalization of their businesses beginning in the year 1890. Salomon Brothers was founded in 1910, and Merrill Lynch in 1914. E.F. Hutton was founded in 1904 as a stock brokerage firm and morphed into an investment bank. These banks do not accept retail deposits but seek large investments from large investors. Their purpose is the bulk purchase and retail sale of T-bills and to aggregate capital and invest in businesses. They will be considered in detail towards the end of this chapter to preserve a continuity in sophistication of the evolution of financial instruments.

**Venture capital** had its roots in the late 1800's when wealthy investors like the Rockefellers, Vanderbilts and J.P. Morgan sought investment opportunities for family wealth. Indeed J.P. Morgan and Vanderbilt were original shareholders in Edison Electric Light Company. Venture capital has evolved today into a source of capital for new or young companies with high earning potential. Venture capitalists do not lend money to businesses; instead they invest money in exchange for majority shares in the new corporate venture. Hundreds of venture capital companies financed much of the "Silicon Valley" of California in the late 1960s and 1970s; dozens more financed many of the dot-com industries of the 1990s, and more financed the Internet bubble which burst in 2003. Today they take the form of "funds" of limited partners, established for a fixed period, usually of 10 years. They usually have four stages of growth, wherein capital is raised from the partners, ending in a final stage of liquidation by "going public."

They are not regulated by any government agency and are responsible for much of the socially productive development of our economy today.

The **quasi-public/private corporations** had their start in the FDR era. They are curious animals, corporations started by federal mandate, sometimes actually federal corporations, but private in their dealings. They often morph into privately held corporations such as the Commodity Credit Corporation (CCC). Not being of the private sector there is no competition to shape them. Their accounting is suspect or worse. Management gets huge salaries. There is always a question whether they are guaranteed by the federal government, and, if guaranteed, to what extent. There is opportunity for untold economic mischief. They include the Federal Reserve, the CCC, Sallie Mae (now SLM), Fannie Mae, Freddie Mac and more. Home loans offered by government agencies such as HUD, FHA, FmHA, FMAC and VA are both poorly constructed and imprudently administered machines. These agencies do no financial analyses. They permitted financial institutions to bundle and sell complex frauds as securities. These agencies didn't even discover the Ponzi scheme of Bernard Madoff when they were told time and time again it existed. They made no attempt to penetrate corporate veils and limited liability partnerships that allowed wrongdoers to go on for decades. When irregularities were revealed, they still slept on the job, letting the frauds continue. Fortunately some state attorneys general got involved and knocked the wheels off the wagon.

Regulatory agencies masked their incompetence and indolence by offering federal guarantees of mortgage loan performance, at unrealistically low cost insurance premiums. This created the implied assurance that investment in these quasis was backed up by government guarantees against investment losses. These assurances created the next round of financial disasters; like the S&L and bank bailouts of the past and the bailouts of the 2007-2009 meltdown. Our politicos are, in effect, subsidizing the next crop of financial disasters with this cheap government insurance. This impacts heavily upon conservative, well-run banks who must compete with mortgage brokers of lesser scruples and ultimately degrades and dilutes the standard of care or attention the careful bankers give their credit analyses. To make matters worse, the well run-banks pay increased FDIC premiums to cover the messes made by their crooked brethren. How is this in the general welfare?

Because these "**quasis**" have a governmental connection, their directors and officers are protected from personal liability. Hiding behind veils of corporate identity, even layers of corporate identities, quickly became a license for abuses and mayhem of all sorts and colors, running from negligence to fraud and deceit. Between shields of corporate liability, insurance and bailouts, officers, directors and managers of these finance operations slip and slide through the cracks and avoid personal liability for the aforesaid mayhem.

Policy wonks rather blandly assumed that real-estate was always golden, that you cannot lose money on real-estate, that the value of real estate will always increase, that putting everyone in his or her home was good public policy, that all people are fit and proper to keep their own homes up, that people will never wish to lose their home and that it will all work out in the end. With such thinking they created one huge mortgage bubble. And the resulting economic damages spread throughout the economy.

Closely related to the "quasis" are **Government Sponsored Entities (GSEs)**, which exemplify government immorality at its apogee. They were created to avoid federal budgetary limitations such as the Gramm-Rudman Act, which is thought to impose limitations on government spending. Because the GSEs are quasi-private in nature, their liabilities are not picked up by the Government Accounting Office (GAO) and so are **off the federal balance sheets.** But often the federal government has to step in to guarantee and indemnify the ill-advised transactions in which they become involved. So they should be included on the balance sheets, because these guarantees of performance are a potential public liability. In 1989 there were warnings that these off the balance sheet liabilities from guarantees were already twice the national deficit. Since 1989 the extent of liability has ballooned substantially. This is, again, nothing but **fiscal illusion.** While the government may guarantee the performance of a mortgage, it does not assure the shareholders or bondholders who invest in these companies of any dividend or return of original investment. Indeed, many banks lost money due to their belief that the stocks and bonds of these GSEs were guaranteed by the federal government. The reality is that some are guaranteed and some are not. Government was fooling with the integrity of the leveraged finance system and destroying public confidence in it. This is tantamount to undermining the "full faith and credit" of the dollar.

The **hedge fund** phenomenon seems to have had its birth in the mind of a financial journalist, Alfred W. Jones, about 1950. He believed opportunities existed that would allow a balance of short sales of assets expected to drop in value against long positions expected to rise in value, and that this approach could remove risk from investments. Several hedge funds evolved using these principles. These devices are rather benign to society.

**Private equity funds** (which recently have taken to calling themselves "investment banks") are groups of investors that utilize *leveraged buyouts* (**LBOs**) to make their money. They seem to have had their birth in 1982 when William E. Simon, former Secretary to the U.S. Treasury, formed a group of investors, Westry Capital Corporation, to acquire Gibson Greetings, a publisher of greeting cards. The acquisition for $80 million was funded by an LBO using less than $2 million of original investors' money. The company was sold soon thereafter for $290 million. *Time* magazine reported Simon made some $66 million on that deal.

Private equity funds have become modern-day pirates and are truly horrific in their actions. An LBO takes a little currently held capital, often offering for sale junk bonds to raise more capital, and purchases a majority interest in a target corporation. Once in control of the board, existing management is dismissed and the LBO players strip the corporation of all assets (including pension plans), pay themselves huge salaries and bonuses, and then sell off the corporation piece by piece. The hope is that the sum of the parts brings more value than the whole that was purchased. Undervalued businesses or prudently run businesses with substantial cash reserves, or those who pay their employees generously are the prime targets. With the LBO there is no need to use your cash to buy control of the corporation thanks to Mike Milken's contribution of the concept to sell junk bonds to finance these acquisitions.

The genius of Simon was his invention of the LBO. In the 1980s there were hundreds of these leveraged buyouts led by pirates, big and small: Carlyle Group, Blackstone, KKR, TPG Partners, Goldman Sachs Capital Partners, to name just a few. But it was Kohlberg, Kravits & Roberts (KKR) that employed the concept big time and acquired the reputation of the "barbarians at the gate." They were far and away the biggest LBO player, destroying over $1 trillion in U.S. capital and numerous U.S. businesses. (See Exhibit 2.)

LBO players use the mantra of the modern MBA that they offer our economy new and fresh views and business tactics. They claim these tactics make companies more efficient and competitive. In reality, cash reserves once held for a rainy day are immediately grabbed by the new owners for bonuses. Hence another mantra: "greed is good." Newspapers promptly parroted the phrase. Once in control of the corporation, pension plans are the next asset of interest. An unscrupulous actuary/financier may opine that the rate of return on investments is unrealistically conservative or low and hence the plan is over funded. These opinions support concluding that millions of extra dollars are there for the taking. These assets are promptly taken as bonuses. If they are wrong, the Pension Benefit Guarantee Corporation (PBGC) will cover the losses. How is that in the general welfare?

Middle management is made "lean." Many are let go. Remaining employees do double or triple duty. Wage earners are pressed harder and salaries and fringes are cut. In-house specialty functions may be replaced by consultants. Jobs, even departments, are shipped overseas where wages are a fraction of the local wage scale. Research and development goes out the window. Inventories are dramatically reduced; "just in time supply" is the fashion. The sell-off of "excess inventory" leads to the illusion of efficient management, justifying huge management bonuses.

But lean inventory means the company is dependent on precarious supply chains. A company could be idled waiting for key parts. Technology is given away for a few years of lower prices. Business interests that are not "core" are spiffed up and sold off. One useful tool is the "off-balance sheet conduits" to remove liabilities from balance sheets, increasing the appearance of solvency.

Private equity funds are not regulated by the federal authorities. But competition has diminished their importance. KKR's takeover of RJR Nabisco was met with competitive bids that may have induced an overpayment. In any case, there was a marked decline in private equity takeovers in 1990–1992, and with the burst of the dot-com bubble in 2000–2003.

The loosening of government regulation during the Bush dynasty caused a resurgence of private equity abuses which in turn caused a dozen of the world's biggest buyouts and finally the credit crunch or meltdown of 2007-2009. "Busts" following "booms" were previously contained within industries or sectors of the economy, but this is no longer the case. There is a real question whether government can contain the 2007-2009 meltdown and how long the inflationary effect of palliative measures will affect the economy.

This will continue so long as people can avoid personal liability for these schemes by operating in the corporate style of business and as long as prosecutions of fraudulent activities receive lame effort by the agencies of our executive branches of government. Unrealistically mild court sentences further encourage these frauds. Meaningful whistle-blower compensation will help right the ship. (See Exhibit 2.)

**Investment banks (continued):** As finance morphs into the investment world, it is time to pick up investment banks and trace the evolutions that have occurred therein. Their services vary from institution to institution, but generally they perform the following:

- Sell government T-bills
- Capitalize and recapitalize corporations
- Advise and manage mergers and acquisitions
- Security activities including:

- Initial public offerings (IPOs)
- Insuring IPOs
- Brokering of stocks
- Proprietary trading
- Market making
- In-house analysis of stock values
- Advising clients on investments
- Portfolio and wealth management
- Bulk divestitures of stock holdings, <u>and unfortunately</u>
- Securitization of junk to fabricate investment grade paper

As can be imagined, willingness to assume all these roles and unwillingness to forgo any chance for profit causes many conflicts of interest. **Proprietary trading programs** are one such example. Within one bank there can exist a retail stock brokerage division and another division that invests bank funds seeking the maximum stock market return for bank or preferred bank customers. The latter division does not share any of the insights of its secret proprietary program with the retail part of the bank. Indeed, preferred customers are sometimes thought to profit from less prudent investment program advice offered to retail investment customers. The **bulk divestiture** example shows how this conflict of interests can occur.

Assume that a huge client, like California Public Employees' Retirement System (CalPERS), wants to dump a huge block of one stock quickly before its value drops. Investment banks, with many well-heeled professional clients keeping IRA and pension plans in their retail stock brokerage division, are the perfect place to dump these unwanted stocks. In-house (captive) stockbrokers who have cultivated the confidence of myriads of these busy professionals advise their clients to purchase these stocks. This happens quickly, unnoticed by anyone but those running sophisticated trade analysis programs. These in-house brokers are motivated by "*spiffs*" or increased commissions for each such stock sale. Is that alone not proof of conflict of interest?

If a retail client notices that the value of the stock declines after purchase, and if they inquire, they are told "that is the market" and are encouraged to hold on and wait for the rise that inflation will usually bring. With the present trend towards purchase of mutual funds, such dealings involving individual stocks tend to be lost in the layers of financial devices, which makes these deals even less transparent and hence less noticeable to small investors.

**Securitization** is the act of bundling paper assets of various grades (recently referred to in the trade as garbage mortgages and junk bonds) and fabricating "investment" grade paper by the application of "new school" business tools such as risk spreading, risk management, variable and fanciful rates of investment return based upon bold but groundless projections of value in the future, supposedly in proportion to risk of defaults. Unfortunately the rating agencies have done poorly at identifying hazards (untoward results) and risks (the chance the hazard will occur; simply a percentage) of these securities. Consequently their ratings are financial illusions, wishful thinking. The reality is "*garbage in — garbage out,*" as proved conclusively by the 2007–2009 meltdown. There is an all too common practice of an investment bank creating garbage, then, on the other side of a "Chinese wall," selling this garbage to its retail stock clients. This is often the strategy of an investment advisor. Recall the wisdom of Aristotle: "*Some think that a very modest amount of virtue is enough.*" This is simply an outrageous but common practice!

Indications of ethical conflict are found when an investment bank holds itself out as an informed and impartial advisor and wealth manager to the retail stock clients. For investment banks are never able to explain why a stock may have a sell recommendation for institutional investors and still have a buy rating for other, smaller investors. An immense advantage is given to large stock retailers when their firm is able to sell these stocks to their trusted investment clients. Secrets known only to the market maker can affect the advice the counselors give their clients. Market makers/investment banks have created a conflict of interest no Chinese wall can possibly address. Customers advised to buy the stock by the retail stock brokers arm of the investment bank are usually at variance with the interests of the investment bank on the hook to support the price of that stock.

**Analyses of stock value** lose necessary impartiality through incestuous relationships analysts form with the very companies they are analyzing. This conflict is tolerated by the investment bank, for the forming of this bond is thought to help to attract lucrative IPOs and more lucrative insuring of these IPO transactions.

**Market making** is a situation where a large investment firm, for a fee, becomes the buyer of last resort for stocks of a single and particular company. This means the market maker must buy and hold stocks of that company when someone on the open market is offering that stock for sale and there is no other buyer.

The function they perform is supplying "liquidity" for that stock. In some stock markets the market is so small there may be no buyers for a stock issue for days on end. The specter of such a possibility depresses the value of stocks and the market as a whole. Imagine the situation of a person who must sell a stock immediately for some urgent personal reason, and the possibility there would be no buyer. Assurance of the existence of a buyer for each and every listed stock of an exchange for each second of the business day increases confidence and adds value to the stock market.

Because there is immense risk in the guaranteed purchase of a stock when a market is falling, the market maker minimizes their risk by quoting a buy/sell spread for the stock they warrant. These prices change by the moment at the speed of electronic transfer. They hope to profit on the spread between the buy and the sell.

Market makers are granted certain privileges, such as naked short selling, and a bit of time delay in stock trading and early information and analysis advantages. There is an economic benefit to the investment bank that keeps a pool of house account stocks that can clear internally not having to go through the floor (the pit). The result is that the fees of buying and selling can be kept or harvested in-house. The client is led to believe he or she is getting market price, but it is not so, because the sale never hit the pit. This can lead to stock price manipulation, facilitated by the in-house retail banking arm of the bank. With huge funds masking individual stock sales, this becomes opaque. No wonder investment managers are keen on mutual funds.

In America, market makers are granted monopoly, for there is a single market maker for each stock. In London there must be two such market makers. The disturbing trend is that with electronic trading more and more sales go through market makers and fewer are performed in "the pit" of the open market in stock exchanges. Openness and transparency are being sacrificed for the convenience of electronic trading. There is more opportunity for shenanigans discoverable only by an electronic sleuth. Administrators will not be up to the task.

## Policy of Investment

The presidential policy on investments, for the average citizen, is that merely the appearance of a return on investment is all that is necessary. A real return (corrected for inflation) is available only to the ultra-rich. Just how is this done? What is the machinery that causes this to happen?

In the Eisenhower years, war expenses and irrational federal government spending led to unacceptable levels of income taxation — up to 90 percent. Tax-deferred IRA and pension plans were thought to be the answer to high taxes. Thrift was to be encouraged. It was thought to promote the common good, the general welfare.

To qualify for tax deferral (distinguished from outright exemption) a portion of earned income was to accumulate in an individual retirement account (IRA) trust in the name of each worker. Actual title, or ownership, and control of each IRA are held in the name of the trustee. The assets and earnings are held until retirement or extreme need. Money is then subject to taxation only upon withdrawal.

There was an assumption that money would have a reasonably constant value and that there would be earnings in real (inflation-corrected) terms and that wealth and prosperity would inure to all, according to the amount each worked and saved. Let us look closely at the machinery that was set up to accomplish this. Let us also note how the laws of unintended consequences had their impact.

Those fortunate enough to have IRAs imagine that their investment funds are actually held in stocks, bonds or mutual funds, perhaps in their name, perhaps in the name of their trustee, in their account, stored in nice, neat, locked file cabinets. Nothing is further from the truth. The accounts exist only on paper. They are simply a list of what the trust firm must deliver at some time in the future. The beneficiary's funds are actually in a house account hard at work for the trustees, making huge fortunes for them

Just as bankers learned years ago, so long as there is no run on the banks, only a small portion of their assets need be held at the bank. The rest can be put to highly leveraged "work" for the benefit of the bank. Bankers soon found that retail savings deposits were a chancy basis for long-term loans that they might make. They invented certificates of deposit (CDs) with fixed long-term maturities and "*substantial penalties for early withdrawal.*"

The pension funds/IRAs stumbled onto something even better in every sense of the word. When the well-meaning Congress created tax-deferred IRA accounts, they created for the trustees managing these accounts huge pools of money, held for the long-term with waves of new cash washing in each year. The trustee has no need to pay interest on the funds raised this way. There is no tax implication on the trustee raising all this capital with which to play. The trustee does not have to pay back a fixed sum of money; trustee obligation floats with the market. If the market goes down, it is the IRA client who loses, not the trust; the duty of the trust fund manager to repay is locked to the listed stocks or the value of the mutual funds. In many pension plans, upon retirement the beneficiary may be locked into an annuity with fixed rates of return in the face of ravaging inflation.

Because retirement occurs late in life and withdrawals are gradual and predictable, the money supply is quite stable and is in the hands of the trustee for the long-term. Investment houses usually do not charge for early withdrawals. The IRS does this for them. The only risk is that clients might move their investments to another firm.

From time to time a trustee might be audited. It is a good idea for a trustee to have sufficient in-house stocks to cover each of the client's positions on those monthly statements. But since stock records are now handled electronically, a rookie auditor will probably not track where the money is, and if there is a shortfall in stock holdings, there is always a computer or a program or a programmer to blame.

Thus vast and ever-growing sums of money are there for the IRA managers to play with, and are there for the long-term. There is little accountability or liability. Those who bring in their funds sign many papers, perhaps in blank. Beneficiaries agree to mediation and arbitration of disputes through private regulatory authorities who are firmly under the thumb of the investment banking houses. Beneficiaries give away their right to a jury trial. They give away their rights to meaningful discovery by a real trial attorney. They are securely wrapped up in a procedure that has no meaningful appeal rights. They consent to letting the fund manager do pretty much whatever he/she wants and without the right to see what is going on. In reality the law of unintended consequences resulted in a huge and unending river of cash for Wall Street to use to create the financial playground with all its excesses and to buy all the privileges they enjoy today.

## Financial Institutions by Function

Recall that in the investment world the following institutions perform the following functions:

**Stock exchanges** or markets: for example, NYSE and NASDAQ, are where stocks are sold and transferred, but not where title to stock is held past event of sale.

**Brokerage firms**: Retail stock sellers may offer investment advice and have in-house holdings of stocks and act like an inhouse stock exchange, including **market making** (being a buyer of last resort for any listed stock). They may offer trust services.

**Trusts** for IRA and pension accounts: fiduciaries where title to assets is held in the interest of beneficiaries, usually:

- Retail or commercial banks
- Broker firms
- Investment banks
- Wealth managers

**Investment advisers**: for a fixed percentage give advice as to asset purchase and asset allocation. Small independent advisers are usually licensed, insured, regulated agents for huge trust management firms such as Fidelity, Vanguard and so on.

**Investment banks**: perform initial public stock offerings (IPOs), are big block brokers, make wholesale purchases of massive blocks of T-bills (which are promptly resold), lend to corporations and governments, design and market derivatives such as CDOs and the like.

**Retail banks:** provide savings, mortgages, and commercial loans; sometimes have trust departments and may provide investment advice in house.

**Stock rating agencies**; Moodys and the like, usually freestanding entities.

**Wealth management firms** (tax evasion specialists): can act as trustees, investment advisers, stock brokerages and even stock exchanges, the most notable being Union Bank of Switzerland (UBS).

Law has long mandated that assets held in trust be isolated from possession of the beneficiary, for the moment the beneficiary is found in actual or constructive receipt, the trust will legally collapse or cease to exist and the assets will be subjected to income taxation. Because a trust is a special legal creation often created for the benefit of minors, the infirm or unsophisticated beneficiaries, it is mandatory that the functions of *holding of assets in trust, brokerage of assets, investment advice* and *rating of stocks and bonds* be separated or in separate business entities. Transparency, accountability, confidence of beneficiaries and those who create trusts demand this.

The law demands that the beneficiaries' interests are primary and paramount to any interest of the trustee or its agents. It is also strictly illegal for a trustee or any agent or employee to engage in self-dealing for profit and at the same time carry out the function of protecting and prudently investing the assets of a beneficiary. The conflict of trustee self-interest against the duty of the trustee to keep the interests of the client paramount cannot be reconciled. It is impossible to serve two masters at the same time.

In reality boundaries and actions between financial institutions are blurred and hence conflicted. As vertical monopolies such as UBS wealth management slowly evolve, conflicts of interest between clients and the house inevitably develop that no artifice such as a Chinese wall can possibly address or cure.

## HOW TO MAKE MONEY IN A RISING STOCK MARKET

First, you have to be in the market. Obviously you have to own shares to make money. Buy low and sell when the stock value is higher. But why be satisfied with that? If you are sure the market is on the rise, why not leverage? You can legally buy **on margin,** or buy twice as many stocks as you have money to pay for. Another trick is to buy **options**, the right to buy stock owned by another at an agreed price at a fixed date in the future. That person gives you the opportunity to harvest the gain for a price you pay today. Your precious dollars could buy the gain (or loss) of many times the number of shares of stock you can afford to buy with an outright purchase. This is called **leverage**.

## HOW TO MAKE MONEY IN A FALLING STOCK MARKET

If you are confident the price of a stock is about to fall you can *sell* the stock that you do not own and that you buy at a later date (after it finishes falling). The way you legally sell something you do not own is to rent with an option to buy from the owner of that stock (usually a broker) to cover the chance that the stock is not available when you need to deliver the stock to your purchaser. This is called a **short sale**. It is politely characterized as a transaction where the sale of stock precedes the purchase of the stock.

Another embellishment of finance is called a **naked short**. Here you sell a stock you do not own and you have made no provision to cover it with a contract for purchase. At this point you are selling stocks on the hope they will be available when you need them. This is an illegal practice. Because it is not supported by a printed share of issued stock, there is no limitation on the number of shares that may be "sold." As the market gets saturated (far more stocks offered for sale than demand) or gets wise (recognizing that there is more sales volume than there are issued shares) the value of the shares plummets and the manipulator can now buy shares for pennies on the dollar. Done in a subtle way, this offers phenomenal opportunities for gain, so long as you are not caught. Usually selling something that you do not own is criminal. But not in the wonder world of finance. Only in the rest of the world do people get in trouble for selling what they do not own. In the world of finance everything becomes relative: how much money and power do you have?

## Tools of Financial Houses

Learning the leverage principle from the banks, financial houses developed new ways to play with your money. UBS, for example, has assembled about $3 trillion to play with (assets under management), all tax-free, interest-free and unregulated. The first tool is **appearance**, the look of prosperity and massive wealth, and is highly desirable. This is why beautiful people are showcased in gorgeous and sumptuous offices as, for example, the massive UBS office building at One North Wacker Drive in Chicago. Compare this to the dumpy, old, red brick warehouse that is the home office to Berkshire Hathaway, and guess whose clients are getting "whacked."

**Market churning** is a practice developed where brokers for unsophisticated or addicted clients constantly turn assets over in the market for no other purpose than to harvest broker's fees. Long ago, before ScotTrade reduced its brokerage fee to $7 per trade, broker commissions averaged between $100-$200 for a 1,000-share transaction. Occasionally trust funds were virtually depleted by such practices. But this practice is little seen today. There are other ways to profit from handling the immense funds at a trustee's disposal.

**Client investment advice** at brokerage houses to all customers is to get in the market and hold for the long-term. They collect management fees only on funds in the market. Those funds in interest-bearing accounts generate no management fees for them.

Compare this advice to what they do with "their own" funds. While dealing with your money, and advising you to stay in the market, they do anything but follow this advice. They are constantly going in and out of the market. Sometimes they are in for only a few seconds. They spend tens of millions of dollars on **trading programs**. They spend more on programmed trades. One third to one half of the transactions on the NYSE are program-driven trades.

Odd is the difference in advice given to big clients and smaller retail clients. At UBS, preferred customers have long been given one list of recommendations to buy and sell while regular retail customers got another, different list. And in-house trading (exclusively for UBS profit) followed yet another "list" generated by an exclusive set of proprietary (secret) programs. Some people maintain the company dumps less desirable shares on both big accounts and retail customers. Some also feel that in-house brokers for small accounts were pushed to dump stock shares the big accounts no longer wished to hold upon their retail customers and the market at large. They were encouraged to dump such stocks with their clients by spiffs.

**In-house accounts**: big brokerage houses maintain house accounts that contain huge inventories of stocks. Such large inventories allow these big firms to internally broker many deals that clients order, and thus to harvest both the buy and sell fees that would be charged were the deal made on the NYSE or other exchanges; it is an internal transfer, no use splitting with brokers at the NYSE. When brokers tell you "we don't follow that stock," are they really telling you it is not a stock we trade "in house"?

## Additional Tools of the Big Firms

The biggest brokerage houses have created their own special playgrounds, with opportunities that occur only when you have your own private stock market. Unregulated fees and charges of every imaginable type and style may found here. In-house transfers are more likely when the firm has trillions of dollars of shares of stocks in its private inventory. UBS has created in New York the biggest stock trading "pit" in the world. It is the size of two football fields. Why would they go to the expense of such an operation just to save a few dollars on $7 trades? Why would big investment firms do all this if it were not very profitable? Are we watching a real market or simply a bunch of puppets at work? What is the price of Exxon today? Whatever UBS wants it to be.

These big brokerage firms have programs that use artificial intelligence (AI) to follow and analyze breaking news worldwide 24 hours per day. These programs have the ability to execute, without human intervention, nearly instantaneous stock purchases in whichever world market is open at the moment. There are programs for trend analysis, programs that purchase stocks based not on any market fundamentals, but that trade for the moment on which stock is selling the fastest. Other programs employ **statistical arbitrage**: the "mining" of data, analyzed by AI to spot any market trend that might be an early buying opportunity.

Big houses employ **front running.** When the computers spot a huge series of trades in progress they **flash trade,** or put their house holdings a few milliseconds ahead of their own clients' orders to buy and resell stocks, to harvest in those moments a small profit, at the expense of their clients. These and more tactics are done with sophisticated computer trading programs and artificial intelligence, action without human intervention. In the words of Richard M. Bookstaber, these practices form a *Demon of Our Own Design.*

While holding stocks in the name of their investor beneficiaries, these investment houses have developed the peculiar habit of using client assets for their own benefit. Some see nothing wrong with selling stocks traders do not own and/or which are not covered with a "rental" agreement. This leads both to illegal profits and deterioration of the market as a whole.

**Market timing** is the art of buying low and selling high. But how can you time the market efficiently and with confidence that you are making the right and timely moves? Why leave this to chance? The simpler, less risky solution to market timing is in owning your stock pit. All the tools to create the fluctuations you need to make money are comfortably contained in-house. Ever wonder why there is a flap, and litigation, when investment bank personnel suddenly change allegiances and go on to other banking firms? Confidential trading programs could be evidence of stock market manipulations. All is settled in secrecy, so we will never know.

**Market manipulation:** it has been suggested that there are those who actually manipulate the market; that certain firms use short sales to diminish the price of a targeted stock, then pay their obligations by purchase of the stock at mildly or wildly depressed prices, pocketing for themselves huge gains. Brokers no longer churn individual accounts; they churn the entire market. Or they create the appearance of genuine popular demand for a stock, or sector, and foster this appearance by building up a trade flow, slowly increasing share price, and then, at a moment they determine, quickly dumping their holdings. With big houses running their own stock exchanges there now exists the possibility for conspiratorial in-house actions to move the share prices as they wish. The tail can now wag the dog. Market manipulation allows big houses to run share prices up, then dump them discreetly. Or the house may suppress the value of target stocks by the device of naked shorts and buying near the bottom. Any attempt at regulation is quite ineffectual. Remember how Nick Leeson took the 233-year-old Barings Bank of England down with his currency speculation? Regulators were asleep.

When UBS has a piggybank with over $3 trillion and Wall Street is capitalized at around $12-13 trillion, there is certainly enough cash to manipulate the market. The rules of the game are different for them. Simply yo-yo the price of individual stocks by market timing and harvest rich rewards. The added benefits with your own private stock market are privacy, secrecy, confidentiality and immunity from lawsuits. Also beneficial is utilizing tools like short sales and the puffery eagerly reported by mindless financial reporters of the press and other media. To make sense of market movements, they personify it with such statements as: "the market wants to move upward," "the market marched upward led by Apple's hot new item," or "the market was sleepy today." Financial reporters are willing co-conspirators.

If a group of smaller investors is orchestrating a drop in price, they rent stock from a brokerage house and then sell short. When the stock price crashes, they buy enough at fire sale prices to redeem the stocks rented from the broker.

But in an investment bank orchestrating a drop in price, there is no need to rent stocks, for it is possible to use naked shorts in safety since they have a huge inventory of in house stocks, with titles kept electronically. There are no printed stocks with names upon them. The audit trail is virtually impossible to follow. There is no smoking gun for lawyers. When the price is depressed, simply buy enough at reduced prices to meet your obligations on your naked short position.

If you are doing a run-up in the price of a stock, slowly purchase plenty, perhaps buy a few more options, and sell off before the chosen stock crashes. Then you can load up again at a bargain price before fabricating a news break. All this is done by computerized trading programs.

In testimony before the U.S. Congress in March 2009, ex-Federal Reserve Chair Alan Greenspan said he was shocked that the "*self-interest of lending institutions to protect shareholder's equity*" proved to be an illusion. Shouldn't the humongous salary and bonus packages for financiers have been his first clue to these goings-on? Obviously they take lots of money and produce no goods or services.

Alan was also puzzled by the "*irrational exuberance*" of the stock market. With the market driven by artificial intelligence, why should there be puzzlement? Did he expect that the computers would develop some sort of synthetic morality? Who left Alan at the helm of our financial ship of state? Why?

## How Investment Houses Avoid Litigation Hazards

Investment houses are insulated from pithy and uncomfortable questions from client's attorneys. Remember, when you set up your account you agreed to give up the right to sue and to be bound by arbitration or mediation by friendly arbitration firms. Investment houses are protected from regulators by layers of corporate veils, corporate sovereignty, offshore rules, international treaties, the doctrine of caveat emptor and enough money to buy any politician on the planet. Often, this is not necessary, for politicians frequently have secret accounts in the same investment firms and are extremely modest about them. So it is that politicians and regulators are willing to look away as financiers do their sleight of hand.

## Indisputable Wrongdoing by Financiers

Wrong by any measure is when **trustees**, with the primary duty to preserve value for their clients, put their personal financial interests ahead of those of the beneficiary. When trustees profit by using trust funds in their own names and make personal gain by trading with these funds, they are milking someone else's cow. How is any of this legal? Brokerage houses continue to harvest rich rewards from stock owned by clients. Some see nothing wrong with the practice, certainly the SEC and the president. Regulation of these firms is a joke. Those interested should read the *Statement of the Security and Exchange Commission Concerning Financial Penalties* available online. Their concern is about civil penalties, corporate penalties, fines and restitution, and how these affect shareholders. They overlook the wrongdoers — officers and directors. There is no talk of punishing them or assessing fines, restitution, disgorgement of salaries and bonuses, and stock options. There is no thought of jail, forfeiture of citizenship, or the like.

In the July 2010 settlement of the case of *SEC v. Goldman Sachs,* regarding the sale of CDOs based on toxic mortgages, a fine of $550 million was apportioned $300 million to the Treasury, and $250 million for restitution. Goldman Sachs had just pocketed most of the $1.2 trillion of the second bailout (the sale of distressed assets or toxic mortgages) or about $1 trillion. Do the math:

$$\frac{\$\ 550,000,000}{\$1,000,000,000,000} = \frac{\$\ 550}{\$1,000,000} = 0.00055 = .055 \text{ percent}$$

To be sheltered from claims of bilked investors by a fine of a mere $550 million or .055 percent of the $1 trillion harvested in the second bailout is a rather rich reward for Goldman Sachs. Did the punishment fit the crime, or is it a whitewash?

All of this clearly demonstrates the Presidential policy that prosperity is only for the wealthy; this is even laid out in the SEC guidelines. Originally, money recovered for transgressions by financiers went to the Treasury as fines. Eventually it was decided to give a portion of the money to the financially damaged parties. Then it occurred to someone that this is just a transfer of money from the pocket of the shareholders to the aggrieved (financially damaged) party. Hence the wrong people were being penalized. Why not punish the officers and directors? They did the wrongdoing so logically meaningful financial reform must start here. Just because they are big contributors to politicos, should they get a free pass? Toothless and witless is the SEC. Presidential policy is clearly revealed: real returns on investments go only to the ultra-rich.

## The Cure

Clearly, investment houses, retail banks and stockbroker houses are different animals. There are inherent conflicts of interests when they merge. For these reasons, mergers of these functions should not be allowed. This is hardly a place for vertical monopolies operating behind layers of privileges and privacy. Instead we need separation of these functions and transparency. Monopoly is never good for the public. Leaving regulation in the hands of the president has done nothing to define or eliminate the unethical and illegal acts of financiers and investment houses. It is an inadequate tool to solve the problems created by grants of privilege. Only public involvement will define and cure the problem. It is time for the courts to take charge and put the review of financial manipulation in the hands of juries.

Finance, like government, produces no goods or services. It produces acquisitions, mergers and derivatives, and worthless paper. It always favors leveraged transactions, which make small problems big and very expensive to the rest of society. When trouble arises in this highly leveraged and unforgiving world, financiers arrange things so they are themselves bailed out and unaffected. Society is left to pay the bills, in the form of higher taxes and reduced property and home values, money again eroded by inflation. Financiers merrily skate on, free to create the next round of financial products. Trustees have lost their way. Administrators have forgotten their purpose or are clearly asleep at the switch. The president has been bought and won't let his puppet regulators work for the common good.

Paying for the mess is left to the public again. Why, then, shouldn't juries review the propriety of investment activities? Citizen participation is the only way out of this mess. Investment has become nothing but privilege. This is obvious to all but financiers and politicos. Retail banks, investment banks and stock houses have separate functions. Finance is central to prosperity, finance demands the confidence of the public and transparency is essential. To allow confidentiality, privilege, nontransparency, vertical monopoly, exemption from meaningful prosecution and restitution for fraud from the taxpayer's pockets simply cannot be tolerated. These must be the basic building blocks of financial reform. And all of this must be supervised by jury trials.

## Finance and the Airline Industry

Airlines were founded by pilots and engineers, good at keeping airplanes flying and keeping them on schedule. The business types approached the airline industry with a scheme to turn unused seats in unpopular time slots into revenue — frequent-flier miles.

Once the airlines were hooked, the financiers expanded the program to include all credit card purchases. Now you don't even have to fly to get frequent-flier miles, you can get them by simply spending with your credit card. So successful were these programs that frequent-flier miles years ago surpassed the greenback as the largest supply of money in the world. That is to say, there are more frequent-flier miles "in circulation" than there are greenbacks, real and counterfeit.

Perhaps much of the present economic plight of the airlines arose from this use of frequent-flier miles, for airlines are expected to provide airline tickets for economic transactions from which they get little economic gain. How does the purchase of a wide-screen TV with a credit card benefit the airline? Remember, the underlying message is: "let us turn those unused, unsold seats on your airplane into benefit for you"; i.e., the economies that should arise from flying airplanes full of paying customers. Like our government, airlines let financiers run the money supply (frequent-flier miles) and thus became enslaved to a monetary system not of their own design or benefit.

Some feel today we have MBA types in the airline industry canceling flights willy-nilly and holding airplanes on tarmacs for hours hoping for one more paying passenger. One wonders what would be the economic condition of airlines if they were not outsmarted and enslaved by credit card financiers? Finance is rarely a good deal for the counterparty.

## Derivatives

At first glance it would seem a difficult task to steal, from under the noses of thousands of trustees, the assets held in life insurance companies, casualty companies, private and public pension plans and IRA accounts; but with the device of the **derivative,** this plunder was accomplished without anyone being the wiser. Perhaps trustees and fund managers are too modest to admit they have bought any of the $700 trillion in derivatives that have been issued. Perhaps they are simply fearful of losing their high-paying jobs, but it is time to ask: who is holding all this worthless paper?

The darling of the investment banks is the derivative. The derivative is a *financial product*, a creation on paper, a contract. It has no tangible value whatever. It is not specie or evidence of title or even a lien on a tangible asset. It derives its supposed value from a possible event or change of a condition or that an event or condition may or may not come to pass or from a notion that the world will never change. Unfortunately we live in a world of change. Think of a derivative as a bet. It is a bet made by an investor of average sophistication against the brightest and most informed persons in the market place. When the investor purchases a derivative he is betting he knows more than the derivative designer about a particular situation. How likely is that? He is also betting he has more political clout than the investment banks, which caused events like bubbles to occur. How likely is that? The investor is the probable loser.

Designers of derivatives have developed a new business model for finance. The theory they pursue is to develop the perfect investment vehicle that provides them with a high return, but which is totally free of all risk to themselves. This means the counter party who pays the money is snookered into assuming all the risks of economic loss and receives only the appearance of value for what is in fact a highly unlikely economic return. The basic premise of the perfect derivative is that the seller assumes no risk and the buyer assumes it all: "*heads I win, tails you lose.*" A totally one-sided contract is a peculiar animal, because when the seller assumes no risk and off loads all risk to the buyer, there is no *consideration* at law. This is the classic definition of an **unconscionable contract** or contract unenforceable at law. Yet this is the central idea behind the perfect derivative.

The derivative is accompanied by a disclosure, a prospectus comprised of hundreds of pages with many subtleties of wording and implications of future value and the numerical projections of what is likely to happen if certain eventualities unfold, carefully written in legalese guaranteed to induce stupor or deep sleep. It is incomprehensible even to those with a Juris Doctor in law, unless they also have an MBA, a master's in finance, years of experience in finance, and an intimate knowledge of a particular market. A most fundamental conflict of interest is that the design of derivatives is proprietary. Information about the true nature of derivatives certainly would do the sale of these derivatives no good should it become public. So the sellers of these derivatives in the retail arm of a bank do not tell their customers about them. One section of the investment bank participates in the design of these virtual frauds, and then another section of the bank, down the hall, recommends the purchase of these products to their trusting retail clients. The Chinese wall is designed to limit insider trading, but is no cure to this problem. In the world of the derivative the trick is selling people a bright and colorfully wrapped empty box, too beautiful to open.

**Derivatives have become fraud masquerading as investment.**

The world of derivatives includes such devices as the **collateralized debt obligation** (CDO), CDO squared and CDO cubed, residential mortgage backed securities (RMBS), and structured investment vehicles (SIVS). But far and away the largest is the family of **credit risk swaps** (CRS) sold through the most prestigious banks and brokerage firms as high grade securities to the unsuspecting public. They come in many styles:

- Fixed for floating interest rate swap in the same currencies
- Fixed for floating interest rate swap in different currencies
- Floating for floating interest rate swap, same currencies
- Floating for floating rate swap, different currencies
- Complicated variants or combinations of the above

## HOW DERIVATIVES WORK

One simple example of a derivative is a future contract, a promise by a farmer made early in the year, to deliver a specific quantity of corn at the end of the growing season for an agreed price. Let us examine another example of derivatives and see how it works.

How about an **interest rate swap**? Let us talk about one based on **bonds.** We each have $1,000,000 in bonds. My lower-grade bonds have a stated rate of interest at nine percent. Your higher-grade bonds are paying three percent. We sign a contract stating that you get to collect the cash flow from my bonds, and I get the cash flow from yours, hence the term "swap." The contract also provides "basis points" and syndication fees and the salesman's ten percent commission for the prospect of increased interest income. For security purposes, you continue to hold your high-grade bonds (let us say AAA rated). I continue to hold my junk bonds. We are both locked in for the term of the contract, say ten years. How can you lose?

At the end of the first month you find you are getting not nine percent but 4.5 percent interest, because half the bonds are in default. The income continues to fall, as more people default. When you find I bought my bonds from the cleaning lady at Mike Milliken's office for two cents on the dollar, or a mere $20,000, how does that make you feel? Remember, you are locked in for ten years. Have we not, by this device, made a negotiable instrument non-negotiable?

The final revelation is that after having neatly excised the value out of your high-grade bonds, having taken over the cash flow for ten years, I now move to my Swiss office and repackage these interest rights in a new derivative which I offload or sell to insurance companies for 50 cents on each dollar of present value, and put my discounted winnings in a numbered account, where I pay no taxes and the stability of the Swiss currency protects my loot. This becomes the capital I can use to buy privileges from legislators, executives and the occasional judge.

For those derivatives that are not pure frauds, in the end you are betting money against experts. They know the system. They have superior knowledge of that small microcosm of the economy. In derivatives based on future grain prices, imagine the advantages that go to that small group of speculators that have earliest access to the U.S. military special spectrum satellite "photographs" of the world, like ConAgra. How do you hope to win in that game?

Derivative designers have special knowledge of the "free market" at the Chicago Board of Trade (now the Chicago Mercantile Exchange or Merc). How transparent is that operation? Problems are usually "resolved" by administrative law judges. No hope for due process of law there. Federal cases based on financial irregularities usually go before one special judge. How convenient is that?

And if, by chance, you end up in the winner's chair on a futures contract, the big corporation is often quite free to ignore their contractual obligations to pay you your advantage by threatening to no longer buy from you the product line of your small specialized company; they often have a monopolistic position in the market place (like Wal-Mart or Nestlé). Or, the corporation trapped in many long-term grain futures contracts can simply slip into bankruptcy court for a period of time, then re-emerge after a "miraculous" turnabout à la Pilgrims Pride. Heads I win, tails you lose. Bummer! Who is next? Step right up and try your hand.

In spite of such "frailties," these financial devices are immensely popular, used by pension plans, insurance companies and hedge fund speculators worldwide. By 2007, credit swaps were 75 percent of the world derivative market. ($309 trillion/$415 trillion). See the way credit swaps alone have grown from the Bank for International Settlements:

2005: about $170 trillion
2006: about $230 trillion
2007: about $310 trillion
2008: about $600 trillion
2009: about $700 trillion

Lehman Brothers went under holding $39 trillion in derivatives. Compare this to the U.S. GDP of about $14 trillion. The world GDP is about $60-75 trillion. Steven Cecchetti, of the Bank for International Settlements says, "*The problem comes when you start securitizing things for which you cannot compute the risk of default.*" (E 5-16-09, p. 12)

How do they make this work; sell something for nothing? How do they get away with this? Municipalities and companies that buy these "securities" have been incurring huge financial losses. The system is beginning to unravel. Derivatives have been sold for trillions of dollars to many people who not surprisingly claim not to have understood them. Lawsuits to recapture billions of dollars are now starting. Investors invariably claim that the sellers of these documents misrepresented the documents. As these incomprehensible documents contain 500 pages or more, one could easily see how even sophisticated investors could be misled. Many big banks, pension plans and insurance companies bought these same derivatives and have failed. In lawsuits on derivatives in America, the judges usually decide against the purchaser before it goes to the jury; that means the jury has no say in the matter. The judge usually rules that you should have read the document before you paid your money. Hence the investment "bankers" usually win.

The supreme stupidity of our politicians is shown in the ease with which Goldman Sachs talked our new president and his political advisers into the bank bailout without any thought on the part of the politicos as to how immense the problem will actually prove to be.

> Why did no one ask how much exposure to derivatives there was? It is $700 trillion!

Even if we spent our entire federal taxation revenues of $2.5-3 trillion, how far would that go to bail out these investment banks? Who asked where that money was going that mostly ended up in the hands of Goldman Sachs?

## BAILOUTS OF DERIVATIVES

Two forms will be discussed: (1) the TARP (troubled assets recovery program), comprised of roughly $700 billion and (2) the purchase of toxic (mostly residential) mortgages by the United States Treasury. The second program involves roughly $1.2 trillion. This is roughly one and one-half the supply of U.S. currency in circulation. Let us clearly distinguish these two programs.

The first program, TARP, was dreamed up by Hank Paulson (ex-Goldman Sachs executive) while head of the United States Treasury in the Bush administration about October 2008. The purpose was the prevention of a meltdown of the banking industry, and a gridlock of the entire economy because it relies so heavily on credit for day to day activities.

It was designed with strong incentives for payback of money loaned to banks and businesses by our treasury. The loans were secured by preferred stocks or by devices known as warrants, which pay high (above market) rates of interest. The warrants are also secured. There were also limitations on golden parachutes, executive total compensation and a "**clawback**" provision (one that limits or reverses a payment or distribution) for excessive compensation. All this was so unappealing to corporate executives, because it limited their liberties to personally plunder corporate assets, that most of these funds have already been repaid. This progress is closely followed by the press and the Internet; Pro Publica is a wonderful database tracking this program.

> The Hank Paulson bailout under Bush put about $700 billion into the economy, more than half of which has been repaid.

The second bailout program was the outright purchase of toxic mortgages by the U.S. Treasury under Timothy Geithner. Former Goldman Sachs employees now working in government designed a new format for the program. Because it is an outright purchase of toxic (thus worthless) mortgages, there is no payback requirement. There is no need to keep track of who sold what for what money. Hence these transactions are not followed by the media; what is there to follow? Even phony numbers are hard to find. There is no clawback provision. The mortgages are purchased at face value, and that is that, the book is closed. Never mind that they were originally acquired by the seller at steep discounts of 10-20 percent of face value; they may even have been acquired for little or nothing in a forced bank merger. Who can imagine what value these non-performing toxic mortgages were assigned? But they are being redeemed at face value by the U.S. Treasury. What a nice markup — nearly $1.2 trillion involved.

The beauty of the scheme is that once the sale is made, there is no going back, no accounting, no accountability. Just oodles of money: $1.2 trillion, quietly changing hands without limitations on executive compensation as were set in the TARP bailout. Because we are not being told who is selling these to the treasury I will take the liberty to assume it is none other than Goldman Sachs. It certainly is not their archrival Lehman Brothers. Bank robbery has a new meaning: it is the bankers who are doing the robbery. And the press just sits there talking about sports, new cars and cosmetic surgery.

The Geithner bailout for Obama put $1.2 trillion into the economy, none of which has been repaid, or is traceable to the seller of the toxic mortgages, and little of which will be recovered by resale of those toxic derivatives by the Treasury.

The thing not discussed about bailouts is that $1.2 trillion is one and one-half times the currency that the U.S. Treasury has in circulation. As observed before, we have increased the money supply by 150 percent with no increase in goods and services. How can economists and politicians say inflation is at 2-4 percent?

## NEW DEVELOPMENTS IN THE WORLD OF DERIVATIVES

In Milan, Italy, the sale of fraudulent derivatives is being handled differently. A huge suit against UBS and J.P. Morgan has been brought as a result of raids by the Italian federal currency police. Millions of dollars of bank and investment house assets were seized and are being held pending the outcome of the litigation. Over 600 Italian municipalities have been "taken." Frauds based upon derivatives are being alleged monthly. Representations by salesmen were often recorded on audio or video or in minutes of meetings. How do you think an Italian court will rule on these claims of the municipal pension plans? How can a lawyer lose that lawsuit? This is quite beyond control of the American courts' approach of "buyer beware."

> Is it not time to ask your insurance companies how many dollars of derivative "investments" they are sitting on?

Derivatives are not understood by politicians; they are not regulated by politicians; they are way beyond the power of politicians and administrators to regulate, and they always will be. With derivatives, slight misunderstandings and miscalculations have been shown to be able to destroy the largest of banks (Bear Stearns, Lehman Brothers, Merrill Lynch), the richest of investors, the most savvy of financiers. Due to such investments CalPERS now totters on the brink of insolvency. How can government regulators hope to understand and deal with derivatives? How do you regulate finance when economists cannot fathom derivatives, let alone predict when and how they will impact the economy or when they will "kick in"? Derivatives, being highly leveraged devices, require quantification of risk and benefit. Small errors become big errors. And it happens quickly. Federal agencies do not have an understanding of what they are dealing with or how to deal with it, plus they move so slowly that they are ineffective. An administrative agency is simply an insufficient engine in every regard to regulate our banks and financiers, or to protect our currency from such things as derivatives. (See Chapter 6.) How will this impact future bailout programs? The Federal annual "allowance" is only $2.5 trillion. They are dealing with hundreds of trillions of dollars of exposure. The investment bankers will be back for more money. Will we fall for it? The problem has continued to grow in scope and breadth. The financial losses are no longer contained within any one investment bank or a series of banks or the investment banking community or even the banking sector. They directly threaten all businesses that hold these derivatives — insurance companies, pension plans, foreign governments and so on. They indirectly affect anyone who has saved money for a rainy day, for this debacle is destroying the value of the dollar and will continue to do so for the next decade or two. How is the general welfare being served in any way by the bailout of these big investment banks? Where is the public need to bail them out? Are we not subsidizing them to continue to dream up new investment "opportunities"?

> The derivative bailout is the ultimate privilege set
> granted by any government to any corporation.

## The Reality of Modern Finance

We have seen a progression of decline in prosperity as privileges take over our economy. We have moved from a baseline of gold and silver to fiat money, then personal checks, plastic money and now finance. In finance we have seen privileges allowing financiers to escape personal liability for fraudulent transactions and accounting, usually involving a series of fictitious corporations that allows them to accumulate vast personal fortunes from duped investors. Not satisfied with that, they have turned to funding their fraudulent actions and business plans with government bailouts, as seen in the savings and loan industry. Thus we have seen finance morph into the investment world, and destroy the average man's hope of any real, or inflation corrected, returns on his precious savings and investment accounts. The privilege of real returns on investments is reserved only for the ultra rich and ultra connected

Big finance has this advantageous relationship with government because of its intimate role in floating treasury bills, which allow the continuations of the fiscal illusions on which government depends. Big finance has nothing to do with the general welfare. Dealing with big finance will leave the counterparty in a losing position every time. Big finance has gone on to dominate the investment world, systematically removing virtually all chance to invest for profit in real (inflation corrected) terms. But for themselves they have used their financial clout to assure personal returns that are risk free, greater than inflationary rates and usually free from income taxation. If you have doubts, skip ahead to the UBS story.

## More Presidential Policies

The next presidential policy is that of incumbency. These are the behaviors politicians employ to maintain their hold on the elected seats of government. Incumbency is policy, because there are no laws regulating it. There is a glaring absence of meaningful, enforceable law on the point. There is no law mandating term limits or career limits. There is no law defining a legal campaign expenditure. There is no law prohibiting the accumulation or personal use of campaign war chests. There is no law mandating meaningful accounting before receiving the immunities and privileges of public office. And once in office, one is quite insulated from jury review; he or she is entitled to a jury of their peers — their fellow politicians.

The principles of the policy of incumbency, though published nowhere, seem to be roughly congruent with the laws of incumbency (no meaningful laws exist). But we can surmise that the fundamental principles are these: don't rock the boat; we're all in this together; I suppose it may be wrong, but we all do it, politicians will judge us (the Senate, a jury of our peers); we are well insulated from jury scrutiny. With proper media management no one will know.

## POLICY OF DENIAL OF REALITY

The next presidential policy is that of denial of reality. This executive policy is made necessary because in the election process there are so many promises made, it is simply impossible find funds to fulfill all of them. Sometimes there are contradicting promises, and both cannot be fulfilled. Herein arises the need for misrepresentation and denial. The policy of denial of reality arises because the public expectations raised by a candidate in electioneering, are met once the candidate is in office with the limitations of economic reality: there is a limit to what money can be confiscated from the public. The public's perception of reality must be somehow managed. The tools of politicos include spin, statistics, studies, distraction, deception, denials, misrepresentation, mislabeling, miscategorizing, big lies, big lies repeated, simply ignoring the question or responding to a different question. The media is managed by gifts of bandwidth spectrum, scoops, tips, and news feeds.

A parade of experts and consultants is displayed because they look good and sound good. On reflection it is usually revealed that real-world experience and common sense are missing. Experts proffer economic theories, long ago disproven, but now pushed as gospel. Education standards are managed with financial grants, toleration of strong teacher unions, and in the universities, the promotion of intellectual incest. U.S. education standards have deteriorated dramatically. But this makes the population easier for the political sorts to manage. Here unproven policy is unquestioningly taught as science or reality. Seniority bordering on senility means that the entrenched remain so. The few students who survived schooling with imagination and critical thinking intact are soon overcome by frustration. The rest of the public is beaten into submissive resignation and in disgust allows the politicians to do as they wish.

## POLICY (PRETENSE) THAT ADMINISTRATIVE DUE PROCESS ACTUALLY EXISTS

Why do we have two sets of laws, two sets of courts, two types of judges? In administrative courts, why is there no jury? Why are decisions, for the most part, not recorded? Why are internal appeals not recorded, published or indexed? (See Chapter 9.) Perhaps the most important dynamic here is that all of this is off the record, beyond the scope of newspaper investigation, beyond court review. This is a blatant sale of privileges done in the most discreet manner. Just as one example, how can there be any justice in an internal revenue service private letter ruling on a taxable situation?

## POLICY THAT ADMINISTRATIVE REGULATION OF SUBJECTIVE BEHAVIOR IS IN THE GENERAL WEAL

First, we must recognize the glaringly obvious: that regulation by administrators is an insufficient engine to do the job. Regulators may be able to monitor objective (scientifically verifiable) behavior, but cannot hope to codify, let alone police subjective behaviors. Thus it is that creating yet another agency, and some new czar, is an exercise in futility.

Second, we must recognize that political forces in the legislative, executive, administrative and even the judicial branches will always intervene in response to campaign contributions. The solution is elegant in its simplicity, requires virtually no new political or governmental employees and can be designed to be beyond most governmental interferences. (See Chapter 9.)

The remedy? A jury trial for financial misbehavior is discussed at the conclusion of the section on limitations on the executive branch.

We need to get rid of the whole administrative law pretext that administration is in the general welfare.

This next section covers the spectrum of policies ranging from prosecutorial discretion, plea-bargaining and paroles, to pardons and diplomatic solutions. All these considerations are outside the view of the court system.

## POLICY OF PROSECUTORIAL MERIT

The executive has the ability, through his agents, the Department of Justice, the Attorney General, and the district attorney to decide to bring charges or ignore a situation, usually without public scrutiny or need for explanation. Again, there is no published code for this policy, but we can surmise the following principles: never big campaign donors, indeed no big fish. And only too often the executive prosecutes transgressors if they are of the opposite political party.

## POLICY OF PLEA-BARGAINING (DEALS MADE BEFORE THE TRIAL)

They are made without public scrutiny or explanation. We must guess what is in the mind of the executive, and his agents, the prosecutors. Is it insufficient evidence or is the defendant too big, too rich or too politically well connected to prosecute? Is it national security? ("We know he kills people, but it is usually for our side." "He knows too many secrets that will come out if there is a trial.") Who really knows what is going on? We cannot peer into the mind of the executive or his agents.

## POLICY OF PAROLE

Neatly packaged and removed from the executive, an administrative parole board, "policed and monitored" only by the media, has the power to decide how much of a sentence someone must serve and often where it is to be served.

## POLICY OF PARDONS

Can anyone explain how the gubernatorial and presidential "sale" of pardons, especially as they leave office, in any way enhances the general welfare? It could be argued that it simply encourages white collar crime. Such persons know that corporate veils protect them. They know that the expense and delay of penetrating the corporate shield protects them. They know how to conceal their ill-gotten gains. They know there is usually a deal offered by prosecutors. They bank on the notion that if caught and convicted, the punishment never fits the crime. Aristotle tells us that in Athens, liability ran from twice the damages suffered by citizens to ten times the damages to the community, and in that case they could well lose citizenship. Here judges only assess a fraction of the damages that wrongdoers cause. And, if they are convicted, there is always the hope of executive pardon. In New Hampshire, pardons are only considered in Supreme Court. How can you improve on that?

## POLICY OF DIPLOMACY: THE UBS STORY

For decades, Switzerland solicited the wealthy to deposit money in its banks. It also created, through international treaties and decriminalized tax evasion within Switzerland, privileges of near absolute confidentiality for depositors in their banks. The Union Bank of Switzerland (UBS) was the second largest bank in Switzerland, behind Credit Suisse, and has given special emphasis to *global wealth management*. This is polite talk for income tax evasion.

**Tax avoidance**, planning transactions to minimize taxation, such as creating trusts or changing residency or taking income not as a lump sum but over time, may or may not be legal. **Tax evasion**, such as failure to report income or lying to the government about the extent of money or value involved in a transaction is a criminal act around the world, but in Switzerland it is merely a civil offense. This means that in Switzerland alone, tax evasion is not a criminal act and thus does not lead to jail time. But it is a crime in Switzerland to disclose the identity of the accountholders unless tax evasion can be proven.

Without the specifics, making that proof has been quite impossible in most circumstances.

With the historic numbered account (pre-1992), it was possible to open a Swiss bank account in such a way that no one within the bank knew who owned that account. Due to a change of Swiss laws, since 1992 a few senior bank officials know the identity of the owner. Without ownership identity, the history of transactions and account balances becomes rather meaningless. Hence the Swiss government historically granted bankers almost absolute confidentiality within the system of numbered accounts. The central tool for tax evasion has become these numbered accounts. More recently, with the use of data processing, some processors have become privy to knowledge of account ownership.

The Swiss policy of strict secrecy has led to them to spurn the euro and instead use their Swiss franc to further assure stability and client satisfaction. Switzerland's unique banking privacy laws have made it one of the world's richest nations and the envy of dozens of other tax haven nations, like Luxembourg, Lichtenstein, Panama, the Cayman Islands, and more. The account minimums are customarily large, usu-ally $1-5 million. Dozens of Swiss banks are thought to hold $2 tril-lion in offshore investments. 11-12 percent of the Swiss gross domes-tic product is purported to relate to banking. And this legendary secre-cy has led to untold national wealth. It can be extremely profitable to banks when wealthy clients die, leaving their heirs in the dark as to the extent of the true wealth of the deceased, and the bank retains these proceeds.

On January 7, 1997, Chris Meili, a night watchman at UBS, dis-covered large bins of WWII bank documents being destroyed. He saved some of them and made them public, to the embarrassment of UBS. This destruction was a direct violation of a new Swiss federal law passed on December 13, 1996, prohibiting the destruction of such documents. This incident promptly led to expensive lawsuits brought by Holocaust survivors and a $1.25 billion settlement. For his candor and honesty, this hardworking father of two was fired.

When UBS bought the American brokerage house Paine Webber in 2000, they had to get approval from American anti-trust regulators. In so doing they perhaps unwittingly agreed to have American transactions be bound by American law practices and trading and banking standards, which proved to be quite different from the Swiss standards.

In the mid-2000s, German intelligence discovered curious communications between UBS bank customers and the bank, which they first suspected to be terrorist related. They later proved to be legitimate, though codified, communications using fruits substituted for numbers. In the U.S. a long, intensive investigation of UBS began based on the United States laws to which the Swiss had consented to be bound. This culminated in a criminal probe leading to the arrest in 2007 of a UBS special account officer, Bradley Birkenfeld, at the Miami airport on his way back to Switzerland with a client's diamonds in a tube of toothpaste. Even though he turned whistle-blower and is claiming millions of dollars in IRS cash bounties, he is now serving a 40-month prison term in the U.S. He was simply following bank orders and protocol; his crime: getting caught following them.

The criminal case leading to Birkenfeld's incarceration had been started in Miami in U.S. federal court (the Miami Case); it became clear to UBS management that they, too, were exposed to criminal charges and the bank was exposed to conspiracy and racketeering charges. Panic ensued in the boardroom at UBS. Criminal sanctions against UBS officers appeared inevitable.

Huge write-offs for losses on derivatives, coupled with the possibility of bank clients withdrawing billions of deposits (a massive run on the bank) due to the criminal charges, led to the possibility UBS would not meet the mandatory reserve requirements. So it was that in 2007, one year before the financial meltdown of 2008-2009, UBS announced a vote of shareholders to accept aid (bailout) from the Swiss government. On Oct. 16, 2008, the Swiss Federation bailed out UBS with $6 billion in special mandatory convertible notes.

> The UBS bailout began over one year before the meltdown of 2008-2009. To what extent did it cause it?

Under the terms of the bailout, loss of liberty for management and directorship was severe. On Nov. 12, 2008, it was announced that various clawback provisions would be instituted: no more than one-third of bonuses would be paid in the year earned, the rest would be held in reserve, and incentive stock shares would vest only after three years and would be subject to reductions.

Then came terrible news from another quarter. HBSC is a large London bank, with many branch offices. In 2008-2009 Herve Falciani, a data processing employee of HBSC-Switzerland, stole data from HBSC showing ownership and account details of at least 109,000 bank customers. The documents were reputedly seized by French authorities at his home. These records involved transfers from other banks, revealing account ownership and transaction details from many European banks.

Seemingly due to international treaties of privilege and confidentiality and threats by the Swiss to reveal secret Swiss bank accounts of the politicians of the various European nations, HBSC claims that most of this data was returned to the bank without attempts by those European nations to prosecute the tax evaders, and they lost few accounts.

This proved not absolutely true. The French are using this information to investigate and prosecute over 3,000 French tax evasion cases. In the United States, Dr. Andrew Silva has pled guilty to tax evasion based on this data and it seems to be the basis for the tax evasion convictions of Mauricio Cohen-Assor and Leon Cohen-Levy, two real estate developers. Oddly enough, someone seems to be selling this data to various governments for millions of euros.

But the difference in American law and procedure and politics soon became apparent. The Miami suit against UBS was started by the U.S. Justice Department in 2007 on the theory that UBS systematically conspired to help U.S. citizens avoid income taxation. Because these proceedings were in open court, the usual attempts to seek a *diplomatic* solution (a cover-up) were less available to the Swiss.

For the Swiss bankers denial of charges of wrong doing and minimizing the impact of bad news in the press was not working. The next attempt to control the problem was threats. On February 15, 2009, the *New York Times* broke the story of "sister" cases involving German collections of taxes evaded by Credit Suisse account holders. This data was derived from the counterparty data produced from the stolen Herve Falciani discs. This means bank account numbers, identities and transaction details of money moved into C-S were revealed. Credit Suisse bank lobbyists threatened to reveal account details of German politicians holding Swiss accounts, explaining that "*if Germany buys stolen data, we will work for a change in the law so that complete Swiss accounts of German people holding public office have to be disclosed.*" The German prosecutors went ahead anyhow.

> Here are public, published threats to disclose the identity and details of politicians and political employees who hold secret Swiss bank accounts.

As evidence of criminal activities and conspiracies by UBS employees mounted, on February 18, 2009, someone at UBS thought it was a good idea to save the bank officers and throw the bank clients to the wolves. UBS enter a deferred prosecution agreement. It agreed in court to pay $780 million in fines, penalties and interest and to surrender account names and details to escape criminal prosecution of bank officers in the U.S., hoping to keep its huge U.S. business portfolio intact. Approximately 250-300 names and "confidential" account details were delivered to American authorities by UBS, as part of this settlement.

On February 18, 2009, two Swiss newspapers reported that a *diplomatic* solution had been reached whereby no money was to be paid by UBS to the United States. All seems well for UBS, but this was just spin.

On February 19, 2009, in the Miami, Florida, federal courtroom, the U.S. Justice department dropped a real bomb on the Swiss, issuing 52,000 "John Doe" warrants on UBS for client account details.

Billions of deposits fled from the UBS bank. Depositors worldwide lost confidence in the secrecy of Swiss banking. UBS cut some 11,700 jobs. Its share value dropped by nearly half. Officers admitted that if they lost the privilege of secrecy, UBS might cease to exist. Switzerland frantically attempted to create a *diplomatic* solution.

About this time President Obama showed interest with a "high level of direct personal involvement." But it seems that attorneys for UBS, in an attempt to protect UBS officers from U.S. criminal prosecution, had made an illegal agreement to disclose bank customer names. The deal is illegal by Swiss laws and exposes the Swiss to criminal charges in Switzerland.

On Feb. 24, 2009, people in America were reported to be losing sleep at night. There were also reports of people paying U.S. officials tens of thousands of dollars to see if their names were on the list of 250-300 persons! **Are any of our politicos on that list?**

On Feb. 25, 2009, U.S. clients of UBS sued the bank in Swiss federal court to prevent disclosure of their names and account details to the United States. It had occurred to American tax evaders that UBS officials had decided to throw them to the wolves, and save themselves.

On March 4, 2009, Mark Branson, UBS chief financial officer (CFO) of the bank's global wealth management division, testified before the U.S. Senate subcommittee on finance and banking that there were, as of September 30, 2008, not 52,000 U.S. tax evaders, but only approximately 47,000 who had accounts at UBS — U.S. citizens who did not pay taxes on assets or income with accounts at UBS.

One wonders which U.S. politicians are on that list?

Evidence adduced at that hearing shows a conspiracy to move assets into numbered Swiss bank accounts to avoid detection by U.S. revenue authorities, to open and maintain accounts in the names of sham entities. It shows the creation of a special division within the bank to expedite and facilitate cross border transfers of money. Within that division, special agent employees make up to 30 trips per year to run lectures and seminars on how to transfer money to avoid present and future income taxation; how to use shell corporations and phony charitable trusts; how to effectively "launder" untaxed income and assets by using numbered accounts; how to withdraw proceeds in secret, using coded language like fruit for numbers; and how to use phony charitable trusts, special credit cards, and payphones to conceal bank directives. In essence, a whole internal bureaucracy was created for these special bank customers to evade taxes.

Branson concludes that most of the accounts are now closed and the bank has done all it can to cooperate. He adds that to turn over more information would subject UBS employees to prosecution under Swiss laws. The conclusion of the subcommittee hearing was that the U.S. was losing $100 billion per year to offshore tax havens, including the Swiss.

> Denial and delay allowed many (most) to transfer
> accounts to other (less-regulated) banks.

On March 30, 2009, panic was rampant among American holders of UBS accounts and there were more threats to sue UBS for breach of Swiss privacy clauses in banking laws. Accounts left the country in significant numbers and amounts. The stock market hit a new low, as the Dow hit 6,500.

On or about July 11, 2009, fearing destruction of their private banking business, the Swiss government prepared to seize UBS data to prevent the bank from handing it over to U.S. authorities, on the basis that the Swiss criminal code makes it a crime to hand client information over to foreign authorities.

Judge Gold, in charge of the Miami tax evasion suit, announced that the trial against UBS for criminal tax evasion would begin July 13, 2009. He was said to contemplate seizure and sale of UBS properties in the U.S., and advancing criminal prosecution. The Swiss were within two days of trial, and . . . the screen went blank.

On Aug. 3, 2009, the *New York Times* reported UBS would escape fines and jail time and release 5,000 names and account details. UBS would turn the names over to the Swiss Government, who would turn them over to the U.S. Department of Justice. They would disclose only the names they wished to disclose, and then only if they chose to go ahead with the deal; there was no binding treaty compelling them to so disclose names or data.

Such a deal can only be covered by a treaty between nations. The Swiss now screamed even louder for a *diplomatic* solution to the problem. The matter went to the Swiss parliament. The lower house approved the disclosure of names and numbers. The conservative upper house blocked the deal. Swiss parliament now decided that any information from Swiss banks would not be made public in court, *but would be transferred from government to government.* Threats to disclose accounts of politicians might be more focused and effective. The upper house suggested a referendum by its people before allowing the data transfer; was this a simple delay tactic? Accounts were transferred to other banks, records were lost daily and the expense of tax collection increased.

On Feb. 24, 2010, the Swiss government levied a $1 million Swiss franc fine on UBS "to cover part of the costs related to the case."

> **Where is the proof that any of the $780 million was paid?**

There then fell a virtual news blackout: no coverage of anything, no reporting on the prosecution of the 250-300 names previously disclosed.

In the Swiss parliament, a bill discussing a treaty went before the lower house, then the upper house. But it had no power to stop American prosecution, except by bribery and threat of disclosure of politicians with secret accounts. Judge Gold has shown no interest in letting this case fall by the wayside. Who has the power to stop court proceedings? Only his boss, the president of the United States.

> **Only the president has the power to stop the UBS prosecution.**

On January 8, 2010, it was reported that 14,700 U.S. citizens used a special amnesty law to avoid criminal prosecution by the IRS. This caused some to ponder the "tax deals" hawked on TV where persons claimed "I settled with the IRS by paying only 10 cents on the dollar."

Fast-forward to July 2010. Nearly one year has passed. There is little news of any prosecution of the 250-300 or so tax evaders in the hands of the Department of Justice. News has simply dried up. No news is bad news. Where is the evidence of any payment of the $780 million in fines and penalties? Where is the proof of payment? Do we have another buyout — a sellout by the president under the color of "*diplomacy*"? These are institutionalized crooks; these are not diplomats by any definition!

Many accounts have fled to other offshore tax havens that may never be discovered; the golden opportunity for justice is lost. Who stopped the federal prosecution? Another campaign contribution? How many American politicians had secret Swiss bank accounts? Anyone smell a rat? The Swiss and the ultra-rich have won again; every day each trail grows colder.

So it is that UBS wins their tax evasion case as American citizens are distracted by other things and simply forget that a few ultra rich evade one hundred billion dollars in income tax every year to off shore tax havens.

Why have a tax code in America if the rich do not have to pay taxes?

## TRANSGRESSIONS OF UBS

- January 7, 1997 Meili employer loses UBS security contract, and Meili is fired. In 1997, the World Jewish Congress (WJC) starts a suit against UBS and other major Swiss banks to recover deposits of those killed in the Holocaust.
- On March 20, 2003, Richard Scrushy, founder and CEO of HealthSouth Corporation, was reported to have falsified the earnings reports of his company since 1996, to meet investor expectations and control the price of the stock in the company, all to his benefit. SEC hearings investigated Scrushy and others including three senior UBS bankers, one of whom left UBS shortly thereafter for "personal reasons."

- From 2000 to 2002 in Connecticut and New Jersey UBS brokers engaged in market timing trading practices, and were fined 5.5 million dollars and loss of license according to the Connecticut Department of Banking preliminary statement to the court dated January 16, 2006.
- In 2005, in *Zubulake v. UBS Warburg*, a discrimination lawsuit, UBS was found to have destroyed e-mail evidence in violation of court orders to preserve it. The judge instructed the jury that these acts give rise to the inference that the missing evidence was unfavorable to UBS. The case was promptly settled in private.
- In 2005, the city of Milan, Italy, encouraged by alleged fraudulent misrepresentations of UBS, Deutsche Bank and J.P. Morgan, bought a 30-year interest rate swap derivative for the years 2005-2035. This deal will cost the city an estimated 300 million euros. Other such deals made with other municipalities by these banks will run over 40 billion euros. A 2007 investigation reported in *Newsweek* that traders for two hedge funds were paying UBS employees for information on impending rate changes on stocks.
- On Feb. 23, 2008, in Brazil, twenty employees of UBS, Credit Suisse and AIG were arrested for money laundering, tax evasion, fraudulent banking practices and operating without a banking license.
- On February 18, 2009, UBS wealth management agreed to pay fines to the USA of $780 million for helping tens of thousands of Americans evade hundreds of millions of dollars in taxes per year for each of at least seven years. Due to the passage of time and movement of money any hope of recovering these taxes is pretty much lost. Amazingly UBS retains banking and investment licenses in most states within the USA.
- On September 23, 2009, the Financial Industry Regulatory Authority (FINRA) fined Deutsche Bank $150,000, UBS $150,000, and Citigroup $175,000, and ordered payment of up to $400,000 in damages in the Vonage securities IPO.

- On November 5, 2009, England fined UBS $13.3 million and in addition, UBS paid clients $42 million in damages for illegal trading of precious metals from January 2006 to December 2007, up to 50 unauthorized transactions per day.
- In 2010, UBS paid €184 million to settle fraud allegations in the financing of Parmalat dairy of Italy.
- On February 24, 2010, UBS agreed to reimburse the Swiss Federal Government 1 million Swiss francs to cover part of the expense of the government hearings regarding the attempted settlement with the U.S. Department of Justice.

It should be clear to anyone but a regulator or a politician receiving campaign contributions that fines and government regulation are an insufficient engine to cure the "black hearts" of big investment banks. Nothing but juries and good old-fashioned American punitive damages will really get the attention of bankers. Why not turn American trial attorneys loose on these modern-day pirates?

These are small fish compared to the meltdown of the financial system in 2008-2009. Step back and look at the big picture; could the meltdown have happened without the puffery of big finance, bankers and offers of stability for the privileged to hold their private assets and other plunder in secret accounts under the guise of "wealth management"? Would any of this occur without privileges for the ultra-rich?

Why is UBS, of all financial institutions, allowed to keep its banking licenses and monumental banks in the U.S.? Their proven track record is that of breaking laws worldwide, yet they seem to avoid the fines, penalties and interest that should accompany such misdeeds. They wish to impose the Swiss privilege of secrecy in banking upon us. It is contrary to the tax code of virtually every other country. By allowing them to keep banks in America, we facilitate their imposition of Swiss secrecy and tax evasion. The ultra-rich do not want to put their money in shaky Third World economies, where a change of dictators could cause them to lose it all.

To leave huge sums of money in the hands of strangers in secrecy requires a special rapport. Much of the appeal of Swiss secret accounts lies in the stability of its government, and its money supply, unmatched by any other country. It is a problem to build the confidential relationships needed for secret accounts with no monthly statements, in fact, little evidence that the account exists. Why do we facilitate building such relationships? Moving substantial assets to a foreign bank with the $10,000 IRS limitation quickly shows up on passports as frequent visits to tax haven countries. Why create for UBS clients the convenience of making personal deposits in local UBS banks? Why are we making it more convenient for UBS and its clients to move money? This privilege is nothing but a springboard to build rapport with clients that offshore banks do not have.

So the Swiss win again, battle after battle. The golden rule is that those who have the gold, rule.

## CREDIT SUISSE

Documents from 2004 show Credit Suisse's officers and directors lament that anti-terrorist laws *"made it more difficult to produce untaxed funds."* The bank likes these deposits of untaxed funds, because *"they require no marketing or service, and contacts with the bank are avoided rather than sought,"* according to *The Independent*, a German financial blog.

In 2009, a Credit Suisse bank employee, Hervé Falciani, sold data disc #1 to the German government apparently for €2.5 million. These data discs showed names, account numbers and transaction details for tax evasion of German citizens. In February 2010, Germany bought a second such disc for €2.5 million. Baden Wurtenburg, a state in Germany, was offered another such disc containing 2,000 names. On February 10, 2010, the state of Bavaria was reported to be considering buying another disc of names and account data, price undisclosed.

On February 15, 2010, Swiss lobbyists retaliate for Credit Suisse and threaten to expose German officials and other public figures as tax evaders. Doris Leuthard, president of Credit Suisse, accuses Germany of creating a market for stolen data, which encourages Swiss employees to steal confidential data.

On March 20, 2010, 1,100 prosecutions were started in the state of North Rhine-Westphalia based on disc data most likely obtained from Hervé Falciani. The prosecutors office suggested there were more than €1.2 billion in these accounts under prosecution.

These discs collectively suggest that 100,000 Germans have untaxed funds in Credit Suisse alone. On October 10, 2009, it was reported that over 3,000 Germans came forward to settle tax bills with Germany.

Hervé Falciani is the reported source of the "Lichtenstein CD." It is not clear if the disc was sold, or simply given to Lichstenstein, but data from that disc was admissible in a German court of law and was the basis for the conviction of Klaus Zumwinkel, who received a €1 million fine.

Note that these actions to enforce tax evasion are not based upon the Paine Webber purchase, and seem to be in violation of specific European intergovernmental treaties granting privileges to bankers. The violation of such treaty terms causes diplomatic problems; the public will not stand for such privileges. The *New York Times* reported that a Liechtenstein court awarded a tax evader named Elmar Bernhard Schulte €7.5 million in damages, saying his bank should have warned Schulte so he could come forward to settle with the German tax authorities.

All is in flux, but faith in Swiss confidentiality is in tatters. So, too, are our income tax laws. It is time to ask: why do we have "big finance" anyhow? How does it benefit the general public? Putting the regulation of banks and finance in the hands of regulatory puppets managed by politicos that are open to bribery has proven to be an inadequate answer. Should not the regulation of finance really be done by juries? Who else better knows the general weal?

When viewed as a totality, the program of presidential policies is easily recognized as a complicated machine focused on administering executive privileges for the ultra wealthy and for corporations. A stark admission of the fact was made by President Obama's pay czar Feinberg on July 24, 2010 when he announced his decision to make no efforts to recoup any part of the $1.6 billion paid to top executives in bailed out banks, those 17 companies singled out for obviously bad behavior. He unilaterally decided that *"shaming these banks was enough,"* because *"a fight with those banks would expose them to lawsuits from shareholders trying to recapture executives' money, and he didn't think that would be fair."* (Associated Press) This is the apogee of administrative **shithead logic**.

## Judiciary Tools: Doctrines of Law

It is the duty of the court to present to its citizens and businesses decisions that are predictable and cohesive. Citizens and businesses alike require this for guiding their actions and business plans. A stable society, the liberty of citizens and prosperity for businesses, hence society at large, demand this.

To this end, our Supreme Court has developed various **doctrines of law,** which are the basis for such predictability and stability. Because the nature of the world, of government and of economies is mutability or change, these rigid doctrines are under constant stress and assault. Because court decisions are under constant and rigorous scrutiny and analysis, even minute changes will not go unnoticed. But doctrines must change with the times, or justice will not be done in courts. The following were once helpful doctrines, but are now out of touch with the reality of the modern world and its econopolitics.

Doctrines of law include *res judicata* and *stare decisis* (the idea that issues were decided once and need not be reheard by the Supreme Court), the doctrine that the **spending powers** of the legislature and the executive are beyond judicial review; **corporate citizenship**; **corporate sovereignty** (making corporate actions beyond judicial review); enforcing the notion that laws granting economic privilege are beyond judicial review; validating the idea that administrative law proceedings are beyond the scope of judicial review; *caveat emptor*, **eminent domain; regulatory due process; delegation of legislative powers** (the notion that legislating can be delegated to agencies, lobbyists and their attorneys); and the notion that money is freedom of speech.

## *RES JUDICATA* AND *STARE DECISIS*

Starting with **res judicata** and **stare decisis:** stability and predictability in law are highly desirable. The court should not be bothered with the same issue again and again, simply brought by different parties. But the fact is that the Supreme Court does change its mind. This means one of the two answers was wrong.

For example, in 1895 the U.S. Supreme Court, in *United States v. E.C. Knight Company* (1895), a case brought under the Sherman Anti-Trust Act of 1890, had ruled that the U.S. Congress *was without* the constitutional power to ban this holding company. Teddy Roosevelt, once in office, promptly challenged the decision in the *Northern Securities Company v. United States* (1904) case. On April 9, 1903, a federal circuit court ordered the dissolution of the Northern Securities trust, and on March 14, 1904, the U.S. Supreme Court reversed itself, or got it right, and affirmed the president. The conclusion: despite *res judicata* and *stare decisis,* sometimes the Supreme Court can and should change its mind.

## CORPORATIONS AS CITIZENS

The issue of **corporations as citizens** has long troubled our Supreme Court. There has evolved a doctrine of corporate citizenship, which has led to the inordinate influence of corporations on our economy. Originally, in *Bank of the United States v. Deveaux* (1807), Justice Marshall wrote for the Supreme Court, which had unanimously decided that corporations were not citizens. They were *"invisible, intangible, artificial beings"* that *"exist only in the contemplation of the law."* It was found they have *"no organ except the corporate seal"* and *"cannot be outlawed."* They were *"certainly not citizens."*

By 1870, corporations were *"quasi-citizens."* Then by 1876 they were full citizens. Clearly the whole doctrine can be junked, and addressed by the commerce clause, which recognizes a free market, meaningful corporate income taxation with penalties for monopoly and, best of all, corporate activity monitored by our states' attorneys general and by juries in courts of law.

## DOCTRINE THAT REVIEW OF GOVERNMENT SPENDING IS BEYOND THE POWER OF COURTS

In 1934, the majority in *Butler* held that: "*A tax, in the general understanding of the term as used in the Constitution signifies an extraction for the support of the Government. The word has never been thought to connote the expropriation of one group for the benefit of another.*"

In *Cuno v. DaimlerChrysler*, the U.S. Court of Appeals said "***we have never squarely considered the constitutionality of subsidies…***" The plain truth is that the court can no longer turn its back on the power of the other two branches to spend money without limitation. The rest of the doctrines will be discussed in Chapter 10, The Judiciary, after a bit of historical and political predicate is laid out in the following chapters.

**We see the presidential policies and Court doctrines, when viewed as a totality are simply that of extending privileges to the ultra-wealthy in every way that they can imagine. The result is spectacular wealth for the ultra-rich, at the cost of prosperity for the rest.**

Jefferson said: "I believe that banking institutions are more dangerous to our liberties than standing armies. If the American people ever allow private banks to control the issue of their currency, first by inflation and then by deflation the banks and corporations that will grow up around banks will deprive the people of all property until their children wake up homeless on the continent their fathers conquered."

With the $1.2 trillion Geithner has given investment banks, and with the hundreds of billions of dollars of offshore tax avoidance documented in the senate banking commission findings, coupled with real estate deflation, these banks are in a fine position to fulfill Jefferson's prophecy.

Aristotle told us that Justice is none of that. Justice is based upon equality, and a government that is not just is as a government that cannot endure.

# Book Two:

# Needed Changes to Bodies Politic

# Chapter 6

# Campaign Finance Reform

D o we attract the wrong sorts of people to political office, or is it the political system as it now stands that corrupts all who are in office? Let us examine the economics of running for office and the "goings-on" once elected to Congress.

Congress, invented by the Founding Fathers, new in the history of government, was designed with care. It was defined with more detail than any other part of the new government in the sparsely written national constitution. Slightly more than half the wording of the Constitution is used to describe the Congress.

The three primary obligations of legislators, then and now, are: to know the constituency and their needs; to search for a consensus, which constitutes the general welfare; and to argue, debate and formulate laws, which are the words that best serve the general welfare of the nation.

"The *real welfare* of the people is the supreme objective. Attaining this objective is the government's only value." (*The Federalist Papers* 45, pp 6)

"The first aim [of government is] . . . to find men . . . who possess the most wisdom to discern the *common good* of the society." (F 57 pp 53)

"Possess a proper knowledge of the local circumstances of their numerous constituents." (F 55 pp 1)

Men with "fidelity to the constituents." (F 57 pp 7)

Those who sympathize with the "feelings of the mass of the people."

"Men who possess the most wisdom to discern, and the most virtue to pursue the *common good of society.*" (F 57 pp 7)

"No man can be a competent legislator that does not add to an upright intention and sound judgment, a certain knowledge of the subjects on which he is to legislate." (F 54 pp 4)

Recall that *"history informs us of no long lived republic which has not had a senate."* (F 63 pp 9) The Senate, the body of elders (30 and above), is important to insure the rights of the minorities and to insure that these rights are not trampled upon by the majority in times when passions run high and reason is not in command. The Founding Fathers were painfully aware that in Athens there were times when a substantial body of less eloquent citizens was ostracized for no other reason than being poor debaters and weak orators for their own cases or points of view. Each was his own advocate, and some simply were not so gifted as others.

Because of the obvious limitations of democracy, the impossibility to put what has now become over 300,000,000 citizens (in the U.S.) in a single arena, government by **representation** was the only solution for giving all citizens any voice in government. And these representatives, each and every one, were to be fiduciaries of the public trust. Simply stated, they were to use the highest level of care in representation of their constituents when seeking and formulating the general welfare of the nation. The standard of care was defined by our Supreme Court as the duty of politicians in their search for the *general weal* to "not only avoid impropriety, but to "**avoid the appearance of impropriety.**" (*Buckley v. Valeo*, 1976)

This standard of care was reasserted in *McConnell v. Federal Election Commission* (2003). Our modern-day Congress falls short of this standard by any test and by any measure. The present work product of Congress is not good. We get laws written by law firms for lobbyists of special interest groups, not congressional persons at all. We get legislation not even read by congressional representatives. We get 91,000 pages of administrative code from unknown scriveners, under the direction of our president. Most of these codes are not reviewable by the courts of law; thus, any issues are decided by those we do not elect to the judiciary. After review of the powers assumed by the executive branch of government (see Chapter 9), we can better see the shortfalls of our Congress.

Why do we seem to attract all the wrong people, for all the wrong reasons to elected office? Or is it that the idealistic are somehow corrupted by the process of getting to office? Is it campaign contributions or the money in politics? Let us look closer at the nature of campaign contributions.

## The Nature of Campaign Finance Today

Campaign finance is the method by which money is raised in democracies of all shades to run political campaigns. Sources run from private money of the candidate, to aggregations of private, corporate, even international corporate funds, to recent experiments using only public funds. Some would argue for banning all private and corporate campaign contributions. Others would argue for banning even campaigners' personal funds; that is to say, that all funds for elections should come from the treasury and only the treasury. According to our Supreme Court, all such notions fall afoul of the First Amendment right of free speech, and an implied right of freedom to associate (assemble). Clearly there are abuses in the present system. We must look to balance the right of citizens to representative government with the first amendment rights of candidates.

Curiously the tax treatment of American campaign contributions is not even covered in the standard authority, the Congress Clearing House a 25-volume treatise on taxation in the United States published by Wolters Kluwer. It is clear that if money is spent on a function that is 99 percent personal and one percent remotely, arguably, related to a campaign, it need not be declared as income, and hence is exempt from income taxation.

It is also clear that unused funds may be treated as a gift, and therefore are not subject to income taxation. These funds can be used for personal purposes in the future without income or social security taxation, which makes them better than a congressional salary. It is also clear that winners are not subject to any meaningful audit at any relevant time. Courts are reluctant to employ administrative audits to undo an election once a candidate has taken office. And, should an audit be undertaken, the candidate can take comfort in knowing that Congress appoints the auditor's bosses, who regulate auditors hiring, firing, job opportunities, pay, promotions and work venues.

Odd it is that there are not temporal limits to making or spending campaign monies. Contributions may be made years in advance, before one even announces candidacy. They may be made while the Congress is in session. They may be made day or night. Contributions may be made by check, credit card or cash. They may be made after elections are won or lost. There is no limitation to say they cannot be made after retirement. Odder still is that there are no limitations as to when they must be spent. They may accrue in war chests after a campaign, insulating the politician from the need to reacquaint oneself with the constituency. And a big war chest full of money can discourage any competitive election bid from others.

Record keeping and reporting of campaign contributions is quite opaque and impossible to audit. Where is a prohibition on cash contributions? Where is any basis for checking the completeness of a candidate's actual receipts? At present it is impossible to determine contributions, expenditures and balances in a meaningful way before a candidate is sworn into office. Where is it defined what a legitimate campaign expenditure might be? Some donors make massive contributions of equal size to both candidates. Why would they do that?

Campaign contributions are a conflict of interest for politicians. Clearly a person can serve but one master. But who is the master? Beyond dispute the master is the one who pays. If the political process is to work, if politicians are to search for the general weal, who should that master be? Who but the constituents at home? Allowing non-constituent campaign contributions simply erodes the allegiance to the constituents back home. To whom is this allegiance owed? A single constituent or the whole? The first campaign donor or the biggest campaign donor? Someone who gave weeks of time in your campaign or the biggest dollar contributor? Do out-of-state donors count? What if your party line conflicts with the interests of the folks back home? What we have in the legislative process seems to be handed down from the Lord Chancellor of England, Sir Francis Bacon, who is reputed to have said:

"I usually accept bribes from both sides, so tainted money can never affect my decision."

Campaign contributions lead to a bookkeeping nightmare. With all the money coming in, how does a candidate track to whom he/she owes an allegiance? What if you accept money from persons on both sides of an issue? How do you quantify your allegiance to an issue? If money is allowed at the moment allegiances are being developed, how can each party get an equal chance to bid or bribe? And who knows or can measure the effect that a political party has upon this "deliberation"? Who knows who is taking how much?

Sanctions are quite ineffective. By the time a problem is noticed, the candidate may be in office and insulated from meaningful review by courts. Fine as juries are, courts do not want to run the risk of undoing elections by a jury. Nor do they wish to have the behavior of politicians in elections tried in a court of law. How could a judge keep "order in the court"? Rather courts take the position that if you don't like a politician, or what he/she is doing, your remedy is to vote them out of office. Then too, once in Federal office, you are entitled to a jury of your peers, the Senate, for the senate shall have the sole power to try impeachments (Article III).

The bottom line is that campaign contributions under present law and practice are nothing but **bribes**. As such they are corrosive to politics. They deflect the politicians from their duty to define and pursue the general welfare of their constituents.

## History of Campaign Finance

The Founding Fathers were suspicious of the common man. In the early years of our country there was a requirement to hold property to be eligible to vote. Only about 20 percent of the United States citizens were qualified to vote from 1775. This practice declined state by state, but existed in some states until the late 1820s. Senators were not elected by popular vote; nor were federal judges or Supreme Court justices. Many forget that our president is not elected by popular vote, but by the Electoral College.

As voters were empowered, politics changed. Andrew Jackson recognized the potential of newspapers for support rather in the mode of *The Federalist Papers*. Perhaps his military background led to his biggest political contribution, the adoption and organization of the patronage system in America, reminiscent of the patron system prevalent in ancient Rome. This was before civil service and the president was permitted to appoint a myriad of officials, basically without consideration of merit. Political appointees were expected to return a portion of their pay back to the political party machine.

In *The Federalist Papers* 54, it is noted that property and wealth also get representation:

"Government is instituted no less for the protection of property than of the persons or individuals." (F 54 pp 8)

"If the law allows an opulent citizen but a single vote in the choice of his representative, the respect and consequences which he derives from his fortunate situation very frequently guide the vote of others to the objects of his choice; and-through this **imperceptible channel** rights of property are conveyed into the public representation." (F 54 pp 9)

Especially in the cities, to build political machines, the purchase of votes was quite common. With hard labor paying less than a dollar a day, reports of a single citizen's vote being purchased for pennies seem plausible. After the Civil War, the new and ultra-wealthy industrialists were routinely solicited for massive donations by federal and state candidates. By 1872, wealthy New York patrons were reputedly making $10,000 contributions. Those in office standardized the practice of collecting money from civilians awarded government contracts. This led to another practice where federal employees solicited money from other federal employees for campaign contributions. This became so extreme it led to the passing of one of the first campaign finance bills: the Naval Appropriations Bill, which prohibited federal employees from soliciting contributions from naval yard workers.

In 1883, the Pendleton Civil Service Reform Act did away with assessing civil servants a portion of their pay for political machines. This was then replaced with funding by extortion, where large contributions from big business were wrung out by threats of unfavorable legislation in Congress. This practice caused political machines to aggressively solicit contributions from businessmen to preserve their privileges through bribery. These privileges quickly turned into abuses as American industrialization expanded.

Post-Civil War industrialization in America led to an unimagined concentration of capital, personal wealth and political power. This power became more streamlined in the late 1800s under Marcus Alonzo Hanna (Mark Hanna), Republican National Committee Chair, when businesses were assessed a percentage of their profitability to support the Republican machine. This powerful machine propelled William McKinley into presidential office over populist William Jennings Bryant. Industrial abuses abounded. Strong reaction by the populists to the effects of this machine now appeared in a literary format. Muckrakers such as Upton Sinclair in his book *The Jungle* exposed the abuses of meatpacking houses. Frank Norris' book *The Pit* exposed trade practices in Chicago and *The Octopus* studied American railroad practices. *Wealth against Commonwealth*, H.D. Lloyd's documentary, exposed the practices of Standard Oil. Sensational journalists (the yellow press) and acerbic political satirists united in declaration that big business was buying political influence and abandoning the general welfare of the nation. Reform notions included women's suffrage, standardized secret ballots, numbers on ballots, voter registration and notions of limits on corporate financing and lobbying. Also resulting from this aggregation of political power was the assassination of McKinley, who was shot by anarchist Leon Czolgosz on September 5, 1901 and died on September 14, 1901.

Teddy Roosevelt, the vice-president, took the stage. Rarely has a nation had a more popular president. His genuine concern for the general welfare focused on trust busting and limiting corporate influences on Congress. He was able to wean himself from big campaign contributions and campaign vigorously against corporate contributions to politicians.

The Tillman Act of 1907 prohibited corporations, including national banks, from making campaign contributions to national political candidates, but the dog had no teeth. It proved unenforceable.

The Federal Corrupt Practices Act of 1925 introduced limits on contributions to the campaigns of federal political candidates. Corporate contributions were banned in federal elections. The loophole: it did not cover state and local elections.

The Hatch Act (1939) prohibited using federal or state assets, including government employee's time, for promoting one party or candidate in an election. It also prohibited promises of jobs, promotions, government contracts or other prospects of financial benefit in order to gain votes or contributions. It has been consistently upheld by the Supreme Court.

The Taft-Hartley Act (1947) extended the ban on campaign contributions to labor unions.

The Federal Election Campaign Act (FECA) of 1971 required the disclosure of campaign financing. In 1974, subsequent amendments to the act established a federal agency to investigate activities and enforce infractions. This act placed *contribution* limitations on federal candidates, political parties and political action groups and was upheld on review by the Supreme Court. It established "disclosure of contributions" requirements (also upheld in court). It placed *expenditure* limits on campaigns, which were promptly stricken by the Supreme Court as unreasonable limitations on free speech.

The position of the Supreme Court was that the free speech and freedom of association protected by the first amendment are basic freedoms and should be protected by a wide construction. For **speech,** the courts allow virtually anything to be said, especially in the political arena. There is no prohibition against libel or slander in the political world. Politicians may tell untruths; indeed it is the norm. On the podium there is no such thing as false advertising. The courts shun policing political goings-on. It is simply impossible to halt an election and have a trial because someone is lying. Politicians know and rely upon this. Hence, it is that, regarding speech, the court outlaws virtually nothing. Anything goes.

In issues of freedom of **assembly** courts allow the executive branch of governments some latitude in policing crowds of persons, but freedom to assemble is still recognized as a basic freedom. The Supreme Court rulings made less and less sense as more cases were considered.

When the issue of the **freedom to bribe (corrupt)** politicians was presented to our Supreme Court, it was presented as questions of freedom of speech and freedom to assemble. The court tried to analyze the behavior of politicians and lobbyists as exercising those basic freedoms.

The burden of proof was high and stringent. Prior to 2003, convictions for *quid pro quo* (cash for a vote) corruption were rarely upheld upon Supreme Court review. There are three reasons for this. First, a crime requires the most stringent standard of legal proof — beyond a reasonable doubt. Second, the Supreme Court wisely protects free speech and freedom to associate and holds government laws that abridge "basic rights" to the highest levels of proof. Third, in an effort to separate or distance court functions from legislative functions, the Court avoided judicial review of legislative processes as much as possible.

This means one must prove an agreement between a person and a politico to pass a law of privilege for a payment and proof of the payment as well as proof that such a law of privilege was passed as a result thereof. There must be proof of an "act contrary to obligations of office by the prospect of financial gain to themselves or infusions of money into their campaigns" *Federal Election Commission v. National Political Action Committee* (1985). Circumstantial evidence of these elements is generally deemed insufficient. Consequently, these convictions have proven almost impossible to achieve. The only thing that stood a chance was a *quid pro quo* deal with proof of payment and a signed confession. Convictions of political bribery just were not affirmed.

The fallacy of the Court's reasoning is that money is not speech and money is not free. Speech cannot store value, money can. With speech you can usually identify the speaker. Money can flow without identities being known. The rulings of the Supreme Court got out of touch with the reality of the political scene.

In 1998 the Senate Committee on Government Affairs held hearings to investigate campaign finance. Those hearings revealed unequivocally that unimagined amounts of money were finding their way into political coffers. Politicians ignored all attempts to limit funding.

Testimony from retired federal politicians, lobbyists and party members showed the *sale* of access to the president and other politicians. And business was big. "Campaign Finance in the 2000 Federal Elections" found federal, state and local campaign contributions in 2000 to be approximately $3.9 billion. It reported political parties selling access to elected officials to be a rampant practice, with "menus" that included pricing for the extent and frequency of personal contacts:

- White House breakfast
- White House lunch
- Dinner with the President
- Sleepover at the White House

*(Pricing was not included with the menu)*

The Senate heard testimony from political organizers bragging that it worked. They found an ex-congressman testifying that this was, in fact, the way it worked. They heard lobbyists bragging how well they worked the system. The Senators concluded that

"soft money loopholes led to a meltdown of the campaign finance system."

In the name of campaign finance reform, Congress passed the McCain-Feingold Act or Bipartisan Campaign Reform Act (BCRA) in 2002. It defined two sorts of contributions: **hard money**, that paid directly to a candidate or his election fund, and **soft money**, dollars contributed or spent to promote an ideal. Such money was to be contributed to, and spent by, a political action committee (PAC) and could not identify a specific candidate, directly or indirectly, nor promote the election or defeat of a specific candidate.

Corporations were prohibited from hard money contributions; citizens had strict dollar limits. Corporations were limited to soft money contributions, but without dollar limitations. The Federal Election Commission (FEC) was to run the whole show. The BCRA was promptly appealed to the Supreme Court in *McConnell v. Federal Election Commission* (2003).

The Court was staggered by the Senate findings in the 1998 investigation and the testimony that supported these findings. Many of these findings were recited as fact for the court decision. The Supreme Court's respect for the legislature was evaporating. **The prior reservation about passing judgment on free speech seemingly vanished. The old case laws and precedents were not mentioned by the court.** The First Amendment rights regarding free speech and freedom of assembly were balanced against the people's right to representative government. For the first time, the Supreme Court of the United States found that:

"The history of campaign financing regulation proves that political parties are *extraordinarily flexible* in adapting to new restrictions on their fundraising abilities."

Things seemed fine until these limitations were imposed on media.

Case Study: *Hillary, The Movie*. In January 2008, the FEC and then later the Supreme Court had to consider *Citizens United v. FEC*. Citizens United had just released a film, *Hillary, The Movie*, a 90-minute documentary about then-Senator Hillary Clinton, a presidential candidate for the Democratic party. The movie was quite critical of its subject.

Because the Bipartisan Campaign Reform Act prohibited corporate spending that advocates the election or defeat of a specific candidate, the FEC ruled it was a criminal act to broadcast the film.

The constitutionality of the limitation on corporate free speech headed up to the Supreme Court. The matter was argued twice. There were 56 Amicus briefs filed (by non parties). The Court found that in 35 years the FEC had identified 33 types of political speech. They had issued 568 pages of regulations, had made 1,278 pages of explanation and had issued 1,771 advisory opinions.

The Court also found that laws require that *"people of common intelligence must [not have to] guess at [the law's] meaning, and differ as to its application."* (*Citizens United v. FEC*)

*"Today Citizens United finally learns, after two years, the fact whether it could have spoken during the 2008 presidential primaries-long after the opportunity to persuade primary voters has passed."* (*ibid.*)

The movie could have been shown. The Court found that media corporations and perhaps all corporations have rights to free speech.

*"There is no basis for the proposition that in the political speech context the Government may impose restrictions on certain disfavored speakers. Both history and logic lead to this conclusion."* (*ibid.*)

Instead of trying to define and administer speech with regulatory agencies and the courts, perhaps a better approach is simply to ban passing and enforcing laws of economic privilege. This would address the real issue head on. And it would solve the problem, for corporations would have nothing to buy.

## Proposed Campaign Finance Limitations

We call them campaign contributions, so how about truth in politics? These proposals are limited to direct monetary contributions made directly to politicos, not money spent on "issue advertisements." First Amendment rights to freedom of speech and assembly rightly place such advertising beyond government regulation. But money paid directly to politicos or funds under their control is different. Campaign contributions were not stricken by the McCain-Feingold litigation. Because of the dominion and control that politicos exercise over these funds, they are little more than huge income-tax-free bribes. To achieve campaign finance reform, let us strictly define and limit politicians' use of these funds to election campaigning as follows:

### 1. CONTRIBUTIONS TO CONGRESSMEN SHALL COME ONLY FROM THEIR CONSTITUENTS.

For *a representative* government to work, the *interests of the constituency* should be first and foremost in the mind of each legislator. By allowing the acceptance of out-of-jurisdiction cash, the allegiance of our candidates is diluted and distracted. Campaign contributions should be strictly limited to citizen constituents. When we allow non-constituents to contribute money to candidates, we allow non-constituents to corrupt the selection of local representatives necessary for democratic government. The formulation and amalgamation of the *general weal*, the *sausage-making* of politics, should happen in the *legislature*, not at the polls. For it is only when representatives and senators begin the political process reflecting the interests of the folks back home that representative government can succeed.

The lobbyist will argue: why not permit out-of-state contributions so we can build a national consensus? Would not out-of-state contributions help unite the nation as a whole? Again, the election process should be to determine representation of local constituents. Consensus making is the political process of legislating. Elections are a process of sorting out proper representatives. Let us not blur the lines of demarcation. Out-of-state money should be scrupulously banned.

The lobbyist might then argue: "What of the corporations? They are citizens, too."

Modern corporations are gluttonous users of infrastructure and shameless abusers of the environment; have a history of constantly leaving governments with huge bills for problems of all sorts; bribe politicians to win subsidies; and do little but shirk their responsibilities to pay social dues (taxes). Are these reasons to allow them to make campaign contributions? This notion has been considered by Congress, resulting in federal legislation (the Tillman Act of 1907) that prohibits corporations, though "citizens," from making contributions to federal candidates. Unfortunately many states are behind and allow corporate money to affect state politics. This is especially a problem in state judicial races, where many states allow corporate campaign contributions, as in Wisconsin. The last Supreme Court race in Wisconsin attracted so much money from the insurance and manufacturing lobbyists that it was noted in an article in *The Economist* magazine published in London, England, which asked what was happening in Wisconsin.

## 2. TEMPORAL LIMITATION

Campaign contributions may be solicited or accepted for the 180 days before the election date for federal office or for the 120 days before state, county or local elections, and never during that time the legislature is in session.

What do we get for all the hundreds of millions of dollars of campaign contributions? Highly charged, emotional, irrational, illogical, patently false representations that are impossible to fulfill; accusations and counter-accusations, slandering and mud slinging and general rhetoric of politicians. It used to be you could make your own relief, by turning off the radio or television, but now they phone you with automatic calling technology and recorded messages. We need some reasonable limitation to the activities of politicians, and they provide us none.

Limiting campaign contributions to a specified time frame is a reasonable limitation of freedom of speech.

## 3. CONTRIBUTION DOLLAR LIMIT

Donors may contribute no more than $50 per election cycle to any candidate's campaign, and no donation may be currency.

Contributions should be reasonably affordable to all, lest the wealthy have inordinate input to the political process. Just as citizens are entitled to the equality of a single vote, why should not there be a reasonable limitation on the money one can contribute to a candidate? Perhaps the amount should be what the average citizen can comfortably afford to contribute. Persons are still free to make unlimited cash contributions to political action committees so their freedom to express themselves politically would be unimpaired.

## 4. CONTRIBUTION RETURN

All campaign contributions must be accompanied by a complete, written *contribution return*, showing residency, constituency, dollar amount and no corporate contributions, sworn to and signed by the donor.

### CAMPAIGN CONTRIBUTION RETURN

Name _____ Amount _____

Address _____

City, state, zip code _____

Phone number _____

Name of employer* _____

Address of employer* _____

*to verify a company isn't using its employees as a screen for its contributions*

*I swear,* under penalty of law, that my residency is the street address shown above, and the source of these funds is my personal income, and not of another person, partnership, or a corporation, and that I have not acted as a conduit for any business interest.

Signature _____ Date _____

There must be a provision that all candidates maintain *contribution returns* and all compilations thereof, expense records and receipts during the pendency of an audit or any legal action thereon, but in any case for at least one year post-election. Lost or destroyed records shall result in a felony charge and jury trial, with a jury instruction that the candidate is presumed guilty for the lost or destroyed records.

Why should we have constituency limitations, dollar limitations and corporate contribution prohibitions unless we have a simple way for the politicians to verify that the contributions they receive are legal? This is a simple way to help our politicos avoid the appearance of impropriety.

Isn't this the minimum information that we need to keep track of money placed in the hands of candidates? Is there any other way we can begin to be confident of money spent and unspent in campaigns? It is either this minimum bit of record keeping or taking politicians at their word as to monies received, and what good is the word of a politician when he or she is campaigning?

## 5. ONLINE POSTING OF CONTRIBUTION RETURNS

Candidates, within 72 hours of receipt, must post online at their candidacy website the following: the name, address and dollar amount for each contributor, in the order received, and the aggregate total of all funds received to date.

This would be a wonderful way to keep in touch with your candidates. It would encourage politicians to keep up-to-the-minute records that are clear and accurate and perform the function of a real time audit. For years politicos have regulated every aspect of our lives. But there is no regulation of theirs. They have granted themselves great liberty to raise and spend money, without any accountability. The damage to our political system and our economy is beyond calculation. Let's help them clean up the system. Let's help politicos show their constituents they have mastered basic financial and management skills before they are given the reins to government.

## 6. CAMPAIGN EXPENDITURES DEFINED AND LIMITED

Campaign contributions may only be used for valid and enumerated campaign expenditures, such as:

- office rental
- phone service
- secretarial service
- postage
- advertising and public relations
- reasonable travel expense
- consulting fees

In no case shall contributions be used all or in any part for personal items. Any such funds used for personal expenses must be declared and taxed as imputed income.

We call them campaign contributions. Therefore they should be spent for, and only on, the campaign. Why not strictly limit candidates to spending campaign money on the aforesaid functions and only those functions? For example, should Milwaukee's ex-mayor Norquist's use of campaign funds to settle his paternity suit/sexual harassment suit qualify for a campaign expenditure? Aren't the paternity settlement funds so personal in nature that they should not be the object of legal campaign contribution expenditure? Or does the fact that she was a campaign manager supply sufficient nexus to make this a valid campaign expenditure? Would we be ahead if we mandated that all male politicians under the age of 75 should be neutered upon being sworn into public office?

Again, in Wisconsin, should Messrs. Flynn and Chvala be permitted to spend hundreds of thousands of dollars of campaign contributions in defense of their alleged felonious acts committed while in office? Funds for criminal defense of politicos are presently valid campaign expenditures. Should this be legal? It is one thing to grant politicos immunity for certain actions while in office, but should criminal acts be subsidized by campaign contributions? Is this sound public policy, to reimburse politicos' attorney fees for their criminal, even felonious, actions? Where is the deterrence in a fine if someone other than the wrongdoer pays the fine? Do you think for a moment that this is what the campaign donors had in mind for the funds they contributed? Is this what we expect from our lawgivers? To allow politicians to use campaign contributions for these transgressions is incomprehensible.

If we continue to allow campaign contributions to be used for general purposes or personal purposes, we must answer, how are they different from ordinary income? How are they not bribes? Why do we allow them to be called campaign contributions?

## 7. WAR CHEST PROHIBITION

Campaign contributions, not legally expended on those enumerated items by the end of that election, shall, within 40 days of the election, be paid to the *public domain,* whichever treasury pays the salary of said elected official. It shall be a felony to retain all or part of proceeds saved in any account (campaign war-chest,) or transfer proceeds to a political party or another candidate, before being sworn into office.

The concept proposed is that contributions should be spent in the campaign cycle in which the donation occurred, and only by the politico to whom the money was given. Not later; not on some other agenda; not on someone else's campaign; and certainly not for personal purposes after retirement. **Public policy** would dictate that those elected in each election cycle should be responsive to the electorate. They should not be insulated from the electorate by the aggregation of a huge chest of funds. They should not have a huge accrued financial advantage over new challengers. It is egregiously offensive to public policy if transgressions in office further reward and insulate incumbents against the meritorious challenger. Too often established politicos never leave Washington or rarely find their way back home. Things change, needs of constituents change, economies of the home scene change. Why insulate politicos from these changes of constituents? How is this a good thing?

Most feel that term limits are a good idea for politicians. What is the point of limiting their terms if they are allowed to amass and retain large war chests when in office? Why allow politicos to keep campaign funds, and after we forget about it, to use them for personal purposes? If these funds can be used for such personal purposes, why call them campaign contributions?

Why allow them to set up bogus charitable foundations to "employ" friends, momentarily unemployed politicos and relatives, for apparent "jobs"? Why allow them to give funds to another politician? If campaign funds aren't legally used (for the enumerated expense categories) and then only in reasonable and necessary amounts, why should they remain in the custody and control of a politico at the end of the campaign? Unused campaign funds should be sent to the public treasury. Apportionment and refund to the donors would be an accounting nightmare. But to pay directly to the public treasury might make politicos less foolish with apportionment and spending of public funds. Would any other place be a better repository for such unused funds? In any case, allowing them unfettered discretion with vast sums of unused campaign contributions, or allowing them to retain such funds at the end of their career, raises the question: How is this not a bribe?

Would it not be better policy to start each campaign cycle afresh, with a more level playing field? Incumbents will still have contacts with government and contacts with political parties. They are still ahead of most challengers. Isn't this a big enough advantage for them? If unused campaign contributions are not returned to the public coffers, the result is simply permissive payola. Freedom to convert campaign contributions into personal use is not freedom of speech. Nor is it freedom of expression. It is freedom to distort the political process. It is nothing but *"the appearance of impropriety"* that the Supreme Court has forbidden in *Buckley v. Valeo* and *McConnell v. Federal Election Commission.*

## 8. AUDIT BEFORE TAKING OFFICE

At the end of any election, for each candidate, an audit will be conducted of campaign income, campaign expenditures and disposition of all contributions not legally expended. They must pass such an audit before being sworn into office.

A problem of the present system is that no one checks on campaign wrongdoing in a timely manner so as to do anything about the wrongdoing. With the computerized record keeping proposed, it would be quite possible to do the necessary audits in the requisite time frame.

Why should our law makers be law breakers? This proposal serves to enforce these new limitations with meaningful sanctions: denial of office, and, where appropriate, mandatory jail time. The right to vote is something many of our ancestors died to create and protect. Perhaps vote fraud and distortion of representative government should be a capital offense, for why should political sorts pander away these valuable rights for dollars?

Without tough sanctions, all the previous limitations are merely like words of politicos: pointless hot air. So let us forget "ethics charges," this is merely a delay tactic and a loophole; political grandstanding. Labeling these as ethic violations, without real sanction and causing another trial in criminal court is a supreme waste of taxpayer's time and money.

Perhaps, upon a grand jury finding probable cause, the politician should be turned out of public office (without pay or generous benefits and with prompt forfeit of ill-gotten funds) so they might concentrate on their defense. Perhaps they should not be granted a trial before a jury of their peers (the Senate), for that body is too completely corrupted for the general welfare. But, in any case, a conviction for campaign funds abuse should be cause for prompt removal from office, a future ban from holding public office, or work within government, a mandatory jail term and a permanent bar from lobbying.

## 9. PARDONS

Power to pardon, especially with regard to political crimes, should be removed from the executive (president or governor) and made, upon showing of merit, by a majority of the relevant supreme court. Hopefully this will not invite corruption on the supreme courts. The present system allows presidents and governors of most states to pardon crimes, including those of a political nature, usually in ways that are behind closed doors. Leaving pardons in the hands of the executive branches of our governments is simply not sound policy.

In the state of New Hampshire, pardons are not in the hands of the governor, but handled by the Supreme Court in open session, and thus insulated from demands for campaign contributions. Why is this sound policy followed only in New Hampshire? In the interest of saving the energy and time of our public servants, let us enact these limitations to protect our politicos from accusations of impropriety.

An absolute ban on cash contributions will conflict with the freedom of expression implicit within the Constitution found in the Bill of Rights. But **public finance** of the election process, in lieu of cash contributions, is an unsound policy. This would doubtless lead to political control of the funds in ways unimaginable. Regulation, accounting, and administration of these funds would be in the hands of politicos and their appointees, and would be beyond public view, and hence control would be within the hands of those in office. One need only look at how politicos handle our federal budget.

John McCain's lament in 2010 that *Citizens United v. Federal Election Commission* means that campaign finance reform is dead, is silly, indeed simply stupid. It is a failure to distinguish between two quite different things:

(1) Limitations on direct contributions to candidates (hard money) [**freedom to bribe**].
(2) Limitations on issue advertising by corporations (soft contributions).

Hard money limitations are still untouched and viable. Soft money limitations are probably barred by **freedom of speech.**

Note carefully that the decision did not touch the various state and local limitations on direct campaign contributions to individual candidates. *Issue advertising* is quite different. The recent decision deals only with issue ads and holds that freedom of speech will not permit limits on advertising expression.

The reality is that these limitations are band-aids. The only possible solution to this apparent conundrum of *campaign finance reform* is the prohibition of the sale of economic privileges by our politicos. With such a ban, what will motivate the business types and corporate entities to squander obscene amounts of lucre on politicos if the politicos are unable to deliver economic privileges?

Think of the cleansing effect upon the political process that this prohibition of the sale of economic privileges would bring. What would politicos have left to sell? This would take much of the fun out of political corruption. Best of all, it is automatic; no need for messy and inefficient regulation or prosecution. Police the ban on economic privileges and all the slimy and behind the scene dealings and complex money transfer schemes, all the corporate shell games will simply disappear. Let us excise the tumor before it metastasizes.

> The beauty of prohibition of grants of economic privileges is this: what will politicos have left to sell?

The limitations expressed above are reasonable and are equally affordable to all citizens. Those who wish to spend more may do so through political action groups, but not by making direct monetary contributions to any candidate beyond these modest limitations. Without the aforesaid nine limitations on campaign finance, we face the enigma posed by John Stuart Mill when he said:

"How can a representative assembly work for the good if its members can be bought?

Our original inquiry was, do we attract the wrong people to the political process or does the political process corrupt good people? The answer to this question is both. If the process corrupts good people, it is necessary to change the system. The nine proposed limitations of this chapter will do just that.

As for solving the problem of the bad persons attracted into politics, this should and must be done by the election process. Removal of the right of politicos to sell economic privileges will probably remove much of the attraction of bad persons to public office.

# Chapter 7

# Legislative Limitations

## Limits of Legislative Powers

Legislatures shall write the laws of our nation, state and federal. Legislators seem to believe their power to legislate is limitless. They feel that the nature of the problems they are called upon to solve may be infinite or unlimited. So they feel why should their powers to address problems be limited? Are there limitations to legislative power? If so, what are they?

**First**, they cannot legislate in defiance of the *natural rights* of man: the primary right being the right to self-preservation or self-defense. Next is the *natural right* of man to possess property necessary for his or her existence. This right extends to the right to acquire and hold surplus property or wealth, for their personal preservation. The next *natural right* is to have some voice in government; to create and enforce laws to define and protect property, and the right to have punishment and restitution for those who break the laws of government. The next *natural right* is that of liberty. It is the right to make personal decisions about circumstances affecting daily life. This right is limited only by the liberties of other citizens. There is also the *right to privacy*: the right to hold personal thoughts, and beliefs in confidence, and make personal decisions, immune from government interrogation.

A man may be judged only by his outward actions. This is to say a citizen need not testify against himself, he has a right against mandatory self-incrimination. This right extends to his home or "castle." This includes religion; governments that legislate a mandatory religion are invariably unsuccessful. There is also a natural right to the pursuit of "indolence of body" or leisure. The final *natural right* is the right of citizens to change, by violent means if necessary, any government that fails to protect their natural rights. While these are not absolute, but relative to circumstances, in a final analysis these rights pose limitations on government's power to pass and enforce laws.

**Second,** politicians do not have the power to simply legislate *prosperity* into existence. They can confiscate and transfer or redistribute property or inflate the money supply, and thus appear to create wealth, but this is mere **fiscal illusion**. Prosperity comes from something different than mere legislating. Prosperity can grow, but only in a proper environment of stable and just predictable laws that reward the hard workers and the creative innovators. The growth of prosperity takes time. Simply printing money to create prosperity inevitably leads to financial and national decline.

**Third,** politicos cannot enact *laws of economic privilege* (subsidies, tax benefits or laws of economic favoritism), without degrading or ultimately destroying the fabric of society. These privileges simply lead to the undoing of a society by destroying opportunities for the remaining citizens. Privilege granting leads to aristocracies of the privileged: economic aristocracy, political aristocracy, educational aristocracy (those who feel they have superior knowledge of the real world events simply because they live in the ivy covered towers of higher learning). It leads to inordinate distribution of wealth. It leads to wealth that is not earned by labor. It leads to resentment by the masses. It will lead to revolution.

**Fourth,** it is pointless for politicos to pass laws in *defiance of human nature;* man always reserves the right to act in a stupid or even self-destructive manner. The prohibition of alcohol consumption is an example of this limitation.

**Fifth**, our legislatures in America are not legally empowered to *abdicate the drafting* of legislative text to lobbyists or to the administrators of the executive branch of government. To surrender the power to legislate, all or in part, or to assign the right to legislate, all or in any part, outside the Congress is simply destructive to the integrity of the tripartite government and thus the balance of powers that is necessary for stable government. Any abdication of legislative power simply leads to tyranny.

The **sixth** limitation for the American politicos is they cannot pass laws that destroy or *degrade the Bill of Rights*. These were never given by government to its citizens, as modern politicos seem to sometimes think. They are not a creation of government. This is in part because they pre-date the creation of the government, but mostly because they are all **inalienable** rights of citizens and cannot be given, assigned, or transferred to citizens, or taken from them. Infringement upon these rights is not only bad government, it is the source of revolution, a concept that those representing the citizens have constantly overlooked.

Other lesser limitations include language use in drafting laws: verbiage should be clear to the common man. There are limitations as to the extent and detail of legislation that is good for a society. And there are the notions that laws should not be in conflict with prior legislation or exceed the limited grants of power given to government in our various constitutions. In conclusion, there are very real limitations to the power of legislators to pass laws. How are these limitations observed in the practices of legislating in our Congress?

The problem with our legislatures is that most laws they pass are grants of economic favor or economic privilege. Now we understand the privilege/opportunity equilibrium: that grants of economic privilege diminish the opportunities for the rest of society, and are destructive to our general welfare, leading directly to the decline of our national prosperity and society in general. We are in a position to see through the smoke and haze of political rhetoric. We are no longer misled by our newspapers, radio and the television. We are in a better position to recognize half truths uttered by politicians as they promote sinister grants of privilege legislation for those who make vast campaign contributions.

The Founding Fathers set the **basic premise of good government** clearly before us in the preamble to the Constitution of the United States:

> "We, the people of the United States, in order to form a more perfect union, establish justice, insure domestic tranquility, provide for the common defense, **promote the general welfare**, and secure the blessing of liberty to ourselves and our posterity, do ordain and establish this Constitution for the United States of America."

And then restated this basic premise in *The Federalist Papers*:

> "The real welfare of the people is the **supreme objective**. Attaining this objective is the government's only value."
> (F 45 pp 6)

They took the ideas of John Locke —

> Life, liberty, and health, indolence of body (leisure), and the possession of outward things, such as money, lands, houses, furniture, and the like

— and recognized them to be our **inalienable rights**: life, liberty, pursuit of happiness. Finally, they took more of his words —

> "an established, settled and known law" (Locke, *Second Treatise on Government*)

> "received and allowed by common consent to be the standard of right andwrong" (*ibid.*)

> "the common measure to decide all controversies" (*ibid.*)

> [laws] "plain and intelligible to all rational creatures" (*ibid.*)

— and together with the principle of the separation of the *inner man* (the exclusive jurisdiction of the church) and the *exterior* man (over which government has jurisdiction) they created our **Bill of Rights.**

For most modern politicians there is confusion regarding the Bill of Rights. They feel that acts of government create or grant these basic rights. But remember the federal government had not yet been granted its existence. It was not until the proponents of the federal government conceded the pre-existence of the Bill of Rights that the federal government was created.

The natural rights of man pre-date our federal government and, as inalienable rights, they cannot be surrendered by people to government. They renew with each generation, with the birth of each citizen, and no generation has the power to bind a subsequent generation to a loss of these natural rights.

## Authority For Granting Laws Of Privilege Doesn't Exist

The Founding Fathers debunked the power of a legislature to grant laws of privilege. Indeed, *The Federalist Papers* promised the opposite. In the words of our Founding Fathers we the people must NOT accept:

"An ambitious sacrifice of the many to the aggrandizement of the few." (F 57 pp 1)

"The elevation of the few on the ruins of the many." (F 57 pp 4)

"An interested minority might take advantage of it to screen themselves from the equitable sacrifices to the general weal." (F 59 pp 15)

"A permanent elevation of the few on the depression of the many." (F 55 pp 1)

"Repressing them from oppressive measures, they can make no law which will not have full operation on themselves, their friends, and the great mass of society." (F 57 pp 12)

"Public instability [gives] unreasonable advantage . . . to the sagacious, the enterprising, the moneyed few over industrious and uninformed mass of the people. Every new regulation concerning commerce or revenue, or any manner affecting the value of different species of property presents a new harvest to those who watch change, and can trace its consequences . . . laws made for the *few*, and not the *many*." (F 62 pp 16)

Have not the Founding Fathers just described **Laws of Economic Privilege**?

## Spending Limits on Legislators

The court has considered the issue of limitations on federal spending. In 1936, in *United States v. Butler*, the U.S. Supreme Court considered the following situation: huge grain surpluses produced by our desperate farmers could not be used domestically, exported or even stored, except by leaving them on the ground, exposed to the elements. The price was so low, farmers could not recover planting and harvest costs. Our president explained we had "too much competition." The federal government began to assess "processing and floor" taxes on grain at the elevator and used these funds to pay farmers for not producing grain, leaving some fields fallow. A grain elevator owner sued the United States in the Supreme Court. The Court held:

"A tax, in the general understanding of the term as used in the Constitution signifies an extraction for the support of the Government. The word has never been thought to connote the expropriation of one group for the benefit of another."

In its analysis, the court quotes James Monroe: **"Have Congress the right to raise and appropriate the money to any and to every**

**purpose according to their will and pleasure? They certainly have not.”**

In *Butler,* the court concluded that the proposed spending was an invalid exercise of the power to spend money and the law was stricken. Unfortunately the Supreme Court backed down in the next year, due to pressure from FDR who threatened to pack the Supreme Court with justices until he got them to agree with his social programs.

Next, our Supreme Court, in *Hood & Sons v. DuMond* (1949), explored the ability of states to grant competitive privileges to their citizens. They explained that the intent of the **commerce clause** was:

" . . . designed in part to prevent trade barriers that had undermined the efforts of the fledgling states to form a cohesive whole following their victory in the Revolution.”

“Our system, fostered by the Commerce Clause, is that every farmer and every craftsman shall be encouraged to produce by the certainty that he will have free access to every market in the Nation, that no home embargoes will withhold his exports, and no foreign state will by customs duties or regulations exclude them. Likewise, every consumer may look to the free competition from every producing area in the Nation to protect him from exploitation by any. Such was the vision of the Founders; such has been the doctrine of this Court which has given it reality...” (*ibid.*)

“The right to engage in interstate commerce is not a gift of the state, and the state cannot regulate or restrain it.” (*ibid.*)

## Public Expectations of the Legislature

In addition to previous limitations, what should the people expect from Congress? Representation! That’s why one house is called the **House of Representatives**. Recall the specific qualifications for membership as defined in the Constitution. It was designed to be the engine to search for and define the general welfare.

> "The aim of every political constitution is, or ought to be, first to obtain for rulers men who possess most wisdom to discern, most virtue to pursue, the **common good of society**." (F 57 pp 3)

The people should expect that legislation that is passed in Congress is for the general welfare of the nation. Precious public funds should not be dissipated for factions, special interests and the like. The people should expect that legislating is done in Congress, not delegated out of Congress to unknown persons not directly accountable to Congress.

Politicians should exercise a professional standard of care while they are in public office. That **standard of care** for conduct of those in public office was defined by our federal Supreme Court in *McConnell v. Federal Election Commission*. The Court said politicos **"must avoid impropriety, and even the appearance of impropriety."** And again, *"Undue influence of an officeholder's judgment, or the **appearance** of such influence."* How can the creation of economic privilege be anything but the appearance of undue influence?

This means that all citizens are to be treated equally in the creation of the law. And that means no grants of economic privilege, no subsidies, no tax forgiveness, no laws creating economic favors for special factions. Because any grants of economic privilege mean the rest of society will not be treated equally before the law, these laws of privilege are unjust.

When laws are written so that we must hire a lawyer to tell us the present state of the law, is this not a poorly written bit of legislation? How can a court tell some poor citizen "you are presumed to know the law"? Yet attorneys spend many billable hours deciphering the meaning of a law, then can give the client only a conditional opinion of what the law may be. Is this not proof a law is poorly drafted? When attorneys must spend half a day arguing in court over which law covers a single point, and judges need a recess to decide which attorney is right, or indeed the Supreme Court needs a year for its decision as to what law controls a situation, is this not proof that a law is indeed poorly written?

The root of these problems is that lobbyists and administrators write most laws, and Congress never reviews any legislation on a law by law basis. Is it not time to clean this mess up so we can concentrate on the business of national prosperity?

## Can Legislating Be Delegated By Congress to Administrators?

Today in America one of our biggest problems is the abdication of legislating to the administration. They have created for us at least 91,000 pages of administrative codes, none of which came from the floor of Congress, none of which has had meaningful Congressional review.

Ours is said to be a representative government. The calculus of representation is spelled out in the Constitution. The House of Representatives is supposed to represent the general welfare of the constituents. (See Chapter 9.) Legislation should be drafted that serves the *general weal.* Legislators alone are supposed to choose words that are appropriate to that end. This is explored in depth in the section on executive limitations.

In brief, representatives and senators are **fiduciaries** of the people, by the people and for the people, placed in a special position of **trust** by the voters. They are empowered with concentrations of authority and power. They are charged with the duty to search for the general welfare of the public and to create legislation in the furtherance of this general welfare.

But too often an agency, an arm of the **executive,** is given permission to draft details of administrative codes. Faceless administrators, with identities unknown to the constituents, seize the pen. They are not responsive to constituents; they are not in touch with the people, their needs or their desires. They have no way to canvass the various districts of the country. They are appointed by the executive, hence they follow executive agendas, which all too often are the result of campaign finance bribery and never generated by the representatives of Congress. These administrators are under the sway of lobbyists; indeed, often the actual verbiage of a law or code is drafted by counsel for trade groups wanting to corner a portion of the marketplace or seeking some other advantage. There is no public or open discussion of the merits of different positions constituents may take on a subject. The administrators create privileges, the opportunities of the general masses are diminished, and *general weal* is in no way served. Political expediency has caused the merger of the legislative branch into the executive branch. Administrators are not responsive to the populace. They cannot be recalled. They cannot be voted out of office.

Often administrators are selected because of some business experience. For example, an appointee to a utility rate commission has a lifetime of experience working in a utility company, and when he/she leaves the commission it is often to go back to the same utility company. While serving on the commission guess how he/she rules on rate increases or on a new power line right of way? Is it any surprise air pollution abatement procedures are blocked time and time again? Is it any surprise rate increases are always granted? We have lost the checks and balances of separation of powers. Administrators are often untouchable and become arrogant. Due process is completely ignored.

Claims are made that administrative bureaucrats are especially qualified because of special education, training and experience to draft administrative codes. Claims are made that they alone are familiar with the intricacies of an industry that no politico could ever master. They are right in one sense, but the cost of merging legislative and executive powers has shown that the practice is destructive to the rights of citizens. This is perhaps an attractive argument, but it is flawed policy.

"The legislature cannot transfer the power of making of laws to any other hands, for it being a delegated power from the people, they who have it cannot pass it to another" (Locke, *Second Treatise on Government*)

Locke also noted it would exceed the powers granted to government by the *social contract*. Administrative laws are usually privileges, favoring factions, not the general populace. The constitution limits the authority of the Congress to the general welfare.

"No one can transfer to another more power than he has in himself." (*ibid.*)

Remember that the act of legislating is a unique and non-delegable duty, like taking a bath or getting a haircut. You cannot have your secretary take a bath for you; you cannot send your aide to get you a haircut. These are non-delegable acts. The legislative power is entrusted only to those elected to represent their constituents. And only these trustees, known by their constituents, are supposed to spend time among their constituents, learning what it is the constituents need. Only those legislators know and are responsive to their constituents and their needs. All the parts of legislating should remain within the halls of Congress.

We now have an easy test to instantly distinguish good law from bad law. We can clearly articulate why "tax breaks" are merely words of artifice, privileges only for the favored few exempting them from taxation. The rest of us are then left to pay all the social dues. Newspapers can no longer make tax breaks and other privileges seem like "good news." Preferential tax treatment in its many disguises is always bad law, it is never in the general welfare. And no amount of rhetoric or irresponsible articles in the business section about subsidies and Tax Incremental Financing (TIF) can ever change the fact that "tax breaks" are privileges, and thus never work in the general welfare.

Nor can politicos ever again convince us that subsidies are good for us. For example we now know that every time a TIF is granted, this is a project that the private sector investors feel is too risky to back with their own funds. This is the acid test for a poor quality investment. It is a project that the public does not want or need. It is probably a bad deal for society or a waste of tax dollars. The only way the promoter can get the deal done is with public funding and tax privileges or guarantees; in effect, free government insurance for the project. To get government backing requires the promoter to make big bribes, "campaign contributions." This is bad legislation: it is never in the general welfare.

We are now in a position to critically judge the wording of laws to see if economic favors lurk in the murky verbosity of ill drafted legislation. We are in a position to instantly recognize that such favoritism can never be in our general welfare. We now have a unified standing on which to judge legislators and legislation. We now have a unified basis to judge our laws. We can now unite in our demands upon our legislators.

We are in a position to recognize good legislative practice from bad: bad legislation creates privileges for factions. We are in a position to demand more from our legislators. We can now agree on what we demand: no more economic privilege of any shade or color. Our demands are simple ones, based on promises found in the Constitution and in *The Federalist Papers*.

Legislatures shall write the laws of our nation, state and federal. This means legislatures must not abdicate the drafting of legislative text or any part thereof to lobbyists or to the administrators of the executive branch of government. Laws shall be in the language of the common man. Each bill shall contain a single proposed law. Legislators shall read each law before deliberation and vote. Each bill shall be voted upon individually. Term limits for legislators shall be a total of six years and for senators twelve years. Campaign finance reform laws shall be observed on pain of immediate removal from office. Most importantly, legislatures shall grant no economic privileges for anyone. There shall be no laws granting "tax benefits." No more grants or funding subsidies. There shall be no other laws of economic favoritism: laws shall treat all citizens equally.

There has been no constitutional amendment allowing the executive branch to usurp the powers of the legislature since the Constitution was adopted. Nor could there be, for this notion would upset the fundamental definition of tripartite government and the equilibrium between the three branches of our federal government. Delegation of legislative powers has been conclusively shown to have no basis in law or politics. Did not our Founding Fathers specifically promise us laws passed for the **public good** (used twenty times) or the **general welfare** (used three times) in *The Federalist Papers?*

How did Congress get distracted from its duty and purpose? By now it should be clear that Congress got wrapped up in the exchange of privileges for special factions, for money called **campaign contributions,** which are in reality spent for campaigning and virtually anything else the candidates wish. (See Chapter 4.) How might we get our politicians back on the task of their appointed roles and duties? Let us study how they have strayed, so we know what to correct.

## Observed Behaviors of Parliament (and Congress)

John Stuart Mill, 1806–1873, was afforded an opportunity available to no political writer before him. He had the advantage of seeing both the American Congress and the English Parliament in action. He was able to see democracy in the form of representative government in action. He noted parliamentary shortfalls with an eloquence not often found today. (Note the similarities to our present day Congress). He found:

". . .insufficient mental qualifications in the controlling body" (Mill, *Considerations on Representative Government*)

". . .crotchety members threatening delay" (*ibid.*)

"inexperience sitting in judgment on experience" (*ibid.*)

"an assembly . . . artificially stirred up" (*ibid.*)

[They were often] "under the influence of interests not identical with the general welfare of the community" (*ibid.*)

"duties left to those who undertake them because they have some private interest to be promoted" (*ibid.*)

". . .incongruous clauses inserted to conciliate special interest groups" (*ibid.*)

". . .clauses omitted which are essential to the working of the rest" (*ibid.*)

". . .specious fallacies may be urged in defense of every act of injustice yet proposed for the imaginary benefit of the masses" (*ibid.*)

". . .and a House of Commons that will not forgo the precious privilege of tinkering with their clumsy hands." (*ibid.*)

"explaining and defending a bill . . . rests upon some minister or member of Parliament who did not frame them...[who] does not know the full strengths of his case....Does not know the best reasons to support it....[hence] is wholly incapable of meeting unforeseen objections" (*ibid.*)

[And we get] "unforeseen consequences of a law" (*ibid.*)

Mill found that those "*fluent of tongue and facility of being elected*" *did not necessarily make them "qualified for legislating"* (*ibid.*), and suggested that:

"every provision of a law requires it to be framed with the most accurate long-sighted depreciation of its effects on all the other provisions; and the law should be capable of fitting into a consistent whole with the previously existing laws." (*ibid.*)

He concluded:

"How can a representative assembly work for the good if its members can be bought?" (*ibid.*)

We are now in a position **to ponder the heretofore unthinkable:** a Congress legislating without any grants of privilege. Can the country be governed without subsidies and tax cuts and other laws of economic favor? So ingrained are grants of privilege that it is difficult to imagine such a concept.

- A government can legislate proper just laws, justly enforce or execute its laws, fairly decide the disputes of its citizens without privileges.
- A government can create the groundwork for prosperity: maintain a stable dependable reliable money supply without privileges.
- A government can buy the necessities to defend its citizens within and without its boundaries without laws of privilege or economic favoritism.
- A government can tax minimally and fairly and spend these precious tax dollars in a reasonable and fiscally prudent manner without laws of privileges.
- Indeed, how is the performance of any of these functions made more expeditious, over the long duration expected by citizens of its government, by grants of privileges or favors?
- How can courts hope to decide disputes fairly, equitably, and justly if some citizens appear before those courts claiming privileges that most citizens do not have? Is not justice merely a species of equality? Therefore must legislating also be a species of equality?

Some may claim we have forgotten the impoverished. How can legislation in the general welfare ignore them? The unfortunate reality is that a gift of money or the equivalent destroys motivation, both that of the recipient and the donor. Socialism is fine until the money runs out. Distribution of opportunity has the chance of going on indefinitely, for it can create the wealth necessary for continued existence of the person and the nation.

What then would be the permissible powers of a legislature in its search to promote the general welfare? This would demand the return of all legislating (and codification powers) to the halls of Congress. Powers of the executive branch would be limited to enforcement and cajoling Congress. This would mean never to subsidize or give preferential tax treatments. Could this possibly work? Will it work? The present system is certainly dysfunctional; our present federal income tax code is irrefutable evidence of that. Is it not time to find out?

The whole idea has a strong appeal. Lobby functions will be dramatically curtailed. The obscene expenses of lobbying will no longer be tacked on to the prices of goods and services throughout the economy, especially in the medical and health fields. It is not the corporations, but we the people who end up indirectly paying those vast campaign contributions. How is that of benefit to the general welfare?

Perhaps less bitter and lengthy fighting will occur in legislative drafting sessions. We may be able to get a better grade of politician. Prohibition on drafting laws granting economic privileges will take the bribes out of politics and the system will be less likely to corrupt good politicians.

With these expenses stripped out of the domestic economy, our goods and services should be that much more attractive on the world market. One thing is certain: campaign contributions are not an efficient engine to measure the general weal. They are too akin to, indeed indistinguishable from, bribery. Mechanically, how might this work?

John Stuart Mill became sour on the obvious incapacity of a legislature to draft legislation. He observed that:

> The numerous assembly is as little fitted for the direct business of legislating as it is for that of administration. There is hardly any kind of intellectual work in which so much need to be done, not only by experienced and exercised minds, but by minds trained to the task through long and laborious study, as the business of making laws." (Mill, *Considerations on Representative Government*)

## The Solution For Legislating In The General Welfare

Allowing any legislative function to the executive and his ministers and agents has proven disastrous for America. All legislative functions must be returned to the legislature. That was the wish of our Founding Fathers. We were warned against the encroachment and pre-eminence of the executive branch.

"The accumulation of all powers, legislative, executive, and judiciary, in the same hands, whether of one, a few, or many, and whether hereditary, self-appointed, or elected, may justly be pronounced the very definition of tyranny." (F 47 pp 3)

In the words of John Mill, "*being popular, handsome or marvelous of wit and tongue*" may get one elected to office, but these qualities certainly do not prepare or qualify one to write law. That requires putting words together to make a clearly written, unambiguous law that dovetails with all that has gone before and offends not the guideline of the Constitution and the Bill of Rights. That is work for specialists.

Hence the conundrum: since all legislative drafting must be kept entirely within the confines of Congress, yet the purity and integrity of members of Congress demand short terms of office, the Representatives and Senators will not acquire the skills, experience and disciplines that legislative drafting requires. It is evident that proper legislative drafting requires a doctorate in law. But there is far more. Proper drafting also requires decades of exposure to, indeed participating in, arguing the meaning of laws to courts. Clear drafting of law requires long hours of reading boring laws and pondering the meanings thereof, learning to avoid the hidden meanings of words, or what counterintuitive meaning a word or phrase has been given by prior decisions in courts. It also requires study and mastery of the Constitution and our Bill of Rights. Essential also is a passion for liberty and an uncommonly found sense of injustice that is outraged by grabs for power and privileges. It requires a rare courage to speak and work diligently in the pursuit of the general weal when surrounded by:

"candidates too little fit to comprehend and pursue great national objects" (F 10 pp 19)

"unworthy candidates who practice with success the vicious arts by which elections are too often carried" (F 10 pp 18)

"that a dangerous ambition more often lurks behind the specious mask of zeal for the rights of the people" (F 1 pp 5)

Mill leaned towards a **commission of legislation** and a **commission of codification** to draft laws and codes leaving the passage to the legislature, giving Parliament *"no power to alter measure, but solely to pass or reject it, or partially disapprove of, and resubmit to the Commission for reconsideration."* (Mill, *Considerations on Representative Government*)

To reconcile the differences between qualifications for election and qualifications required to draft legislation and to permit some degree of delegation, the creation of *legislative commissions* will be required. Here are the desirable features:

**First,** a commission should be comprised of one senator, one representative, and three such aforementioned legislative attorneys, to be chosen by Congress. Numerous Congressional Legislative Commissions shall sit for each proposed bill for a fixed term set by Congress at the outset of commissioning. Terms shall run from one month up to six months. The branch of Congress establishing any commission shall define a mission statement delineating the need of the law to be drafted and any special requirements. *All bills must be drafted in the language of the common man.*

**Second,** the two designated members of Congress must be present for drafting and for all discussion and deliberation of texts and reactions to the proposed text. That member of Congress shall be the person presenting the bill to each respective house.

**Third,** each commission shall promptly establish a *website*, with photographs, office phone numbers, email addresses and office locations of all commission personnel. The website shall have the mission statement of the commission and the current draft of proposed legislation, all organized in such a manner as to be easily found. All communications from citizens or associations or businesses or lobbyists to the commission, or to any member thereof shall be by email. Congress persons may be in contact with any commission in any manner they see fit.

**Fourth,** all bills presented to each branch of Congress shall be done only by the aforementioned presenter. Each bill must be read in its entirety by the presenter in person, before a quorum of that congressional branch while televised on public television, on a bill-by-bill basis. Each presentation must be followed by discussion and a vote thereon. Votes shall be on a roll-call basis. The voting process shall also be televised.

**Fifth**, each house of Congress shall have the power to accept or reject any proposed bill in total. Congress may only suggest changes be made in the verbiage of bills. Neither house shall have the power to rewrite, amend or add text to any bill. It must be sent back to the legislative drafting committee for any redrafting.

**Sixth, absolute prohibitions on legislative powers**: legislation shall contain no grants of economic privilege, especially subsidies. No law shall give funding to any law of economic privilege. No law shall grant or encourage monopolistic trade practices. No law shall grant tax privileges.

**Seventh, all laws and enforcement of laws shall promote the free market in all ways possible.**

After careful legislative review, Congress should retain only the bits and pieces of the federal administrative code that promote the general welfare of our nation. Congress and the courts should unite to toss the vast bulk of our existing federal administrative code in the dustbin where it well belongs. Congress should retain only those laws which, after scrupulous review, have been found to contain no grants of economic privilege; this is to say, keep only those few passages that are in the general weal.

There are those who say that these suggestions are too onerous for our Congress. Is there anyone who can say our Congress members work too hard, or that we have too few laws? Who complains that we are in desperate need of more laws to read? Would it not be a good thing to actually see Congress members at work? To hear them actually propose laws in words that we can understand?

Our new understanding of the prohibition of grants of privilege shows us how unintended and unforeseen consequences of our laws are generated within the system. Well-drafted laws can be perverted or undone by loopholes, hiding in the middle of big words, or long ponderous sentences that are not clearly written or by amendments to the law. Or it is possible that well-written laws can be undone by selective or just plain demented enforcement of laws, usually through administration. Lets tidy up our laws by ridding ourselves of most of them. About 90 percent of them are ambiguous, ill-fitted, unjust laws granting privilege: none of which are in the common good.

## Law of Unintended Consequences

The final reason governmental actions should be restricted to the enumerated powers granted each branch of government by the Constitution is that when politicos and bureaucrats act outside those powers, they are misdirected: either doing the wrong thing or doing the right thing in the wrong way. This occurrence is so usual, that economists call examples of it "laws of **unintended consequences**" or, in the words of Mill, *unforeseen consequences.* A classic example of the law of unintended consequences is student loans.

**Case study**: Wishing to allow Korean war veterans without financial means to pull themselves upwards through college education, Congress passed a Guaranteed Student Loan Program. In 1972, the Student Loan Marketing Corporation became known as Sallie Mae (SLM). It was a quasi-private government sponsored enterprise, featuring low-interest student loans. These loans were to be without interest until graduation and then at a low rate of interest until paid. They were to be only for certified educational programs. The idea was that students would enhance their earning capacity with education and repay the loan with their increased earnings. Society would benefit by the increased production and the greater education of a larger number of persons. Sallie Mae was to evolve into a private corporation on or before 2008. It was privatized in 2005. It was purchased by a small corporation for $25 billion. At that time it had a student loan portfolio of $147 billion. It promptly blossomed into a Fortune 500 company with numerous subsidiaries: Sallie Mae Inc, Nellie Mae, Sallie Mae Service Company, SLM Financial Corporation, and others. It sells student loans, graduate school loans and mortgages, and has a credit card line. It has started a proprietary and lucrative collection practice, able to bill whatever attorney fees it wishes, with assurance that those bills will be paid as part of the guaranteed debt.

In a sense, the federal government is subsidizing the violation of many state unfair collection practice laws. Coinciding with Sallie Mae's privatization, huge campaign contributions to politicos got Congress to raise the cap on interest Sallie Mae could charge on credit card debt. Sallie Mae has a list of reasons to raise interest rates, make additional charges and fees, accelerate liability for payment of principal, renegotiate outrageous interest payments, make outrageous upfront charges for loan novation, and the like that would make your banker blush. More campaign contributions and Congress changed the bankruptcy laws so school loans could no longer be discharged. Congress backdated this provision to loans signed before 2005 in violation of the prohibition of *ex post facto* laws as found in the U.S. Constitution, Article 1, Section 9. SLM got Congress to legislate that SLM was not liable for violations of the unfair collection practice laws (loan shark prohibitions) of various states. Now it can employ any brazen technique for collection, at any time of the day or night, and there is no remedy for the hapless debtor. It persuaded the U.S. Supreme Court to rule that Social Security proceeds can be attached in payment of school loans. Because SLM can assess the fees it pays its attorneys for collection attempts, it is financial suicide to contest these terms if you are in arrearage, for you are paying both sets of lawyers. Now the higher education industry has the president hawking college loans as part of his stimulus package. Many college grads are having trouble finding jobs based upon their present college education.

SLM is under investigation by the Attorney General of the State of California for fraud: charging excessive late fees, undisclosed late fees and using abnormally aggressive collection practices. Since 2008, Sallie Mae has been indicted in Florida for unscrupulous business practices for the way it pays colleges to direct students towards them for loans. Sallie Mae settled its New York student loan probe by paying $2,000,000 in fines to be used to create a board of ethics for student loans.

Sallie Mae is now pressing for the federal government to indemnify them for *any* loss incurred by bad student loans. They bought the program for $25,000,000,000 and it had a portfolio value of $147,000,000,000. They paid 17 cents on the dollar. But with the bailout frenzy, they are not too proud to ask for more money. They want a bailout, too.

Sallie Mae was started with the intent to help and has turned into a program of oppression. Instead of students raising themselves by their bootstraps, they are likely to be mired in poverty. The reality of a Sallie Mae loan is anything but beneficial to the student. It makes loans for unaccredited courses, many of which lead to no prospect of gainful employment. Many students enter the job market with uncertified, worthless, unmarketable degrees shackled by student loans (often exceeding $100,000), which charge loan shark interest rates and collection fees. And that debt is now non-dischargeable in bankruptcy. With the sour job market we are likely to see a new brand of indentured servants, comprised of middle and upper class students forever unable to get out from under their college loan debt loads. How is this in the general welfare? This was hardly what Congress originally intended, but is a sad example of the law of *unintended consequences* and the law of *inverse* consequence. The **unintended consequence** today is stress, anxiety, depression and indentured servitude.

## Term Limits and Career Limits

The cornerstone of good government is term limits. The Founding Fathers explained it so well with these words:

"Frequency of election is the cornerstone of free government" (F 53 pp 2)

"They will be compelled to anticipate the moment when their power is to cease, when their exercise of it is to be reviewed, and when they must descend to the level from which they were raised" (F 57 pp 11)

Remember the example of the Greeks of Athens. The general rule was a term limit of one year. And they put a limitation on the number of terms. A citizen was limited to one term, except in the council of 500, where there could be two single-year terms so long as they were not consecutive. They chose amateurs over professionals when it came to politicians and civil servants. This is the only way to hold politicos truly accountable for their actions.

**The Athenians chose career limits over term limits.**

The policy behind tight term limits is that politicos should be returned to the general population to live with the results and consequences of their laws. Left in office too long, they create and enjoy too many privileges for themselves. We should create immediate and frequent opportunities for successors to office to investigate and to judge what their predecessors have done, so they may be called to task for poor work before the passage of time causes the populace to forget.

In conclusion: the primary duty of the legislature is to write laws in the general welfare: no more subsidies, tax privileges, no more laws of economic favoritism. The secondary duty is to write the laws in Congress, not to delegate any writing outside the halls of Congress. The third duty is to write laws in the language of the common man. Finally, they should not establish their positions as a full time permanent job.

All of this is, of course, subject to the campaign finance reform, because again, in the words of John Stuart Mill:

"How can a representative assembly work for the good if its members can be bought?" (Mill, *Considerations on Representative Government*)

# Chapter 8

# The Marketplace:
# Corporations, Subsidies, and Monopolies

## Econopolitics Revisited

The marketplace is where three elements of **econopolitics** — the individual, business and the government — all meet in the fourth element, its marketplace. It is time to remember the penetrating observation made by Lord Keynes:

> "The ideas of economists and political philosophers, both when they are right, and when they are wrong, are more powerful than is commonly understood. Indeed, the world is ruled by little else. Practical men, who usually believe themselves to be quite exempt from any intellectual influences, usually are slaves of some defunct economic theory."

Let us examine **how** the elements of individual, business and government meet in the marketplace. Markets pre-dated formal governments. Then, it was a barter economy and its natural state was that of a free market — free from government interventions and grants of privilege. The free market is probably an inalienable right of mankind, for whenever government tries to control or regulate its marketplace a black market inevitably pops up and persists in spite of government actions to prevent it. This leads to the conclusion that the free market is a fundamental human right.

> "The right to engage in interstate commerce is not a gift of the state, and the state cannot regulate or restrain it." (*Hood & Sons v. DuMond,* 1949)

> The free market is another inalienable democratic right.

The marketplace is the most democratic institution in the world because elections are constantly ongoing. The polls are always open. The ballots are dollars or the currency of the land. All are equal, citizens and non-citizens. It is democracy in its purest form, unblemished by political devices like republic representation, political parties, gerrymandering, political campaigns, political speeches, policy ad lobbying, terms of office and the like. But it is touched by politicians, because government was created to define and enforce property rights. Unfortunately governments do more than this. Failing to recognize the limits of governmental power and its inevitable consequences upon the free market, politicos attempt to "improve" on the free market. Because of their overconfidence and their wish to harvest vast campaign contributions, politicos have created economic privileges (subsidies and tax exemptions for the privileged few) and laws of economic favoritism of all shades and colors for their privileged factions. Politicians speak half-truths claiming to improve the marketplace.

The Schumpeter hypothesis suggests if the free market forces are so powerful, they will automatically override the forces of bad governance and correct any wrongs that politicians make. Some will argue there is no need for the Department of Justice (DOJ) to police monopolies. Over time this is true, but in the short run the constant government acts to subsidize and grant laws of privilege to business favorites are sufficient to corrupt the democracy of the free market. This is terribly expensive to our economy.

## Canadian Drugs

Canada has a national health service that sells prescription drugs for roughly one quarter the price of U.S. drug prices. Is this because of subsidies? Not really. It is a result of the freed marketplace. Canada notifies pharmaceutical companies and their wholesalers of the opportunity to sell Canada in a single order a large quantity of a type of medication for a specific health problem; for example blood pressure medicine. The company that has the best price for that type of medication gets to supply their brand of pharmaceutical to a whole lot of the nation. As a result of this bidding, Canadians get drugs identical to those sold in the USA for perhaps 25 percent of our domestic retail drug prices. Consequently, many U.S. citizens are buying their drugs from Canada over the Internet or through the mail or through "drugstores" located in the U.S., for a third of our domestic retail prices. They are usually made by the same laboratories, and are in every way identical to drugs sold in America, except perhaps in color.

For example, a neighbor buys his pills in Canada for $70 per month; the same pills made by the same factory used to cost him over $600 per month at the stateside corner pharmacy. The massive campaign contributions made to our politicians assure that with our new health reform plan, none of this "ruinous" competition will occur, and that our drug prices, masked by government payments, will continue to be the highest in the world. These government persons think they can run a national health service in the general welfare?

## The Free Market Defined

A *free market* assumes there are finite yet variable supplies of goods and services. It also assumes that demand for goods and services is variable and relates to price, and that price can relate to demand. It assumes transparency — that buyers know the qualities and shortcomings of goods and services. New ideas have no barriers to enter the marketplace. A free market assumes that the price buyers are willing to pay for goods is flexible. As demand for superior products rises and exceeds the supply, the price is driven upward, rewarding the producer and encouraging more production to meet the rising demand. If the supply exceeds the demand, the price will fall, discouraging excess production.

This equilibrium is the self-regulation of Smith's *invisible hand*. So long as a free market is maintained, the wants and needs of the population are supplied at the most reasonable price. Producers are able to gauge the prospective market with accuracy, and anticipate the markets and demands. Failure is punished by oversupply of unwanted goods, which means bad prices and possible economic ruin for an imprudent business. Accuracy of forecasting is rewarded by prosperity. A free market penalizes those who create unwanted goods.

Recall the definition of **competition.** Competition is "1. striving or vying with another or others, for profit, prize, position, or the necessities of life; rivalry. 2. A contest, match, or other trial of skill or ability. 3. Rivalry between two or more businesses striving for the same customer or market." (*American Heritage Dictionary*, 1975)

Competition, as described by Darwin, might be natural selection of goods and services by the marketplace.

**Competition** in the free market rewards those who work hard or smart. Persons and businesses that do not work hard or smart are not rewarded, or may succumb to Joseph Schumpeter's *"perennial gale of creative destruction."* Businesses innovate to keep or gain market share. Competition is found only in the free marketplace.

Resources, too, are apportioned by the free market. **Competition** for resources translates into price bids. Resources are moved from one sector of the economy to another according to bid prices. **Competition** between suppliers keeps the price of a supply at a reasonable level, for when prices get too high, other suppliers come into the market, in search of profit. Alternative methods of production become more attractive. Perhaps different materials are substituted. But prices remain at a reasonable level only so long as there are multiple suppliers. Monopoly cancels downward price pressure and allows the prices to get out of equilibrium and unreasonably high. It is the only economic mechanism that can do so. Price control adds huge expenses for administration and compliance, which inevitably add to cost of production, which finds its way into price of goods. And price controls simply upset supplies, usually creating shortages and black market prices that are higher than the government set price.

These dynamics can maximize the general welfare of a society. Nothing is faster than the free market. No government agency is as accurate or precise as the free market. No consultancy is as insightful. No court of law is as thorough or as just. So long as organizations do not lie to the market and so long as politicians do not skew the market, there is no better way to evaluate goods and services, or to allocate labor resources as the free market.

In its ideal form, the free market is our most *democratic* institution. Democracy is defined as a social condition of equality and respect for an individual in the community. The free market is responsive to everyone. The valuation of goods and services is the sum total of the collective experiences of the total population. It takes into account all insights and all anticipations. Factored in are inventions, in all stages of development including new technology. The desirability of a new drug is anticipated by speculators, then further refined by market forces of appreciation or depreciation of the price originally set by speculators. The quality of business is accounted for. **Competitive** developments promptly impact price, as does the granting of patents. FDA approval or disapproval promptly affects price. And all evaluation is taken into account by a universal standard that is both recognized and uniformly prized by every member of every society in the world. That standard is presently the U.S. dollar.

Let us consider the mechanics or internal workings of **central planned** economies. Some examples are North Korea, Cuba and the old USSR. They have fixed price structures. Prices are fixed for set periods, often five-year blocks. Demand (black market aside) does not affect price. Consumer interest, or lack thereof, is not reflected in higher price, for the price is set centrally. Government or central planning replaces **competition. The democracy of the marketplace is destroyed.** Prices do not reflect demand. Hence prices are never at a realistic level, and cannot act to increase production of desired goods or models, nor can they fall to discourage production of unwanted goods.

Central planners also set production quotas, years in advance. They must be set independently of market demand. The result is that the bulk of production is invariably out of fashion, out of date, technologically inferior, or all of the above. These products are not desired by buyers, who chase goods available elsewhere. The marketplace shows it is more powerful than dictatorships, even those with huge police forces. If prices are set unrealistically low, farmers will not produce or will refuse to sell at the government price.

It is not that manufacturers and farmers are not patriotic; they simply cannot afford to produce crops and goods when they cannot recover their costs. Laborers, not being paid reasonable wages, are not motivated to work hard or efficiently. Party slogans soon lose their ability to motivate workers. Production quotas and party speeches soon lose appeal. Having your name on a poster or plaque on the wall only works so long. Without the incentive of reasonable pay the efficiency of production plummets.

Black markets for desired goods quickly pop up and endure. Price structures independent of the centrally planned prices quickly evolve. Foreign currency becomes more popular than the currency of the central planned economy. Good money chases out bad money. Where money is not a reliable store of value, or is scarce, or is not realistically valued, people turn to barter. The police or even an army can do little to change that.

Does **the planned economy** have a mechanism to allocate supplies and resources? To set prices? To change prices as conditions in the marketplace or world change? How does the centrally controlled market poll the citizens to see what is needed, what is wanted? Who establishes product design? How is creativity judged? Who decides which is the better design? Who sets production goals? What is the basis for these decisions? What is the timing of such decisions? Who bears the loss for late or stupid decisions? How is creativity rewarded? How is productivity judged and rewarded? How are individual accomplishments rewarded? Who decides which competing business should survive and which should slip under the water? Who decides which enterprise gets how much money? What is the basis for such a decision? The wishes of the general public? Or cronyism, nepotism, secret stock offerings or other forms of bribery? What inspires new product design? What encourages innovation? What encourages extra effort and extra hard work? What encourages a more efficient way to perform a process? What motivates persons to use extra care in production? Who is in charge of quality control? How are bad decisions punished? How are wrong decisions punished? Who bears the financial loss of "bad" and "wrong" decisions? What is to be the severity of such a punishment?

Legislation that sets unrealistic prices by some central system invariably finds that the legislated market is undermined by a black market that springs up. Economic democracy prevails. In the same manner, an onerous and unfair tax system riddled with privileges finds itself undermined by barter and an underground economy.

Is private investment to be encouraged? How does a business raise capital? How does it allocate capital? How is a well-run company to be rewarded? How are investors to be rewarded? In what amount? A medal from the state presented in public? Or good old American profits and financial success?

Who should make these decisions, an all-knowing czar, a committee of politicians, or, worse yet, political appointees? How will they survey the market? How will they know what the public wants? Will they seek centralization of each industry to facilitate the control of each sector? With diversity and multiplicity gone there is no competition. There are no hedges against loss or interruption of supply. The whole process is extremely susceptible to political influences and intervention at every stage and every level. The fall of the Soviet Union and the static economies of Cuba and North Korea suggest the inability of such an economy to compete for prosperity in the modern world. Those who wish to control a market by regulation can never achieve the efficiency of a free market.

The biggest criticism of the controlled economy, or any controlled market, is that there is no meaningful device to control increase in prices. The best that those who attempt to regulate the marketplace can come up with is the strong prejudice against profits. Attempts to set prices destroy the equilibrium of production. When prices are set below cost of production, production immediately stalls, demand sky-rockets and black markets appear, all of which overwhelm the clumsy government attempts to set prices. In the controlled economy there is no meaningful device to propel the development of new goods, novel services, new methods of production. The incentive system is lacking. Profits supply incentives in the free market. The goal of regulators explicit or implicit is to reduce, then remove profits, thereby reducing prices. With the profit incentive removed, where is the incentive to create new goods and services? Yet this is deemed a worthy goal and in the general welfare. In addition, in the controlled economy, there is not any efficient way to allocate creative spark, materials, and labor to be utilized in the production of products the public actually wants. The idea that a central group can forecast the wants and needs, the tastes and desires of consumers, the extent of same or the most efficient allocation of resources years in advance is ludicrous. The misallocation of time and natural resources will prove staggering and the result can be the collapse of a world power such as the Soviet empire. This is the history of mankind. But regulators don't read history. The controlled economy is simply a "copycat" economy. The lead in the race towards prosperity is necessarily conceded to other nations who allow free markets. An indispensable function of government is to prevent monopoly and protect the free market. Is this happening here in the USA?

To repeat: the Schumpeter hypothesis states that monopolies, like Standard Oil, did not need to be broken up by governmental action. Modern libertarians argue that Ma Bell did not need to be broken up by the DOJ. They reason that free market forces would have done the job. They argue that the free market system eventually is all powerful. Over time the free market has shown the ability to topple governments that impose their will on their marketplace. They argue that the government has no business policing monopoly.

These arguments are totally wrong. Government intervention in the form of a constant shower of tax cuts, subsidies, administrative laws and other laws of economic favor overwhelms the natural tendency of the free market to overcome monopoly.

All of this is lost on politicos and political advisors, policy wonks, utopian thinkers and the liberal educators of today. Being unfamiliar with budgets, living within budgets, the cost of goods sold, gainful employment, the concept of fiscal illusion, and probably balancing their own checkbooks, they continually search for buttons to push, knobs to spin and levers to pull so as to control or "improve" the free market. They have become detached from reality, yet we find them at the helm of the ship of state. The public knows they are unrealistic, that "the emperor wears no clothes." But politicos intoxicated with "*more confidence than they deserve*" are mostly unaware.

Government actions that tolerate concentrations in the market are examples of poor government. It is our government that allows, indeed promotes, the consolidations of business that destroy the freedom of our markets. These consolidations are mergers, acquisitions, takeovers, buyouts and the like. Indeed, the government actions subsidize and promote these activities. They allow subsidies to flow to the biggest industries which then allow those industries to use economies of scale to crush competitors and obliterate competition. In the final analysis politicos simply cannot keep their hands off the marketplace, always to the detriment of the general weal.

## Birth of The Corporation

Historically, most taxation was **indirect** or hidden from the view of citizens. Tariffs, duties, imposts were the norm. These were intended to be indirect but some were quite visible. The stamp tax was not a tax on stamps, but a stamp on a good to prove payment of the tax, like the state tax label on liquor bottles. Because this was visible and evident to the citizens, it was a focal point and quite inflammatory. Such a tax stamp on tea led in part to the American Revolution.

**Indirect taxation** was taxation not visible to the public.

219

There was never a thought towards **direct taxation** of income in England until about 1799 or in America until the Civil War. But revenues generated by indirect taxation were generally insufficient to keep pace with government spending. There was also revenue from burgage or the purchase of special trading rights for geographic areas or special events like trade fairs. Eventually it was realized that these trading privileges could produce serious revenue, and without the administrative complexity and resentment of taxation at the individual level.

> With **direct taxation,** the levy was obvious to the public; for example, the sales tax added to the price of goods today.

Corporations seem to have been invented in England. They evolved from royal grants of privilege or "charters" to hold markets and fairs, dating back to perhaps the 1100s. Formal incorporation may date to the Merchant Adventurer Act in England in 1390. It was soon followed by the Baltic Trade Act of 1404. In 1570, Queen Elizabeth I granted a charter to the Eastland Company. And on December 31, 1600, she granted articles of incorporation to The East India Company, therein granting a monopoly on trade east of the Cape of Good Hope for a period of 15 years. The charter was amended in 1609 under James I to last "*for ever*," though with a proviso that it might be revoked "*on three years notice if trade should not prove profitable to the realm.*" (E.B. 1956, vol. 7, p. 869) Successor corporations lasted until 1858.

The East India Company was immensely profitable from the beginning. It was soon a major source of revenue for the Crown. By 1757, the East India Company had become the ruling power in India after a victory at Plassey. But the Crown began to reassert control; in 1773 it appointed a governor and approved a supreme court and lesser judges, and by 1784 England took control of political, military, and financial affairs in India. Under government pressure, the East India Company steadily declined. By 1813 its monopoly of exclusive right to trade, which had been under legal assault since 1683, was finally lost. Meanwhile, taxation of other corporations was generating lots of revenue, without much public notice.

A corporation is defined as a group acting as a single entity granted a charter by a government that recognizes that it has a separate existence, with its own rights, privileges and liabilities distinct from those of the separate members of society. Corporations are a grant of privilege to a citizen or a group of them to conduct business in a special way. So long as certain rules are followed, the corporation shall have perpetual life, and the incorporators, officers, directors and employees are protected from personal liability for legal corporate business activities, should the corporation fail. Corporations provided fractional units of ownership that were easily traded, called stock shares. In good times shares would pay *cash dividends or stock dividends* to the holder. Originally stocks had equal or uniform rights; all shares were identical. Then corporations started granting certain stockholders privileges. Some stock shares (*preferred shares*) were given guaranteed rates of return. Other shares were given the privilege of power to vote (*voting shares*), which allowed control of the corporation to be held within a few hands.

## Proprietorship Mentality

Sole owners had sole and unfettered discretion to use business assets, and employees were left to be satisfied with whatever amount the owner chose to pay them. The owners had taken the risks; they had built the business. Owners had unlimited dominion and control over business assets, and were accountable to no one except tax authorities and the law.

As corporations evolved into larger businesses, management was no longer confined to the founder or his family. Other persons found their way to the helm of the business. At the same time, the characteristics of shareholders were changing. Private individuals, unrelated to the founder, were often buying shares as investments. But curiously, the **ownership mentality** was adopted by the new managers who did not create the business. It is no surprise that in small corporations this ownership attitude survived unchanged. Shareholders quickly came to be treated arbitrarily. Management treated shareholders more like employees than equity owners in the business. Even though the new management might own no shares and thus have made no contribution to capital, they treated the business as if it were their own and acted as though they were accountable to no one. Predictably this led to problems.

In response to these problems, a **board of directors** was established to look after the interests of shareholders. Legally, the board of directors are **trustees**. Legally they are charged with the non-delegable duty to look after the interests of the shareholders. And legally, most managerial transgressions can be laid at their feet.

## Anatomy of a Corporation

A schematic looks like this:

| Sole proprietorship/small business | Corporation |
|---|---|
| Owner | Management |
| Employees | Board of directors |
| | Shareholders |
| | Employees |

## Directorship Dysfunction

Instead of taking a watchdog role, often the board of directors become tyrants, practically speaking, controlling the power to nominate candidates, explained in Chapter 10. In corporations, while all shares of stock have the power to vote for directors, the **power to nominate candidates** is held within the existing board of directors. Meetings were held periodically, but too infrequently for any meaningful oversight. As corporations grew in size and complexity, many bad acts and bad practices were never discovered by the board of directors. Many directors overlooked or did not examine closely corporate actions. Inaction on the part of the board was the accepted norm. Secrecy in board meetings prevailed; secrecy from shareholders, the public, the law. Directorships became highly paid. Directorships often became **interlocking**; one person could and did serve on several boards, an incestuous monopolistic practice. Often the board of directors was either ignored by management or filled with weak-minded or aged directors, or, worse yet, directors who were compromised by huge paychecks and fringe benefits for a few moments of their time. Director **errors and omissions liability insurance** (paid for by the corporation) facilitates, indeed guarantees, shareholder abuse by directors as they will experience no personal loss for fraudulent and collusive acts.

Worst of all, case law leaves within the hands of the board the power to decide if action should be taken against any errant corporate officer or employee. Fraud committed by officers can be discovered by directors and the board of directors can decide it is not in the interest of the business to prosecute that fraud! In most states it is very difficult to overturn that decision of the board.

**The inevitable conclusion is that the privileges of limits of personal liability soon lead to abuse and are not in the public interest.**

Minority shareholders in corporations are at risk of being ignored; corporate assets can be siphoned off as management fees, leaving no money to pay minority shareholders any dividends. A shareholder bill of rights to remedy such abuses is suggested in Appendix Two. This provides that "whistle-blowers" will receive a lifetime annuity of 125 percent of their compensation in the event the evidence they provide leads to a felony conviction; such annuity shall be paid from the assets of the convicted corporate officer.

## Advantage of Incorporation

Sole proprietors have finite lifespans and finite work life expectancies and may become less focused or dedicated as their lives progress. In a sense, they are the business. Succession can be a real problem, as the heirs generally have different preferences or desires, and usually have not been raised in the environment that hones skills necessary for business success. Family problems, underqualified children wishing to run a business, divorces with property settlements, or bad health of the principal or spouse can compromise a sole proprietorship.

Partnerships must die and reform every time there is a change in membership. Renegotiation between partners can be quite messy, with promises and expectations not being lived up to.

Corporations usually are of indefinite life-span and allow the accumulation of wealth without limitation. They can grow to incredible size. If one were to insert the annual sales of our three largest corporations in a listing of nations' Gross Domestic Products (GDP) for the year ending December 31, 2001, we would see:

| #20 | Belgium | $229 billion GDP |
| #21 | **Wal-Mart** | $221 billion sales |
| #22 | Sweden | $201 billion GDP |
| #23 | **Mobil-Exxon** | $191 billion sales |
| #24 | Austria | $188 billion GDP |
| #25 | Saudi Arabia | $186 billion GDP |
| #26 | **General Motors** | $177 billion sales |
| #27 | Poland | $176 billion GDP |

Or, more startling, combining **Wal-Mart, Mobil-Exxon** and **General Motors** sales at U.S. $589 billion, for the year ending December 31, 2001, exceeds the GDP of:

| #10 | Spain | $581 billion GDP |
| #11 | Brazil | $502 billion GDP |
| #12 | India | $477 billion GDP |
| #13 | S. Korea | $422 billion GDP |

When dealing with national governments, corporations' highly paid talent and massive budgets allow them unimaginable liberties. When dealing with local governments, their legal resources, secret agendas and large budgets assure that local politicos will be overwhelmed and make bad bargains.

Corporations, with this ability to accumulate unlimited wealth, have an inordinate ability to recruit and pay talent (especially trained and experienced) for all levels of management functions, simply not paralleled in sole proprietorships. **Corporate immortality** allows for specialization and division of managerial functions that sole proprietorships rarely have time to develop. Often the brighter stars of the business world look past sole proprietorships and explore only corporate employment opportunities, which they judge to be more stable. Corporations are not family dependent, and fractional shares of corporations are often publicly traded, so shares of stock and options have value that minority interest non-corporate forms of business simply do not have.

## Corporate Citizenship

Jurisprudence granted corporations citizenship by accident. The Supreme Court of the United States first considered corporate citizenship, in the case of *Bank of the United States v. Deveaux* (1807). Justice Marshall wrote for the Supreme Court, which decided unanimously that corporations were not citizens. The court found corporations were *"invisible, intangible, artificial beings"* that *"exist only in the contemplation of the law."* It was found they have *"no organ except the corporate seal"* and *"cannot be outlawed."* They were *"certainly not citizens."*

The limitations of the **doctrine of the law of corporate citizenship quickly** became apparent. Corporations were usually granted existence by individual states. Soon corporations started doing business outside their native state. These "other" states in which corporations did business tried to regulate and tax the corporate behavior, but ran into jurisdictional complications and troubles enforcing their judgments outside their borders. And citizens of "other" states had trouble bringing suits against "foreign" corporations, problems doing discovery involving persons outside their own state's jurisdiction and enforcing their judgments on assets of corporations of "foreign" states.

Some attorney turned to the federal courts because the Constitution gives them power (1) where the United States is a party,

(2) in actions between states, (3) in actions between one state and citizens of a different state (4) or in actions between citizens of different states, (5) or in controversies involving federal laws. But corporations still seemed to evade the law by falling somewhere outside the practical power of state courts, and yet not being subject to the jurisdiction of federal courts, because they were not citizens. So the Supreme Court by 1870 "solved" the problem by holding that corporations were "*quasi citizens.*"

Then someone noticed the Constitution required **diversity of citizenship as to all parties.** The general practice of attorneys, just to be safe, was to sue corporation by name and the officers and directors personally. Because officers and directors were usually citizens of the state of incorporation, this destroyed diversity as to all members of the lawsuit and the federal courts could not hear the case. Out of state corporations seemed to escape again.

By 1876 the Supreme Court "solved" that problem by reasoning that since the corporate entity usually protected officers and directors from personal liability it was proper to sue corporations, but improper to sue officers or directors personally. The diversity of citizenship test could now be met.

> Corporations were granted citizenship to bring them within the jurisdiction of federal courts.

Corporations had been granted full citizenship. They had gone from "*certainly not citizens*" to citizens. But this "solution" simply created more and bigger problems. In granting full citizenship to corporations they were given the fundamental rights of free speech, freedom of assembly, and freedom of religion. As the only tokens of corporate existence are the articles of incorporation, the corporate seal, the corporate minute book and the corporate checkbook, they needed a mouthpiece to exercise their newfound freedoms. These spokesmen were paid attorneys, then lobbyists. Soon money was flowing directly to politicians as campaign contributions and payola had become legitimatized.

> The corporate right to freedom of speech led to hiring
> "mouthpieces" by which to speak, and soon led to
> money flowing into the hands of politicians.

No case has explicitly granted corporations freedom of (or from) religion, but corporations were free to worship the dollar and profits with complete disregard for other citizens of society. They take an oath to no God. They cannot be put in jail. They do not perform military service; indeed we fight trade wars for their benefits. They are only subject to monetary fines, loss of license or dissolution. The wealth they have accrued, and the willingness of government at all levels to sell privileges makes corporations quite immune from the laws that control the rest of us. They have become above the laws that ordinary citizens must follow.

> Corporate "citizens" soon became, in the words of
> Orwell, "more equal" than mortal citizens.

## Corporate Sovereignty (Tyranny)

By granting citizenship, and by insulating officers and directors from personal liability, the court laid the foundation for **corporate sovereign entities**. Just as complaints against elected public officials should not be the basis for a court lawsuit, but should be addressed by elections, courts developed the notion that the business dealings of the corporation are only the business of the corporation. The courts held that corporations should be governed by the board of directors, and only the board of directors, and not in any way by the courts. If the shareholders do not like what is happening within the corporation, their exclusive remedy is to change the board of directors, but not come to court. The courts generally will not peek under the petticoat of a corporation.

Given this liberty, corporate boards of directors quickly seized on the notion that actions against corporate officers were an exclusive right of the board and were not to be questioned by shareholders, that a board might ignore the most grievous transgressions of officers of the corporation, reasoning that public disclosure of such crimes would damage stock share prices, and hence not be in shareholder's best interests. It is the board, and only the board, that can decide to prosecute officers for their actions.

An outsider running for the board of directors is usually an exercise in futility. Shareholder lists, unlimited funds, glowing recommendations of approved director candidates in quarterly reports are all there, but only for the insiders. The stark reality is far worse. It has gotten to the point the board of directors can even disqualify a properly nominated candidate to the election of the board because the candidate has the wrong ideals: perhaps they are "too green." Appeals of such decisions and actions lie not in a court of law, but in the hands of the board of directors.

So we find what attorneys now call **shareholder derivative suits** is little but delusion. In reality the rights of shareholders are limited or crushed in court by the doctrine of **corporate sovereignty.** Taking corporate behavior to court produces little but huge attorney fees. Evidentiary rulings usually favor corporations. Shareholders, who are in fact the owners of the corporations, have few rights or remedies and corporate officers are free to be tyrants, free from oversight by courts. Predictably officer and director compensation in America has risen to heights never before imagined. Officers are free to backdate stock options, intimidate whistleblowers, take compensation net of taxation, leaving the corporation or shareholders to pay taxes (essentially doubling their pay packets), have corporate (exclusive) jet airplanes, and contrive complicated international contractual dealings to move personal assets to offshore tax havens in manners that appear to be normal corporate business dealings and the like.

Congress was first to catch on to the unjust actions of corporations. Recall the history of Mark Hanna and the Tillman Act (1907), saying corporations could make no cash contributions to federal elections. (But these prohibitions didn't cover state elections.) And, unfortunately the Supreme Court routinely wiped out most legislative attempts to limit campaign contributions with the broadest interpretations of free speech imaginable.

With the McCain-Feingold Act, this problem was "solved" by attempting to limit the free speech of corporations. The absolute prohibition of cash campaign contributions was removed and replaced with a distinction between "*hard money* campaign contributions" and "*soft money* campaign contributions." Congress left in a loophole: there was no meaningful and timely accounting for soft money. The result was a positive avalanche of corporate campaign contributions. So it is that the solution to the problem of corporate citizenship led quickly to another and far bigger problem, the apparent validation of the corruption of our entire political system.

The Supreme Court did not catch on until the *McConnell v. FEC* decision discussed in Chapter 6. A careful reading of the case shows that the freedom of speech tests are never mentioned by the majority of the Supreme Court. Most limitations on cash contributions to candidates are upheld. However, corporations are free to spend unlimited amounts to make "issue ads" so long as a particular party is not identified or clearly inferred.

## The Corporate Citizen Revisited

Corporations quickly became gluttons for infrastructure: the best ports, canals, highways, airports, railroads, telegraph and telephone service, fiber optic and radio/television bandwidths. They desired the best education for their workers and research from the universities for product development, design and marketing. Modern corporations enjoy the benefits of citizenship and enjoy benefits of law and order protecting their assets. Of course, corporations have no duty to serve in the military and though they may be referred to as citizens, they have no right to vote.

Businesses exist simply for profit. The corporation that does not maximize its opportunities for maximum profit runs the risk of being devoured by a competitor who is more profitable. Corporate behavior too often includes such acts as hiding toxic production waste products in abandoned water wells; selling tainted food products; failing to pay decent wages; demanding outrageous and ever increasing workloads of employees; plundering pension plans for exorbitant management bonuses; failing to place mercury scrubbers on electrical generation plants; phony entries in corporate books to justify huge management salaries, backdating stock options for officers and directors, reckless oil drilling practices by British Petroleum in the Gulf of Mexico — and many other such practices, the list is endless. How can any of this be called citizenship?

The concept of *corporate citizenship* imposes costs on the civic corporation that unethical, unencumbered competitors don't assume. This allows the bad "citizens" to become more competitive than the corporation that self imposes costs of citizenship. The solutions to such problems are beyond the powers of legislation

Part of the answer is to not promote such behavior with subsidies and laws of economic privileges, sold by our politicians. The rest must be addressed by informed consumers in the marketplace. Businessmen argue that when government imposes "*costs of citizenship*" on corporations within its jurisdiction, it tends to drive those corporations outside of its jurisdiction, thus removing them from the tax base. We must recognize this argument for what it is and not buy that fable. They are simply seeking privileges to cover their own laziness and greed. Tell them: fine, move out; then tax them at the borders as they try to import back to the USA.

It is not surprising that as corporations matured, they became huge and a bit arrogant. Competition in the marketplace and the drive for profits were central and primary values. Public interests, scruples and even laws began to matter little, if at all. Shareholders, the owners, were treated no better. A special **code of irresponsibility** to shareholders and society developed. These attitudes and devices are taught at the more prestigious universities in the master of business administration degree programs. Under the guidance of high power staff attorneys and MBAs, laws came to be bent, or "to be meant for others than ourselves" or even broken but only if it was profitable to do so. A standard calculation became cost of compliance versus costs of breaking the law: What are the chances we will be caught? What are the chances we can beat them at trial? What would the fines and forfeitures be? What damages in civil suits could be expected? Will it be profitable to follow the law or to break the law?

## Corporate Cannibalism

Corporate cannibalism was infrequent until William E. Simon invented private equity funds utilizing LBOs in 1982. These funds quickly became the darling of the advanced business courses and then Wall Street. Admiration and dread swept corporate boardrooms as these "raiders," assisted by judicial apathy in the form of the doctrine of **corporate** sovereignty, devoured corporation after corporation using little or none of their own funding.

Once cash reserves, surplus inventories, generous pension reserves or other assets held in reserve for "rainy days" were found, the corporate raiders attack was launched. They replaced officers with themselves. While proclaiming they were freeing under-producing surplus or capital and putting such funds to more productive uses, these **raiders** disassembled the victim corporation and took for themselves exorbitant salaries, and bonuses. They used bits and pieces of the victim for the next deal. For a while, **Kravits, Kohlberg & Roberts** bragged on their website about how they plundered about $1 trillion from the American economy. Much of this was from the funding for pension and profit sharing plans. The web pages are no longer there, but are reproduced in the appendix as Exhibit 2.

Small businesses have long been noted as the font of new jobs. The signature of big business is lower wages, demands for higher production and higher stress in the workplace. Why are we so anxious to promote mergers, consolidations, takeovers? Why do we purchase newspapers that tout all this as progress, or somehow in the common good? Isn't this simply monopoly in the making? The export of jobs, technology and opportunity is un-American, but is subsidized heavily by our politicians following the new mantra "greed is good." Everywhere newspapers trumpet mergers and acquisitions as some sort of progress or societal benefit. How are newspapers working for the general welfare? When will we get wise?

The concentration of manufacturing into fewer plants plays nicely into the hands of financiers and speculators. The concentration of businesses makes disruption of production from storm damage, fires and employee strikes more of a risk. Diversity is lost; reliance on supplies from manufacturers on the other side of the world coupled with minimal inventory invites disaster. But disaster is good; one man's disaster is another man's opportunity. Employees and investors lose while management and speculators thrive.

The main focus of business today is the short term. Business plans stress daily production, monthly quotas, quarterly results. A long-term business goal is next year. Where do you find a five- or ten-year plan in the American business scene? Our businessmen seem entirely too willing to sacrifice the national future for next year's bonus. The export of jobs and technology may make little sense to the prosperity of the nation, but makes perfect sense to corporate types focused entirely upon bonuses for quarterly profits.

Corporate "royalty" next got the idea that management compensation should be net of taxation, leaving the tax repercussions with the corporation. Your salary should be tax-free. This means a $1,000,000 annual bonus is really $1,600,000 and the shareholders, press and public never catch on. Load up on fringe benefits: home, security systems, bodyguards, armored limousines, multiple condos for vacations, servants, private jets, all tax free. Staggering salary packages are paid to corporate officers, who move them to offshore tax havens. Will we ever learn the names of the 52,000 American citizens holding UBS accounts in Switzerland?

As corporations went international, elaborate facades and convoluted accounting systems were crafted to show that high expense procedures were performed in global locations with the lowest tax structure. It became possible to use imaginative accounting practices to move profits out of one nation to a nation where the rate of taxation was low. Instead of paying social dues, corporations spend huge amounts of cash and effort seeking subsidies: tax breaks, tax credits, TIFs, low interest loans, special laws of privilege in the marketplace favoring their product over others and the like. They seek subsidies far in excess of the little tax they pay. Why do we subsidize these activities? Why do we give them fancy tax breaks? Why do we let them keep United States citizenship? The Athenians would have ostracized such persons.

Wealth remains concentrated in corporations and dodgy book-keeping avoids corporate tax liability. When there is blatant tax evasion, our politicos, motivated by campaign contributions, refuse to prosecute them for these acts of tax avoidance. (See Chapter 11: Taxation and Reform Thereof.)

The final paradox is that corporations pay little or nothing in the way of social dues. Over time corporations have developed other attitudes towards taxes or the social "dues" for amenities. They are viewed as wasted dollars by the corporate types. They feel any society should be happy that corporations employ citizens and not expect tax payments as well.

**Is any of this citizenship?** It is a bit paradoxical that corporate charters, devices originally created to generate business and generate tax revenue for the Crown, have become the biggest gluttons for infrastructure and have evolved into the biggest tax evaders here and in England, indeed around the world.

## The Marriage of Corporations and Finance

In 1711, England was again at war with Spain. Public debt was mounting. All of England anticipated both victory and lucrative trade concessions to follow. Based upon these expectations the Lord Treasurer, one Robert Harley, Chancellor of the Exchequer, dreamed up a scheme to absolve the Crown of the national debt (then consisting of £10,000,000), to raise money to fund the war, to raise additional revenue for the Crown, and to make profits for himself and shareholders. Following his plan, that year England granted incorporation to the South Seas Company and gave it the privilege of exclusive trading rights with the South Americas (soon to be won from Spain) and an annual annuity payment of some £600,000 from the Crown, *if* the Crown would be absolved of its debt. The company had persuaded holders of that £10,000,000 Crown debt to trade that debt for stock shares in the new company. Parliament expected tariffs from the trade to the South Americas to fund the £600,000 interest payments and more. Any excess tax revenue would be the property of the Crown.

Politicos were given stock at discount, to make the deal go through Parliament. Appropriate hype drove the stock from £100 per share upward even before the war with Spain was won. The hype led to a gigantic bubble as share price increased. There was a frenzy of mortgaging homes and estates to get in on the increase in share price, which got up to £1,000 per share.

But the trade concessions from Spain were not as generous as anticipated. Even government and private manipulation of the stock prices could not sustain share valuation and the share price plummeted to a more realistic £175. Financial ruin was widespread. The director's personal wealth and property were forfeited, but were vastly insufficient to pay debts.

In 1719 the Bubble Act (the Royal Exchange and London Assurance Corporation Act) was passed, limiting and regulating corporate practice in England. Notwithstanding this tragedy, the South Seas Company was kept alive, bilking English citizens out of investment dollars, until 1850.

Thus it was that corporate abuse of granted privileges was recognized on the Continent early on as evil, by any measure. Corporations were the preferred device for fraud, convenient shields from liability for misrepresentations. Corporations created difficulty in knowing whom you were actually dealing with: a person, a partnership with financial responsibility, or an incorporated business where a person was acting in a limited personal liability role. Corporations became vehicles of speculation and fraudulent schemes of all sorts and colors. They were being condemned on the Continent as the cause of economic "fluctuations." All this could have lent foresight to our Founding Fathers. But it was beyond their power to foresee the scope or magnitude of the role multinational corporations would have in the modern business world.

## Monopolies, Cartels, and Trusts

**Monopoly** is a word with Greek roots: *mono* meaning single and *polein,* which means to sell. Monopoly was recognized in Greek and Roman times as not good for the public. *The Domesday Book* of 1086 (its name comes from the Teutonic "doom" meaning legal decision of a judge, most often in criminal matters) was a listing of all lands and livestock in England so that William the Conqueror might know what rent to charge nobility. Described in the book were the prohibited trade practices of forestalling and engrossing, which pre-dated that book. **Engrossing** was the practice of buying up a commodity to establish a monopoly and then reselling the goods at a higher price. **Forestalling** was the act of buying grain and future contracts for grain and then pushing the price upwards by spreading false rumors. These actions were punishable by forfeiture of the grain. By the time of Henry III, the penalty was forfeiture and two months imprisonment. For the second offense forfeiture was twice the value of the grain; the third offense was penalized by pillory and financial ruin. Compare that to the puny reparations demanded by judges today.

Monopoly results in fewer competitors or impaired competitors, which usually leads to higher prices, lesser service and goods of poorer quality. Monopoly can take a vertical form, as in an oil company that controls everything from production at the oil well to sale to the customer; or a horizontal form, the control of all or most of one sector of an industry. Examples are pipelines, refining and well drilling. A monopoly can take the form of a single buyer for raw materials or a single seller of finished goods or services in a marketplace. But a monopoly can exist if as little as 20 percent of a sector of the economy is in the hands of a single business. Hence a monopoly is simply any concentration that can make the price for goods or services higher than would be found in a free market.

> A simple working definition of a **monopoly** is "too big to fail."

A **cartel** is an explicit, though not written, agreement among *multiple* firms that supply similar goods or services. While they are thought to be in competition, the agreement means that they are not. The purpose of the cartel is to increase revenue and profits not by innovative manufacture or product design, but simply by diminishing competition and thus increasing price. Agreements can cover price fixing, customer allocations, production or even sales allocations and division of the market by geographic allocation. Some studies have found that national cartels raise prices on average 18 percent and international cartels raise prices 28 percent.

A **trust** is difficult to understand by definition, but easier to comprehend by example. Think of it as a mask of ownership. Trusts are sometimes cited as an English invention. In America the practice is attributed to John D. Rockefeller. Actually the concept of trust dates back to Roman times. Roman nobility was to have no interest in businesses. Nobles were to govern and govern for the good of the Roman society. Romans devised trusts to allow themselves to receive profits from businesses and have the titled interest in business enterprises held "in trust" or in the hands of a *trusted* friend.

Today, a trust is defined as placing legal ownership of an asset in the hands of one person (the trustee) with the duty or obligation to pay the benefits or incidents of ownership to another person, the beneficiary. By forming **trusts,** corporations can act in concert to exert monopolistic forces in total secrecy. A trust has many advantages, as the discretionary power to run the corporation can be separated from stock ownership. Corporate control remains in the trust, where there need be no minutes or disclosures, no evidence for lawsuits or criminal prosecutions.

By 1882, John D. Rockefeller had come under criticism for his high-pressure, predatory practices of buying or controlling his competitors. With the devices of trusts and interlocking boards of directors, he was able to secure discrete concentrations of control of the oil industry in companies that appeared to be separate, competing companies. Many of his practices would today qualify as racketeering. He found it beneficial to deflect notice of his acquisitions by the use of a corporate trust where controlling interests of his corporate acquisitions were held in privacy.

Ida M. Tarbell, muckraker and author, wrote *The History of the Standard Oil Company*, which led directly to the Sherman Anti-Trust prosecution of Standard Oil in 1911. When that trust company was "busted," it held at least 64 percent of the petroleum market share. It was broken into 34 new oil companies, including Amoco, Chevron, Conoco, Exxon, Mobil, and Standard Oil of Ohio, now part of British Petroleum (BP).

An early regulatory agency, the Federal Trade Commission (FTC), was created in 1914 to bust monopolies. It was buffeted by political privilege granting and hamstrung by the Department of Justice. It has been a dismal failure at preventing monopolies. We have simply to recall the DOJ guideline:

"In order to compete in the modern markets, **competitors sometimes need to collaborate**. Competitive forces are driving firms towards complex collaborations to achieve goals such as expanding into foreign markets, funding innovation efforts and lowering production costs . . . **such collaborations are often not only benign but pro-competitive**."

The DOJ is telling us that monopoly promotes competition!

Our governments have created corporations by their largess and have nurtured them with subsidies and tax exemptions and privileges of all sorts and kinds. Every privilege granted diminishes the opportunities of the rest of the citizens. Every subsidy raises citizens' taxes. Corporations are adept at avoiding taxes. (See Chapter 6.) It is time to pulverize these large corporations, and spread opportunity around the economy. Prosperity demands this. There is no other way.

## Subsidies Defined

Recall the Schumpeter hypothesis: that government action to break up monopolies is not necessary, for free markets will do the same thing without government intervention. The fallacy is that the constant government interventions (subsidies, tax breaks to the favored few, and the laws of favoritism) defeat free market forces.

Let us examine subsidies more closely. A subsidy is defined as a **direct cash payment** to a citizen or business or economic sector, to encourage a business that might fail, or to encourage economic activity that politicos feel might be beneficial to society. Subsidies can take the form of **financial assistance** to the individual, business or sector of the economy: trade barriers, tax exemptions for business, tax credits for business, tax advantages (write-offs of income to be taxed or even credit for use of a product), advantageous price differentials, regulatory preferences. Or a subsidy can take the form of administrative actions; for example allowing someone cost-free pollution cleanup, yet charging his competitors for cleanup, or less stringent inspection of imported goods for one company than another.

A country that has a free market coupled with a democratic government should be the most desirable place in the world in which to live. The free market should be the goal of legislation, administration and court adjudication. Yet governments have caused many interferences with the free market.

## Characteristics of Subsidies

Subsidies sound so beneficial and seem to have such lofty goals: to protect our infant industries, to encourage local production (protect domestic jobs), to equalize income differentials, to secure the supply of a commodity, to guarantee high quality, to promote developing industries. They have the sound of the general welfare. They sound desirable. They sound necessary. They sound logical. They sound cost-effective. Let us look closer.

The basic nature of subsidies is that they **allow an unprofitable business to exist** in the marketplace. If the business was a startup or if there were some compelling social or perhaps military need, it might be justified. However, to prop up an existing business that is floundering in a normal marketplace has several serious implications.

If a business is not doing well, there are probably reasons for it. To simply pump money into the business without diagnosing or treating the malady is foolishness. And why should a government be playing favorites? There are probably competitors. They may be doing well. Where is the fair play in cheapening capital cost to the failing business? Doesn't that penalize the well-run businesses? Doesn't that also mean that the well-run businesses are taxed more to support the subsidy that will allow the unfortunate competitor to continue in existence? Doesn't this also put the better-run business at a competitive disadvantage? It may have to contend with the unrealistically low price structures of a desperate or disorganized business, price structures that are affordable only to the poorly run business because of the subsidies. The poorly run business will probably make poor management decisions and continue to operate in its losing ways. Poor performance is rewarded and the **well-run business is penalized.** And society as a whole loses the benefit of lower-priced goods. Is that sound public policy?

**Who chooses which business** to prop up, Smith Trucking Company or Jones Trucking Company? What parameters will control this decision? If the business is a losing venture or a declining style of business, why encourage it to continue in its present form?

What are the impacts on competitors in the same sector of the economy? Should they, too, receive subsidies? What about other competitors in parallel sectors of the economy? For example, railroads and air freight companies, to be fair, should both get subsidies.

How much should they be given in subsidies? How is this amount determined? When does the subsidy end? Are we delivering goods and services the public actually wants? Are we rewarding innovation and invention, or simply encouraging and institutionalizing another big, entrenched, aged, rigid, inflexible, unresponsive, uncaring, stodgy, dependent, monolithic beast with perpetual existence?

Perhaps the most ridiculous extreme is the **cross-subsidy.** Congress helps motor carriers by subsidizing them. Then Congress gives tax breaks to the cargo-carrying airlines, to help them get started in business. In addition, the railroads, historically the carriers of freight as well as passenger cars, are an anomaly and are chronically in need of helping programs. Each is too valuable to let fail. Congress loves the campaign contributions. Lobbyists love the business and the rich fees. With all that expense what is achieved? No goods are produced. Costs rise all the way around. Where is the benefit to the public? Why not let the market sort out its preferences? What insights can politicos add to the picture?

If well-run businesses experience momentary bad times, they, too, feel they must turn to the politicos for subsidies. So it evolves that poorly run businesses and well-run businesses alike turn to politicos for subsidies, in one form or another. Subsidies are not permanent; they must be renewed, with constant attention and expense. Year after year, the expense of lobbying is added to the expense of doing business; the cost of goods sold. The whole sordid process adds to the expense of goods and services. How can a marketplace so encumbered possibly produce low-priced goods and services? Is this the best use of our tax dollars? More importantly, is this any reason to run annual deficits, to run up the national debt?

Who are politicos to decide who should survive? Why on earth do political sorts believe they know better than the democracy of the free market system (the voice of the people) which businesses should live and which should die? What unique insights do politicos possess? What special skills do they have? The myopia of bribery? Special insights bred by high campaign finance? Special insights that being absent from their home districts for extended periods of time might gainsay? Special insights that breathing the air of Washington, D.C. might breed?

Politicos have a miserable record at recognizing winners in the business field. Look at corn-based ethanol for motor fuel, look at the AIG bailout, look at the general agriculture subsidy mess, look at the national health plan. Until they stop granting privileges and allow competition in the health care industry there will be nothing but endless expense and deterioration of health care. Imagine witless, clueless administrators defining surgical codes of conduct or trying to decipher what constitutes medical malpractice.

Often a subsidy is an economic program to make goods the market is not willing to pay for or to make more of a good than the market is willing to purchase. Subsidies simply **encourage production of unwanted goods**. They are given to a business in which no capitalist wishes to invest. Indeed, they support business plans that the venture capitalists are not willing to back. Even for ventures in which speculators fear to invest, for a political bribe, subsidies suddenly appear. In short, it is a business the private sector is unwilling to embrace that benefits from a subsidy. Subsidizing such a business to go forward or to continue in business is a perversion of the free market.

Subsidies induce a misallocation of resources: for example alcohol from corn (ethanol) upset food prices and is destroying the quality and quantity of our aquifers. Tobacco is dangerous in any form. Why has its growth been subsidized until recently? As a result of pressure from the farm lobby, 50-year water leases (subsidies) were renewed in California by George H.W. Bush. This led to rates so cheap that farmers felt water could be wasted. Thus water is moved in open trenches in sandy soil, where much of it evaporates or soaks into the soil instead of flowing in more costly pipelines that conserve water. Further evidence of waste due to cheap rates is found in the fields where farmers use more wasteful sprays rather than (water conserving) drip irrigation. Meanwhile the western states are anxious to pipe water down from the Great Lakes due to local water shortages. Subsidies are more likely to promote waste than conservation. Where is the general welfare in that?

Corporations do not act like citizens. Corporations are tax shirks and infrastructure hogs and pay little tax, if any. Why give them cash or credits from our treasury? Subsidies are driven by bribery, usually in the form of cash. Some of the cash is from foreign corporations, seeking privileges and advantages. Because it is the form of cash, it is untraceable. Why are we helping foreign corporations like Honda and Toyota?

The message of subsidies is that everything is up for sale, including politicos and the courts! If politicos have the power to grant cash subsidies, don't they have the power to grant tax exemptions? If so, there can be no fair taxation. There is nothing good for the public to be had from subsidies.

## Laws Permitting Subsidies are Unconstitutional

It is contrary to the general notion of democracy that any government based upon democratic principles would ever create or permit laws of privilege including those of subsidy. A privilege is defined by Webster as **(1) a special advantage, immunity, permission, right or benefit granted to or enjoyed by an individual, caste or class (2) such right or advantage as a prerogative of status or rank**. All these notions are inconsistent with democracy and citizenship.

We have learned Athens had citizens and noncitizens. Among citizens there was equality; any citizen might be chosen by lot to be tomorrow's assemblyman. Even generals were chosen to lead for only a single day. There was no such thing as a king, a senator, a representative or a judge. Different citizens might have differing trades or professions, but all had equality of opportunity.

The Aristotelian definition and theory of government did not suggest that representative or republican government could lead to laws of privilege. Aristotle wrote:

"The object of political rule is the benefit of the subjects of the state" (Aristotle, *Politics*)

"No government can stand that is not based upon justice" (*ibid.*)

"What is justice if not a species of equality, the right to be treated equally." (*ibid.*)

"Should the rights of citizens be decided by their handsomeness, or athletic prowess? The amount of property they possess?" (*ibid.*)

[Justice is] "based upon the principle of equality and similarity among its citizens" (*ibid.*)

"Should not equals receive an equal share?" (*ibid.*)

Or is "liberty to be enjoyed by all, alike?" (*ibid.*)

242

How can one justify one class receiving subsidies of cash when the general masses do not?

Certainly in English common law, the government had the right to grant economic privilege. The King could do anything. Grants of charters were common examples. Indeed the king could force a widow to marry a court favorite or forfeit her deceased husband's estate. But where does the federal government get the right to grant economic privilege? And what are subsidies and tax cuts if not privileges for the few, not enjoyed by the many?

Our Founding Fathers told us they were creating a government that would:

". . .make no rule of law that will not have full operation on themselves, their friends, as well as the great mass of society"
(F 57 pp 12)

And the new government would not pass "laws made for the few, and not the many" (F 65, pp 15)

It would be a government where all spending would be in the general welfare.

The Supreme Court in *Hughes v. Alexandria Scrap Corp.* (1975) was presented with a novel issue: **subsidies**. The *facts* were the State of Maryland passed a law granting a subsidy, or bounty for motor vehicles that were scrapped in the state of Maryland, the moment they were "processed." This allowed its scrap yards to pay higher than normal prices for abandoned vehicles. The state also fined scrap yards that kept motor vehicles over one year. The intent was to clear the Maryland landscape of the aesthetic problem of abandoned vehicles. The *issue* was examined from the point of view of the Commerce Clause, which prohibits a state from erecting a barrier to free trade or the flow of goods and raw materials so as to keep a business within their state boundaries. Until the Hughes case, it was clear that trade barriers took the form of uneven taxation or grants of license or regulatory burdens such as requiring milk to be pasteurized before leaving a state, fruit to be packed before interstate shipping, that shrimp must be decapitated and cleaned before leaving a state, that domestic producers of natural gas must supply domestic needs before shipping out of state. In the Hughes case, seven of 16 scrap processors were from Virginia or Pennsylvania, so the benefits of the subsidies went beyond Maryland's boundaries.

Living in a simpler time, America being prosperous and powerful, and not having witnessed the ravages to our economy of the MBA and business type onslaught, the majority of our court innocently stated:

"Nothing in the Commerce Clause . . . prohibits a state from participating in the market and exercising the right to favor its own citizens over others."

The three dissenters could perceive the future problems with infringing the free marketplace, but were unable to clearly articulate, hence persuade the majority. The majority of the court failed to understand that any subsidy skews the free market. It introduces a competitive gradient in the marketplace that is unnatural. Eventually subsidies become a restraint on the free market. The majority could not see the unforeseen and unintended consequences of their decision: they could see only the obvious immediate intuitive consequences.

This was inexcusable because in 1861 John Stuart Mill coined the term **unintended consequences** in his book *Considerations on Representative Government*. He explained how these consequences arose in the legislative process. He wrote that unintended consequences were created:

". . .under the influence of interests not identical with the general welfare of the community"

And when:

"Duties left to those who undertake them because they have some private interest to be promoted" (*ibid.*)

"incongruous clauses inserted to conciliate special interest groups" (*ibid.*)

"clauses omitted which are essential to the working of the rest" (*ibid.*)

"specious fallacies may be urged in defense of every act of injustice yet proposed for the imaginary benefit of the mass" (*ibid.*)

And he did not take into account the forces of unjust regulation and administration of the law to create distortions on the behalf of special interest groups. The Supreme Court should have foreseen all of this. Permitting any interference with the free market, with government selling privileges will never be in the general welfare.

> But in spite of the advice of John Stewart Mill, the federal courts still do not get it. Proof?

In *Cuno v. DaimlerChrysler* (2001), eighteen taxpayers of Toledo, Ohio, challenged the right of the city of Toledo to grant $280,000,000 in tax exemptions (a TIF) to Daimler to induce it to keep its Jeep production line in Toledo. The federal district court found the subsidy legal.

On appeal, in *Cuno v. DaimlerChrysler* (2003), the Federal Court of Appeals wrote: "***we have never squarely considered the constitutionality of subsidies***" and found the TIF unconstitutional, hence illegal.

The case then went to the Supreme Court: *Cuno v. DaimlerChrysler* (2006). The court was able to avoid deciding the issue of subsidies by finding that tax payers had no "standing" to challenge the power of the city to spend money: that it was a political decision, not one for the courts. So the legality of subsidies has not been answered and the haunting words of the Hughes court —

"Nothing in the Commerce Clause . . . prohibits a state from participating in the market and exercising the right to favor its own citizens over others."

245

— yet remain on the books. So let us examine what subsidies hath wrought.

## Subsidies: The Dollars Involved

$4 trillion is received as tax revenues by federal, state, and local governments per year. $2.8 trillion of that is allocated to non-discretionary spending (salaries, pensions, military spending, Social Security, Medicare and Medicaid payments and the like), leaving $1.2 trillion for discretionary spending. Mark Zepezauer in his book *Take the Rich Off Welfare* calculates that the federal government spends annually $72.7 billion on direct cash payments, mostly to big businesses. That is roughly six percent of the discretionary budget. Approximately twice that amount is spent administering the disbursal of these cash payments.

| | |
|---|---|
| Agribusiness subsidies | $ 30.5 billion |
| Media handouts and subsidies | $ 15 billion |
| Nuclear power generation | $ 10 billion |
| Airline subsidies | $ 5 billion |
| Mining Subsidies | $ 4.7 billion |
| Oil and gas | $ 1.7 billion |
| Corn ethanol and gazol for motorfuel | $ 3 billion |
| Others | $ 5 billion |
| TOTAL | $ 72.7 billion |

And now

| | |
|---|---|
| TARP funds (some to be repaid) | $800 billion |
| Geithner bailouts, mostly to Goldman Sachs | $1.2 TRILLION* |

(*same as $1,200 billion)

**TOTAL EXPOSURE**          **$2.72 TRILLION**

The magnitude of such spending numbs the mind. But with ethanol subsidies rising dramatically, TARP funds one year, the Geithner bailout the next year and the new health program coming on line, $1-2 trillion subsidies and social programs will consume most of the 2.34 trillion tax dollars collected by the Federal government in a typical year. Where is the Federal government going to get the money to redeem the trillions of dollars it has borrowed from the Social Security program? Where is the Federal government going to get the funds to cover future Social Security payments? It should be noted that these numbers do not count tax "credits" which are invisible to the accounting system now in place. Nor do these numbers show the preferential tax treatments or "tax cuts" granted to factions and special interest groups.

Let us look at specific subsidy dollars paid to specific recipients. Below are figures from a database of subsidy checks paid to U.S. farmers from 1995 to 2003 compiled by the Environmental Working Group (EWG/Farm Subsidy Database) under the Freedom of Information Act. They found:

| | |
|---|---|
| Riceland Foods Inc. | $ 519,000,000 |
| Producers Rice Mill Inc | $ 288,000,000 |
| Farmers Rice Group | $ 134,000,000 |
| Cenex Harvest States Cooperative | $ 40,763,896 |
| Tyler Farms | $ 37,000,000 |
| DNRC Trust Land Management | $ 29,000,000 |
| 1st National Bank Sioux Falls | $ 27,168,000 |
| Pilgrims Pride | $ 26,000,000 |
| Missouri Delta Farms | $ 25,000,000 |
| Ducks Unlimited Inc | $ 20,392,000 |
| Mt Board of Investments Sep | $ 18,799,000 |
| Cargill Turkey Products | $ 17,593,000 |
| Bureau of Indian Affairs (B.I.A.) | $ 15,000,000 |
| McNulty Bros. Dairy | $ 13,000,000 |
| Morgan Farms | $ 12,268,000 |

Agricultural subsidies are said to make up over 40 percent of the European budget. This does not count the expense of administration. The madness of subsidies is not confined to the United States.

## Dynamics of subsidies

- They are privileges.
- They are irrational. They tax the hard workers; they tax successful businesses.
- They reward mismanagement.
- They are expensive and produce nothing.
- They prop up dinosaur businesses and business practices.
- They destroy all cost benefit analysis; who knows what true costs actually are?
- They misdirect business managers, resulting in waste.
- They misdirect investors in businesses, resulting in wasted capital.
- They induce a misallocation of resources.

## Case History: Archer Daniels Midland

Let us examine what subsidies have done for one specific business: Archer Daniels Midland (ADM).

There are a few large "players," the "black Barts," in the agribusiness industries: Archer Daniels Midland (ADM) a U.S. agri-chemical giant, Con Agra, Cargill, and one of the quasis, the Commodity Credit Corporation (CCC). All have a long history of interesting political connections. Theirs are stories of extreme modesty; Cargill is a privately, not publicly, held corporation, so penetration into its workings is nearly impossible. Disclosures are not mandated. As for the others, what they do is a confidential "trade secret."

But a peephole into the agricultural sector was opened by ADM in the 1990s. This was documented by James B. Lieber in meticulous detail and in a wonderful narrative style. His book *Rats in the Grain* is a must-read study for economists, political scientists, business types and attorneys. It recounts ADM's corporate activities in the 1990s, as "the supermarket of the world," run by well connected president Dwayne Andreas, his son Michael Andreas, Dr. Mark Whitaker, James Randall and Terry Wilson.

In 1994–1995 they, along with several other corporations (Ajinomoto, Bayer and La Roche), were indicted for rigging the price of the food additives **lysine** and **citric acid.** Whitaker had agreed to and did wear a wire to over 237 meetings where two international multibillion dollar conspiracies were designed and executed that resulted in the price of lysine being driven from 36 pence to 62 pence and the price of citric acid driven up 41 percent. The tapes of these meetings were revealing; they were evidence of the best documented price fixing conspiracies to date. Terry Wilson said on tape, among other things:

"Competition is our friend, remember? Customers are the enemy."

"We are going to get manipulated by these g-d buyers. They are not your friend. They are not my friend. All I want to tell ya again is let's put the prices on it."

On June 27, 1995, 70 Federal agents with search warrants raided ADM headquarters and the three other defendant corporations. These aforesaid officers and others were charged with felony conspiracy to fix prices and the officers faced arrest warrants. Ajinomoto, Bayer and La Roche promptly pled guilty and paid fines totaling over $195 billion and paid restitution of damages totaling $326 billion to their customers.

## THE EXPOSURES FOR ADM

Because of the volume of compelling evidence, ADM faced near-certain exposure to several hazards: hundreds of millions of dollars in corporate fines; loss of the right to do business with the federal government in the future; loss of billions of dollars of tax credits for the growing ethanol motor fuel additive business; shareholder derivative suits (a lawsuit brought by a shareholder on behalf of a corporation against a third party, often an insider of the corporation) for officers misconduct; payment of hundreds of millions of dollars to reimburse customers who were overcharged; the expense of business disruption and a drop of stock share price if a new management team was put in place.

The officers faced the prospects of years in jail, huge personal fines, lawsuits from disgruntled shareholders and financial ruin. Instead of paying the fines, ADM directors decided to use corporate assets to pay the attorney fees for the corporation and for its officers, except Whitaker. He had to pay for his own attorney and all of his other ruinous litigation costs.

ADM retained none other than Edward Bennett Williams, power broker and **trial attorney** from Washington D.C. to represent the corporation and the four defendants. *Rats in the Grain* describes the proceedings that follow. Williams, though a defense attorney, took charge of the prosecution, to limit the exposure to his clients and to dump on Whitaker.

The personality and reputation of attorney Williams was such that the son of the judge, a law student, sat in on the in-chambers proceedings to watch and learn. It was a highly experienced trial attorney versus a team of young government attorneys with slight litigation experience. By force of charm and guile Williams got:

(1) Immunity from prosecution for James Randall and CEO Dwayne Andreas (the father of Michael).
(2) A stipulation from the federal prosecutors that there would be no further investigation into allegations that ADM stole trade secrets.
(3) A waiver of criminal charges against ADM for price fixing for corn sweeteners, which business opportunity was worth approximately five times the business value of the lysine conspiracy.

Already he had won the keys to the bank vault before the trial was started.

The trial went quite well for Dwayne Andreas and Terry Wilson, as compared to the "mole" Mark Whitaker. They were found guilty.

Each was fined a mere $350,000, for what was characterized as the biggest price fixing conspiracy in recent years. Odder still were the short prison sentences. Dwayne Andreas and Terry Wilson each received two years of jail time. An appellate judge later bumped each sentence up to three years. One wonders what amount of time was actually served and the nature of the institution in which they were incarcerated.

But the trial did not go so well for Mark Whitaker, for Williams made him a scapegoat. Williams was able to present evidence that Whitaker embezzled millions from ADM. Whitaker, with limited financial resources, could not effectively present evidence showing that imaginative and illusory bookkeeping had become the norm for corporate executive types. Paying for investigation of confidential corporate tax returns and discerning murky corporate bookkeeping were too high a burden for his limited budget. His counsel could in no way compete with Williams, especially on his budget. As a result, the judge sentenced Whitaker, the whistle-blower, to nine years for embezzlement, doubtless dampening the enthusiasm for future whistleblowers. How is that in the public good?

Note the proposed whistleblower protection offered in the proposed Shareholder Bill of Rights, Exhibit 1.

ADM still faced the possibility of huge fines. Look at the fines paid by the other co-conspirators:

| | |
|---|---|
| Hoffmann-La Roche Ltd. | $500 million |
| BASF Aktiengesellschaft | $225 million |
| Ajinomoto Co., Inc. | $ 10 million |

ADM was clearly the perpetrator and had the greatest exposure under the Sherman Anti-Trust Act. Remember, ADM was the ringleader; the others were merely co-conspirators. Attorney Williams went to work again. When the smoke cleared, **ADM paid only $100 million.** There were additional damages. ADM has paid over $120 million dollars to shareholders and customers. It has paid Canada's largest fine, $16 million Canadian (U.S. $11 million). It was fined

€43 million by the European Trade Commission. Re-enter attorney Williams. There is a law prohibiting trade with the U.S. for three years for any company found guilty of price fixing. Somehow the U.S. DOJ dealt away applying this limitation to ADM at sentencing.

Where does ADM get the cash to pay the millions of dollars of fines and other civil damages not described? From the federal government of the United States! This is because ethanol gasoline additive has been legislated as a mandatory fuel additive in all states for the "major" gasoline sales companies. By law, ADM should have been banned from this highly lucrative ethanol market for three years. Instead a combination of lavish tax credits, favorable government contracts and other subsidies assure ADM nearly half of the billions of dollars spent on ethanol production each year. These subsidies totaled $3.7 billion in 2003, and rose to $5.5 billion in 2005.

The bottom line: it was the U.S. taxpayers who got to pay ADM's fines and a whole lot more. The youthful Department of Justice attorneys were completely outmaneuvered, again and again.

What does this have to do with subsidies? The whole ADM empire was built on subsidies. What did that empire entail? The 1999 annual report for ADM shows that it owned and operated:

- About 335 process plants
- Over 500 grain elevators
- 2,250 barges
- 13,000 railway cars
- 100 oceangoing ships
- 50 percent interest in Alfred Toepfer, largest grain trader in Europe, which processes about 10 percent of the world's grain and produces about 35 percent of the world's animal feeds.

All of this empire is simply built by **subsidies** and administrative destruction of competition as detailed in *Rats in the Grain*. This is a classic vertical monopoly, carefully built and maintained by the USDA. It is built on subsidies, laws of economic privilege and administration of laws and codes to create economic privilege. The subsidies provide the money to use economies of scale to grind the hardest workers in America, farmers, into dust. It's the supreme example of privilege limiting meaningful economic opportunity and destroying the dream of prosperity for America. Imagine what the USDA is willing to do for agribusiness in the area of organic farming.

The free market is the best way to allocate resources and produce high quality, lowest price goods and services. The multiplicity of suppliers created by a free market is the best hedge against catastrophic interruptions of the marketplace. Any government intervention short of trust busting is counterproductive. This is to say most regulation has been perverted to simply degrade the free market, as explored in the next chapter. All subsidies degrade the free market. Other laws of privilege degrade the free market. We must free up our markets and minimize government intervention to succeed. The survival of democracy itself in America is at stake. But the most important consideration is that taking the right to grant subsidies from politicos will clean up politics: what will the politicos have left to sell?

Let us restore our free market. Let us spread opportunity broadly among our citizens. It is the only proven pathway to prosperity. Would not we be further ahead if two-thirds of government employees were doing something productive, even raising turnips?

"The right to engage in interstate commerce is not a gift of the state, and the state cannot regulate or restrain it." (*Hood & Sons v. DuMond,*1949)

Let us re-create a free market, free from government regulation and laws of economic privilege.

# Chapter 9

# The Executive Branch —
# Administration and Regulation

The admitted complexity of this chapter is necessary, because this problem is deeply imbedded in our econopolitics, and is routinely overlooked and misunderstood by economists, attorneys, judges, justices, politicos of all shades and colors, and "political scientists," if any there be.

## Effectiveness of Administrative Agencies

How effective have administrative bodies been in pursuit of the general welfare? Let us examine a few cases. The airlines were regulated by the Civil Aeronautics Board (CAB), now part of the Department of Transportation (DOT). Their regulatory power covered rates, routes, airport spaces and all critical aspects of the business. Since airline deregulation in 1978, we have seen a 40 percent decrease in **airfares,** after correction for inflation. (*Regulation,* Spring 1998, Vol. 21 #2, p. 18) Air flight, once a luxury, has become available to all citizens.

In World War II, America invented the **cell phone,** then called the "walkie talkie." After World War II, Ma Bell did not want anything to disrupt its extensive and expensive landline communications network monopoly. America's history of the regulation of telecommunications was the most incestuous relationship between government and any single business (the Bell company) we have seen to date. The result of such regulation was the destruction of competitive and inventive forces in that industry. The country that invented the "walkie talkie" gave away 40 years of lead time in the development of the cell phone . . . to Finland.

With the deregulation of Ma Bell and the creation of the five "Baby Bells," the cell phone was developed and cell phone use exploded in America. But the Bells were still fixated on analog signals. Finland never regulated its phone services, and there was blistering competition among some 100 "ma and pa" phone companies, some of whom saw the future. They ventured into digital technology, where the Bells did not wish to go. The 40 years of lead time gifted to Finland allowed the Finns to work, experiment and develop digital technology. Nokia, which started business about 100 years ago with raincoats and rubber boots, alone, holds perhaps 30 percent of the cell phone patents. Today we must pay homage to the patents of Nokia with every turn in the road, as they harvest the benefits of these patents and their extensions. This is the heritage our regulators gave away.

### Regulation rarely serves the general welfare.

With the partial deregulation of stock and bond sales that led to the abolition of fixed rates of commission for **stockbrokers**, the commissions for such transactions promptly dropped at least 70 percent in all markets. (*Regulation*, Spring 2002, Vol. 25 #1, p. 60) Today trades that would cost hundreds of dollars at any of the big stock houses are done for less than $10 at numerous discount broker firms, like Charles Schwab, Scottrade, and Ameritrade.

Within a year of the deregulation of **taxicab fares** and practices in Indianapolis, the number of cabs doubled, time for pickup by cabs was cut in half and fares were ten percent less, to remain down seven percent after two years.

New Zealand deregulated its **telephone service** and the wait for phone installation dropped from three months to three days or less; the cost of residential phones dropped 54 percent, 64 percent for business phones, choices for phone options multiplied beyond description. Why? In part because prior to deregulation, repairs always required the presence of three persons, because of the union agreement. (*Regulation*, Winter 1998, Vol. 21, p. 34-36)

New Zealand also deregulated its agriculture. Their subsidies to their farmers are the lowest in the world. Diversity of crops and profitability immediately took off. Ingenuity was allowed to blossom, because they were not frustrated and thwarted by regulation. Now New Zealand farmers are the most prosperous in the world. (*ibid.*)

> De-regulation usually lowers the cost of goods sold as competition is restored to that sector of the economy.

Regulators brought upon the state of California the electricity crisis and magnified the scope of that disaster many-fold. Regulators perpetuated the injustices of the Bureau of Indian Affairs; they created, and maintain, the agricultural/agribusiness subsidy debacle. They set the stage for the stock market meltdown of 2007-2008. The list is endless.

> Regulation usually amplifies the economic shock of any economic crisis, be it real or contrived.

This brief overview shows us that administrative regulation raises the price of goods and services and degrades their quality. With deregulation, huge compliance costs and enormous savings of time and effort from pointless acts of compliance are no longer part of a particular economy.

## Other Economic Impacts of Regulation

Agency regulation usually **destroys competition**, resulting in increased prices and lower quality of goods and services. In addition there are huge indirect costs to the public for maintenance of that administration. This shows up as **higher taxation** and **government borrowing** or simply government **printing of money**. In addition to increased taxes and inflation, these costs show up as **license fees** and various **assessments**, like a $1,000 federal grain elevator inspection fee for a process that often requires 10-12 minutes. Here are some reasons why administration by agency is expensive:

(1) **Expense of supporting administrators:** wages, offices, cars and trucks, not even counting their generous pensions. For example, USDA meat inspectors get salaries of up to $200,000 per year. The Federal government has over 400,000 employees, mostly in administration.

(2) **Attorney, consultant and accountant fees** at $250-500 per **hour** to read and explain 91,000-odd pages of the arcane, often conflicting, gobbledygook that is our U.S. Code.

(3) **Inane, pointless and expensive record keeping**, usually in the most irrational and detailed way imaginable. It is frequently obvious this data cannot lead to conclusions of any value whatever. Here is "jobbery" in its poorest disguise. Often this must be done electronically in some bug-infested cumbersome format that seems to change quarterly, requiring hours of time to decipher. Help lines, if available usually route calls to India, where polite but unsophisticated persons waste more time.

(4) **Costs of compliance** with occasional reasonable, rational, administrative orders are valid, but most are needless, irrelevant and pointless and hence generate needless expense, which is passed on to the consumer.

(5) **Occasional intentional dilatory tactics**: Delays and expense of needless checking and rechecking, which throws scheduling of projects "out the window" due to inability to proceed until an inspector finds time to show up. Try to run a business with your labor force idled by bureaucracy. All of this causes costs to skyrocket and invites payola. Sometimes local inspectors won't show up until paid off upfront and in cash. The time lost because of pointless delay, means progress in not measured in months but frequently is measured in years. Upon questioning local builders, it seems a house built in Madison, Wisconsin (a

highly regulated area) appears to cost about twice as much as the identical house built in a remote (and lightly regulated) county of Wisconsin.

(6) **Expense to contest unjust regulatory demands.** While writing an unfair compliance order takes only moments, the expense and delay of fighting one takes a long time. When you do get to court, you are in an administrative law court where proceedings are plainly rigged to support regulators. "You can't fight city hall." This is to say, there is a lack of meaningful review of administrative decisions and procedures.

"Patient obfuscation will outlast the fitful resolve of any individual." (Mill, *Considerations on Representative Government*)

## The Emotional Toll Taken By Regulators

**Absence of meaningful appeal to courts of law:** Courts of law can neither entertain nor resolve stupid regulatory acts and outrageous penalties. As a result, you are trapped in the administrative law court system.

**Frustration of being completely at the mercy of political powers**; you don't know and have no idea who is on the other side, or what their "connections" are.

There are 14 agencies that have jurisdiction over food products. It is very expensive simply to find out which one is really in charge of an issue. Yet it is extremely risky not to do it right. Any and all will say they are in charge of the issue, in hopes of expanding their little empires. Eventually one regulator will be found to have jurisdiction, but if you guess and get it wrong, you incur the wrath of the little tyrant you offend by not paying him or her "proper" homage from the onset, and your dealings with this agency are likely to be difficult.

**Anxiety and expense of dealing with vindictive regulators**, knowing that uneven enforcement of laws can crush you and your business while competitors can skate free, unscathed.

**Anxiety of drawing and having to deal with the occasional irrational, half-witted, poorly** trained but senior administrative stooges, who sometimes misread or misrepresent regulatory code, "explaining that is the way we do things here" and often make inconsistent compliance demands as regulators *from the same agency* occasionally substitute for each other, and who, when challenged, resort to making draconian threats of prosecution. There is no check on administrative power exercised in a tyrannical fashion.

**Delays in the field** while cretins ponder the blatantly obvious and make compliance demands that are contrary to the wishes or orders of another agency. Imagine the delay and expense of dealing with multiple agencies, often engaged in petty turf wars. For example, we have 15 "intelligence agencies." They are:

- Central Intelligence Agency (CIA)
- Air Force intelligence surveillance and reconnaissance Agency (AFISR)
- Army Military Intelligence (AMI)
- Defense Military Intelligence (DMI)
- Marine Corps Intelligence Activity (MCIA)
- National Geospatial-Intelligence Agency (MGA)
- National Security Agency (NSA)
- Office on Naval Intelligence (ONI)
- Office of Intelligence and Counterintelligence (OIC)
- Office of Intelligence and Analysis (OIA)
- Coast Guard Intelligence (CGI)
- Federal Bureau of Investigation (FBI)
- Drug Enforcement Agency (DEA)
- Bureau of Intelligence and Research (BIR)
- Office of Terrorism and Financial Intelligence (TFI)

All these are in charge of preserving our national secrets and finding out the secrets of others. Breaches of secrecy are routine. Most of the science of our military secrets is in the hands of foreign students in the laboratories of the graduate schools of our most prestigious universities. What do you think happens when they go home for vacations or upon graduation?

## Case Study: Gary McKinnon

Something is secret because you don't tell. Secrecy is maintained by security, good locks and strong walls. The integrity of secrecy is the duty of those who wish the preservation of the secret; it cannot be delegated away, especially to the curious. Something cannot be made secret by stamping **TOP SECRET** on it.

Gary McKinnon, between 2001 and 2002, allegedly "hacked" into at least 97 American military and NASA computers. The government types created a big cookie jar, filled with delicious cookies. They made its location quite well known. McKinnon lifted the lid and looked at the cookies. He did this time and time again. He smelled the cookies, time and time again. But he did not taste the cookies, not a crumb. The U.S. government claims his hacking caused $700,000 in damages. U.S. government officials seek his extradition from England. The crime? He made the government types look stupid. That in and of itself is not a crime. They bring this upon themselves daily. They have chosen to make this stupidity public knowledge. Gary should be given a medal. The intelligence bimbos are grumpy that a single hacker made it through all their firewalls. Did they not set up their computers with deficient and insufficient protection? Why is someone else responsible for their deficiencies? Are they not attempting to cover up their deficient designs for data protection by some curious legislation making outsmarting them some sort of crime? What kind of a law is it that holds outsmarting our "intelligence" people is illegal? How would this foolish law protect us from some imaginative and industrious terrorists in some cave in Afghanistan taking what they wish from such poorly secured databases? Are these computers not undergoing constant assault from hackers round the world? Why do they have the right to attempt to crucify one so successful at revealing their glaring deficiencies? Should they not be retaining his services to perhaps prevent such future embarrassments?

The only secrets in this world are the names on the Swiss numbered bank accounts. Will we ever learn how many Senators and Representatives names appear thereon? Oh, the Swiss, they know how to keep a secret.

And in the end, all this expense of government, of time, of compliance; the loss of citizens' liberties, simply results in additional increases in cost of goods and services within the society as shown above. Too often there is no benefit to society, excepting jobbery — employment of those who can find no meaningful job.

What is worse, citizens often place trust and reliance in agencies to do a good job and protect us. Instead, government bureaucratic bumpkins drop the ball time and time again. An example would be the food recalls wherein tons and tons of food are recalled because those $200,000-a-year food inspectors didn't do their job. Society is left to pay for all the food that must be destroyed. There was a case of peanut poisoning in which the processor had a five-year history of substandard processing. The result was five people dead and millions of dollars of peanut butter discarded, which the consumer ultimately pays for. There have been dozens of food poisoning cases involving beef alone, more tons of food dumped. We have seen spinach with *E. coli*, multiple chicken salmonella poisonings, and toxic green peppers. Rising cancer rates suggest there are many other undetected problems just yet not recognized.

What is the cost of administering this bureaucratic mess? A rough estimate: the USDA gives farmers some $20 billion in cash subsidies. Their annual budget is $72 billion. The cost of administering them is 4.1 times the cash subsidies. The federal government gave out $72 billion in subsidies and the expense of administering these gifts is then an additional estimated $290 billion.

In addition, **regulation** is terribly costly for government to administer.

To calculate the costs of compliance is difficult: the cost of regulations; the expense of keeping a business going while regulators induce delay; the considerable expense of contesting administrators' pointless regulations; their draconian fines for punishing non compliance. The

Cato Institute believes it costs the U.S economy $400 billion in needless expense for unnecessary administration which they projected would increase to $800 billion in 2000. (*Regulation*, Vol #4 1997) The cost to our competitiveness can't even be calculated. Destruction of the democratic principles in our government is also beyond calculation. Try to put a price on the loss of our liberties. And these guys want to run medicine.

## Why We Have Administrative Agencies

Why do we have regulations in the first place? Because some regulation is **essential**. Up to a limit, some regulations actually work. Known, reliable weights and measures, coinage easily recognized and of standards of quality and value, precise volumetric measures are all **vital** to trade and **critical** to economic planning and prosperity. But there is a limit to the effectiveness of regulation: human behavior.

What is the **public** appeal of administration? People accept it because intuitively the public knows of the basic need for fundamental regulation. Everyday they rely on money to function properly, for goods to be sold according to legislated norms. They want 16 ounces in a box labeled one pound. And they don't want to go to court for the ounce or two of cereal that is missing. The public feels a need for protection from big businesses, many of their practices and some of the nasty extremes of the business world. Citizens are overwhelmed and feel the need for some protection that is effective and affordable.

The **president** loves agencies, because regulators report directly to him. Any agent not following his directive is reassigned or is out. Regulations are a handy tool. No one knows where a bit of code comes from or who wrote it. The regulation simply appears on the books. It is fast, very fast, no begging in Congress for approval, no political debts to repay in the future. A very handy tool indeed.

Also, the president wants to expand his power and control. He feels competent to do so. He feels that he is in control, that the system is working and will respond to his dictates (to date, we have had over 13,500 executive orders from our presidents). He feels that the

Cabinet and the approximately 4,000 appointments he has made to his administrative branch are competent, experienced and to up to the tasks he gives them to do. And he hopes the 300,000 civil servants that make up the civil service are especially competent and motivated to do their assigned jobs. He also hopes the same for the 450,000-odd military personnel he has inherited.

Unfortunately, he also feels compelled to create jobs for the persons who have propelled him into office. The qualifications and motivations of these people are often *suspect*.

"The minister who thinks himself not only blameless, but meritorious if the man [he appoints] dances well" (Mill, *Considerations on Representative Government*)

"When a minister makes what is meant to be an honest appointment...[but awards a job]... for his personal connections, or his party...[rather than] try to give it to the person best qualified" (*ibid.*)

"Appointments based upon party connections . . . because he has a reputation, often quite undeserved . . . or for no other reason than he is popular" (*ibid.*)

"Unless a man is fit for the gallows he is thought to be as fit [for appointment] as any other people . . ." (*ibid.*)

But the *suspect* still become administrators and regulators and **czars.** Whenever has a czar been a good thing for a society? Unfortunately administrative regulation is stretched beyond the capacity of regulation and into **subjective human behaviors.**

**Politicos** seem to like regulatory agencies, for they relieve the politico from the dull work of legislating. Politicos think they are doing the right thing. It seems they think the damn things actually work. But they do not see, understand or know the subjective/objective limitation of regulation. And they do not know the overweening false confidence of the regulator. They do not understand that agency, and reliance on the agency, simply magnifies problems when they arise. We tend to rely on regulators to do their jobs, so that banks stay solvent, that currency maintains its value, that investment value does not evaporate, that pension plans will be there, funded, and solvent when it is time to retire, that life insurers did not buy derivatives and will have money to pay policies.

Nor does the **public** understand the fallibility of regulation. The public does not realize that administration is too puny an engine to deliver workable regulation for many human behaviors. Nor do they realize that those in charge aren't really up to the task. They are, after all government employees. Competency here is rare. Motivation is suspect. There is no motive to solve a problem; the regulator would be out of a job. In the end you can count on political favoritism and intervention to derail the best of intentions and actions of the occasional good regulator.

> Administration is too puny an engine to deliver meaningful regulation for many human behaviors

While federal regulators snoozed, the financial types were allowed to hawk trillions of dollars in derivatives, devaluing everyone's pensions and savings and the dollar at large, yet financiers skate on, subsidized, not chastened; for they are the big campaign contributors. We the people take the beating; our dollar plummets against all other currencies. And the financiers continue to sell derivatives.

Why do people place trust in the regulator? With all these people on the job, why are there still regulatory failures? The record of regulation is peanut poisoning, tainted beef, tainted chicken, unsafe water, airline crashes, numerous pharmaceutical recalls, failure at banks, savings and loans, home mortgage debacles, private equity firms masquerading as "investment banks" and their bailouts, monopolistic growth of the big three auto firms (and bailouts of two of them); perhaps a new economic depression created by systematic regulatory failure?

Administration is nothing but the tentacles of the executive branch, which have spread into the legislature and the judiciary. Most of the federal government is based upon a *myth of regulatory effective-*

*ness.* The simple truth is, in almost all instances, administration dramatically increases costs to the public by any measure: taxes, expense of compliance, loss of competitiveness and so on, for no measurable gain or benefit to society; they just don't work. More tragically, the public reliance on dysfunctional regulation and regulators usually creates and magnifies disasters, such as the financial meltdown of 2008-2009. Regulation of weights and measures is for the public good, but there is a limit beyond which regulation of human behaviors is impossible.

## Pedigree of Administration

Clearly the biggest "branch" of government (most employees) has to do with administration. But where in the Constitution is the "branch" of administration to be found? The Constitution describes what has been called a tripartite government, consisting of the legislative branch (Congress), the executive branch (headed by the president) and the judiciary. The powers of each are clearly laid out.

What is the pedigree of administration? Is it a creature of the Constitution? It is not explicitly found therein. What then is its paternity? Clearly not the legislature, for administrators are not elected officials. And it is equally clear this is not the judiciary, there are no courts, juries or robes. Its origin is clearly the executive branch.

Recall briefly the powers of each named department of government. Congress, the lawgivers, is where legislation is to be drafted. The executive branch is where the laws of the land are enforced. The executive branch has the power, indeed the duty, to preserve, implement and enforce the laws passed by Congress, to defend the nation and its citizens, and to preserve the nation. The executive has no legal power to legislate, to dream up new laws, or enforce his or her agendas. His or her legislative function is limited to veto, which can be overridden. The executive has no power to assign to administrators the powers to legislate or to act in a judicial capacity. The judiciary is where laws are judged to be within constitutional limits, or to have exceeded these limits, and where laws are fitted together, if possible.

And what are the functions of administration? With the powers of legislation and adjudication elsewhere, what is left for administration?

## Administration Defined

The history of administration dates to the Chinese where the foundations of meritocracy-based civil service were laid. The Latin roots of the word *administer* are *ad*, meaning motion towards, and *ministare*, meaning to be an aid to, or to serve, a servant. The meaning of *ministerial* is more helpful: it designates a mandatory act or duty on the part of the government agent that requires no personal discretion or judgment in its performance. Administrators are agents of the executive, without decision making capacity or the need to make discretionary choices. Their universe is a simple one: receive the money, collect the toll, issue the license, permit entry to the museum or allow boarding the train. Just do the job. All are equal before an administrator. There is no screening to see if the applicant is properly suited. The goal should be efficiency. Service should be expedited, helpful, non political, without agendas. They are the servants of the citizen. This area of government should be "user friendly."

## Regulation Defined

To regulate is: 1. To control or direct according to a rule. 2. To adjust in conformity to a specification or a requirement. 3. To adjust a mechanism for accurate and proper functioning.

A regulator has no legislative capacity or power. That is to say that the regulator should not make the rule, specification or requirement. The setting of standards is a power that is reserved for the legislature. Enforcement is not regulation. Prosecution is not regulation. Judgment is not regulation. A regulator has no judicial capacity. Those powers are reserved for the courts. Regulation is setting the clock to the proper time.

## Regulation versus Administration

Recalling the definition of **administration**, *moving to aid or serve*, it is clear that there is little judgment required to administer. The act of **regulation** is more complex, for the regulator must identify the act to be regulated, select the proper rule, or norm and measure conformity to that rule, then record and report the results to the executive. It is the decision of the executive, not the administrator or regulator as to whether or not to prosecute.

Clearly the decision of guilt (a jury question) or extent of penalty (a judicial question) is beyond the scope of an administrator and should be no part of an executive decision. It is for the executive to decide whether or not to prosecute and whether or not to pardon.

Modern government has perverted the classic meaning of *ministerial* where all are to be treated equally. Executive functions have been assumed by modern administrators where discretionary decision making should have no part. When administrators start interpreting rules, troubles begin. "This guy looks suspicious. This guy may be a terrorist. This guy is acting strange; should I detain him?"

All people are no longer equal before administrators. When thinking, or evaluation or judgment is required we have passed from administration to regulation, enforcement, prosecution or adjudication. Administration is none of these. Modern administration has expanded into the act of legislating (writing administrative code) and more formal judgment (administrative law judges).

## Horrors of the Modern Administrative Process

What are the powers of administrators? Their function is simply to investigate and enforce the laws and to follow any legal order of the president. Yet they form their own police forces, investigation agencies and act as prosecuting attorneys. The administrator should have no role in deciding if, how and when to prosecute infractions. Administrators should exercise no legislative function. They should have no judicial powers whatever. Judicial powers should remain with the judicial branch.

Administrators are insulated from elections to office, although they may survive presidents' elections. They usurp legislative functions and have executive power; their decisions are beyond court review, cheap and easy to implement. They act with facility and speed, yet are terribly difficult and expensive to challenge, then usually to no avail. The wealthy have hope of access, by way of campaign contributions, while the poor do not have the money to bribe.

"The accumulation of all powers, legislative, executive and judiciary, in the same hands, whether of one, a few, or many and whether hereditary, self-appointed or elected, may justly be pronounced the very definition of tyranny." (F 47)

## Administrators as Legislators

An examination of the administrative process reveals, curiously, that **administrators now have the power to legislate**: to create laws or code. How did this come to pass? Presidents create regulators, they are arms of the executive branch. Congress passes an incomplete law, without details, then authorizes, by an "*empowerment clause*," the executive to create an agency to write the details of the code. They send the administrators off on a mission to write laws, and hope for the best, intending for a knowledgeable agency to fill in the blanks. It simply never occurs to Congress that legislative duties are not delegable. Perhaps they think that we don't have enough laws, or that liberty is created by passing more laws.

To reiterate the discussion in Chapter 7: when administrators write code, there is a major *due process* problem. They have none of the special attributes of a legislator. The Founding Fathers specifically designed Congress with numerous features to delve out and define the general welfare. The legislative power is entrusted only to those elected to represent their constituents. They are **public trustees**, known by their constituents. Legislators are supposed to be knowing of, and responsive to, constituents' needs. They should be available to the constituents. These public trustees are a special class of citizen, carefully chosen at tremendous expense and fanfare, given special recognition and a "title," and placed in special office. Society has given them limited immunities and privileges of office. Society grants them virtually unlimited expense accounts to do their business, that of searching and formulating policy to maximize the *general weal.* They want not for staff or for necessities of life. They are granted special retirement benefits. Celebrity is theirs, if they so wish. In private life, doors closed to many are opened to them.

Because they are **trustees**, the act of legislating is a unique and non-delegable duty, like having a haircut. You cannot send your secretary out to get a haircut for you. This is a non-delegable act, for legislators, and they alone, have been empowered to act as law givers. Legislation should be drafted that serves the *general weal.* Legislators are supposed to choose words appropriate to that aim. They should know their constituents well enough to do what is in the general welfare. It is the legislator, and the legislator alone, who is charged to do legislating.

A big problem with administrators as legislators is that when an agency is given permission to draft codes, it is too easy to deviate from the general welfare. A faceless administrator, unknown to the constituents, seizes the pen. These executive appointees are not responsive to constituents. They are not in touch with the people, their needs, or their desires. They have no way to canvass the various districts of the country. Not being elected, they have no reason to be responsive to the electorate.

Some may say that administrative bureaucrats are qualified because of special education and training to draft administrative codes. Technology wonks are familiar with intricacies that no politico could ever master. This is as wrong as wrong can be. Is this not like having a surgeon phone in from the golf course telling a surgical nurse to go ahead with the operation without his presence? The function of legislating is a non-delegable duty. The duties of trust and of office cannot be assigned to unqualified, unlicensed, unknown, unidentifiable persons.

Administrators are often untouchable and become arrogant. Often they are selected because of some business experience, for example a lifetime of experience in a utility company. The idea perhaps is who knows the jargon, dynamics, and needs of a utility company better than an insider. But after a short term, they leave the commission usually going back to the same utility company. Guess how they rule on rate increases or new power-line rights of way or expensive scrubbers that cleanse the air of pollution? Is it any surprise when they are on a commission or agency that they block proposals for expensive air pollution abatement procedures time and time again? Any increase in costs is detrimental to profits and their stock options. Is it any surprise rate increases are always granted? Due process is completely ignored. We have lost the checks and balances of separation of powers. Again, the general weal is shortchanged.

Administrators don't write code. Scriveners could be policy wonks, inexperienced in the real world, weaving fabric of air. Or they could be lobbyists and their attorneys, concocting laws motivated purely by self-interest and having no regard for the general weal. In any case there is no deliberation, discussion, compromise and formulation of laws in the general welfare by the duly empowered trustees (Congress) chosen by the people to perform this unique job of creating laws.

Indeed, often the actual verbiage is drafted by attorneys for trade groups, wanting to corner a portion of the marketplace. There is no public or open discussion of the merits of different positions constituents may take on a subject. The administrators create privileges for the campaign contributors, opportunities for citizens are thus diminished, and the *general weal* is in no way served. And these are the laws we the public get to guide our lives. Have these laws not become:

[laws passed in] "irregular passion or stimulated by some irregular passion, or some illicit advantage, or misled by the artful misrepresentation of interested men" (F 63, pp 7)

"unreasonable advantage....the sagacious, the enterprising, the moneyed few over the industrious and uninformed mass of the people. Every new regulation concerning commerce or revenue, or any manner affecting the value of different species of property presents a new harvest to those who watch change, and can trace its consequences . . . laws made for the few, and not the many" (F 62, pp 16)

Drafters of code may publish proposed code before codification, *asking for public comment*. But this is an illusory gesture, for where does the public, often working two jobs or a single parent with children, get time to review the torrent of blather thus produced? And usually the deal is "done" before asking for public comment. With Representatives and Senators "out of the loop," how do citizens make their wishes known? Newspapers only occasionally note some of the most outrageous proposals being aired. But too often they dilute or misinterpret passages or miss subtleties entirely. Often they parrot the claims of lobbyists and political media managers, seeking a silver lining in outrageous injustices. Publishing too much on these outrages simply creates frustration, despair and hopelessness to the point of inaction, which is precisely what the executive wants.

The extension of executive powers into legislating functions is insidious. Administrators are not elected representatives. They are appointed by the executive, at the whim of the executive. They do not serve for fixed terms; they can be removed summarily, again at his whim. Their compensation is determined by the executive. As they do not have fixed terms, they serve only so long as they please the executive. They are puppets on a short string. Their allegiance is to the executive; they salute the wrong banner. They are not responsive to the populace. They cannot be recalled. They cannot be voted out of office. Administrators are appointed by the executive, hence they follow executive agendas, which too often they are the result of campaign finance bribery. They are under the sway of lobbyists.

"Gradual preeminence in government finally transforming it into tyrannical aristocracy." (F 63, pp 15)

"It is in the interest of kings and aristocrats to keep them at a low level of intelligence and education, foment dissention among them and even prevent them from being too well off lest they should "wax fat, and kick" (Mill, *Considerations on Representative Government*)

As a result, Congress and the public are confounded with 472 regulatory agencies, which have created 31,854 documents covering 75,798 pages of administrative code in the Federal Registrar; as of 2003.

Have they not created *"laws so voluminous they cannot be read"* and *"laws so incomprehensible they cannot be understood"*?

The agency, once born, grows, whether needed or not, like a malignant tumor. But agencies are clearly not cancers, for they are immortal; they never die. Ronald Reagan once said that "*the nearest thing to eternal life we will ever see on earth is a government program.*" Nor do they solve problems; they have no motive to, lest they be out a job.

A final, fatal due process flaw is that these administrative laws do not see the meaningful scrutiny of Congress, nor do they get explicit presidential review. They are run through in a huge package that makes reading and understanding the implications of what they say quite impossible, like the numbers on the boxcars of a high speed train.

When laws are being properly created in the constitutional process, there is a huge advantage in being the scrivener of a law that is under deliberation and discussion. That person alone is privy to policy considerations, pro and con, and subtleties that may not be obvious. The insights that would be gained from active participation in law drafting remain with the scrivener. If the scrivener is not the one presenting the bill to Congress, all these insights are usually lost to Congress. Meaningful deliberation is not possible. Words of art are missed. Meaningful discussion after the fact of writing is likely sterile. Due process is impossible. The **general weal** is lost, buried in details.

In conclusion, the idea of allowing delegation of the power to legislate to some deputy or administrative agent is not constitutional or in the general welfare. These people are not awarded the station of legislator by the voting public. The legislator may ask assistance, may seek consultation, may seek technical advice, but the act of legislating is simply not a delegable function. By merging legislature and executive we have created the tyranny our forefathers warned us about.

All of this leaves the judiciary, often under unreasonable executive pressures, with unneeded problems of interpretation and the task of aligning the meaning of the statute with the statutory intent. Politicians don't like investigative reporters or investigative reporting. They loathe accountability and responsibility. The general weal causes a real conceptual problem for them, especially when compared to the political favors they grant. They would prefer that newspapers atrophy and that they, the politicians, be free to do what they please, without public scrutiny.

The realm of administrative code is the playground for the lobbyists, with their insights on particular players; their connections with the right administrators; familiarity with which agency controls what; which person has the power; who simply pretends to have power; who is on the way up and who is on the way out; which agenda will trump which agenda. These lobbyists are the true power brokers. How far we have gotten from a Congress deciding what is the **general weal** and how to implement it!

## Regulators as Judges

There is, at present, a "judicial" side to administration. It may have its own tribunals, or courts, the administrative law courts, complete with administrative law judges. Generally the work products of agencies only go to administrative law courts. Here the Administrative Law Judge (ALJ) roots for the "home team." The agenda of the executive as formulated and codified by the agency gets the blessing of "law" by the

ALJ. The result, practically speaking, becomes beyond appeal. Here is how that works: the ALJ is free to make any decision he or she wants, based on evidence that would be irrelevant, improbable or of insufficient weight in a court of law (real court). On appeal, ALJs are almost always upheld. (The mechanics of this are explained on the following page.)

These "judges" sit for hearings rather like trials, but on closer inspection, one sees that there are no juries. This means sensitive fact issues can't be removed from the hands of a "judge" and determined by a jury. Persons have been jailed for "infractions" by administrative law judges! The right to a jury trial goes right out the window.

When dealing with an administrative law court, the lack of due process starts immediately, since administrators control the docket. You could be called for trial before you can prepare or your case can be adjourned indefinitely.

When dealing with administrative law judges, there are more problems. They are not elected to office; they are appointed by the executive. They are not in office for a set term, they can be replaced at will, by the executive. There is no required public filing showing an administrative law judge's business interests. There is no disclosure of his past business dealings. There is no disclosure of political leanings. Most decisions are not published and compiled, so it is impossible to study his or her "leanings" until it is too late for your particular case. There is no right to substitute out a judge for cause shown, as in most real courts. (This is a one-time right of either party in a lawsuit in a court of law). There is no right to demand a recusal (causing an administrative judge to step down off a case) if a conflict of interest can be shown. ALJs are usually attached to a department (for example, Department of Natural Resources) and simply become an adjunct thereof. There they tend to develop a rapport with the department, and become "team players." How cozy is that?

Discovery for trial preparation is "streamlined." Usually there is no right to depose witnesses or experts. Reports are simply exchanged. The expert is free to disclose just part of his opinion or part of the basis for his opinion. This way the expert can later change or expand his opinions in "court." In a real court of law, at a deposition an attorney can ask: "Are these all your opinions? Are these all the facts you have considered? Where have you testified before? What opinions did you give there and then? Who pays you? How much? How much have you received for testimony in other cases? How much of your annual income does this represent?" None of this is possible in the administrative tribunal. This makes a proffer of contradictory evidence problematical, for one does not know with assurance what will be said and what the basis for opinions will be.

Impeachment by prior contrary statements or contradictory testimony, contradicting reports, patterns of testifying for one side or the other, business interests, political connections, lack of training or experience to qualify as an expert, false credentials, bad science, poor science or no scientific basis whatever — these traditional avenues of attack are impaired or gone. This makes it difficult for an attorney to select appropriate witnesses to offer contrary opinions.

Surprise is quite common, but there is no adequate remedy. This severely compromises a trial attorney's attempt to cross-examine and impeachment is unlikely as there is no prior record of inconsistent statements with which to confront the witness. Since there is little prior knowledge of the contentions or basis for opinions, it is virtually impossible to research and prepare questions for impeachment. The testimony in court can be immaterial, irrelevant, illogical, unscientific, unproven, unaccepted, highly in dispute or even disproven by legitimate science, but it all goes into the record. And it goes in with pretty much equal weight to valid science. Even learned treatises have little place in the administrative courts. And the weight, or lack of weight, of evidence is not to be revealed to the "court" or to the appellate body.

In courts of law, issues of fact, such as the believability of witnesses, are usually the sole province of the jury. While an occasional verdict of a "rogue jury" may be set aside, and a new trial ordered, English and American law has long held that the credibility of witnesses is for juries to decide, not judges. The judgment of the aggregate of weight, or convincing power, of evidence, so as to meet a burden of proof is also the exclusive domain of a jury (unless waived by parties).

The jury gets to look the expert witness in the eye, to see how convincing he or she is upon cross-examination. Because there is no jury in an administrative law proceeding, this valuable function is lost. And in administrative proceedings the record simply cannot capture the looks of insincerity, dismay or embarrassment, as witnesses proffer their incredulities. All evidence of candor disappears.

This makes an appellate review virtually impossible, for there is little basis for an appellate court to determine the reliability of evidence. Disciplined and insightful appellate judges quickly become frustrated. Neither a jury verdict (the basis for credibility of witnesses) nor effective impeachment (the usual calculus of appellate decision making) is found. The appellate courts' test of whether or not the preponderance of convincing evidence is in the record cannot be fairly addressed. The traditional bases for decision making are not in the record of administrative "courts" proceedings.

Appellate courts under pressure from big caseloads simply throw up their hands in desperation. They look for the thread or scintilla of evidence to support the foregone conclusion of the administrative law "judge" and go on. The tyranny of the executive has become beyond appeal to courts of law. Politics has displaced due process in these administrative law "courts."

## Absence of Civil Procedure and Due Process

In administrative law courts civil procedure is virtually non-existent. In a **court of law** where a jury is present, evidence that is simply prejudicial or based on emotional appeal, with no rational connection to an issue, may be kept from the jury. This is done by objections as to immateriality or irrelevancy.

In **administrative law courts**, the thought is that there is no jury present so there is no need to "filter" the record. Indeed, the "judges" here, not having been exposed to aggressive trial practice, have simply forgotten admissibility and relevancy tests. When in doubt about evidence, (and there usually is), the "judge" usually allows everything and anything into evidence (or into the record). The result is a shambles for appellate review. In administrative tribunals, evidence of the oddest sort finds its way into the record. The relevance of some evidence tendered is often dubious. Key causal links of facts to conclusions are frequently nonexistent. Probative value of much that is tendered is dubious at best, arbitrary or completely vacuous at worst. The record is so full of drivel and blather, any logical flow of evidence is lost. Briefing appeals becomes more problematic, and meaningful review is virtually impossible.

Returning to the procedure of the real **court of law**, there is a right of either party to have a review of a real court decision *by another set of eyes.* Judges from law courts are careful to state for the record their *findings of fact* and *conclusions of law.* If a jury was present, the written *jury verdict* is part of the record. The judge then utters his or her *judgment* based upon the record. The evidence in a court case must support the findings of fact. The history of case law must support the conclusions of law. The jury verdict must be supported by the preponderance of credible evidence on **all** elements to the cause of action, which must be found in court record. The *burden of proof* in a real court is that you must prove each and every element in the case with a preponderance of clear and convincing evidence. This is analogous in football to getting to the 51-yard line. You must cross the middle of the field. You must have proved more evidence than presented by the other side. You must tip the balance of the scale of justice in your favor to meet your burden of proof.

Not so in administrative law courts. There is no explicit burden of proof. All the parameters for judging the weight of evidence have been forgotten about or, by design, ignored. All measures of due process have been removed from the system. The administrative law judge can find whatever he or she fancies, so long as there is any sliver of evidence in the record. The administrative law judge is affirmed on review by any thread of credible evidence!

## HOW TO APPEAL FROM AN ALJ

Forget about it; you or your client is doomed. The *due process* failure in an administrative law proceeding is that, with the loose standard of admissibility, all evidence goes in *"for what it is worth."* This permits a flood of drivel into the record, regardless of its weight or value. The burden of proof is now a mere **scintilla** of evidence that might under any light support the administrative law judge's decision, and with everything allowed into the record, something can usually be found to defeat an appeal. This means upholding the administrative law judge's decision is virtually assured; his decision has become appeal proof.

Given the wide breadth of issues before the ALJ, and given the frequency with which the ALJ's decisions affect everyday transactions, and given the abject lack of due process at every level in these proceedings as compared to proceedings in real courts, why should the decisions of the ALJ be so impossible to overturn on appeal?

The fact that *real judges* in *real courts* are on occasion overturned on appeal speaks to the fallibility of judges, both real and the administrative sort. The work of the judge from the court of law is far more scrupulous and professional than that of the ALJ. Why on earth then is the work of the ALJ given such credence? Can it be anything other than to support the privileges for the favored few?

For a while it looked as though the courts of law would give meaningful review to administrative law proceedings. In 1968 they said: *the construction put on a statute by the agencies charged with administrating it is entitled to deference by the courts, and ordinarily that construction will be affirmed if it has a reasonable basis in law. . . . But the **courts are the final authority on the issues of statutory construction** . . . and are **not** obliged to stand aside **and rubber stamp** their affirmance of administrative decisions that they deem inconsistent with statutory mandate or that frustrate the congressional policy underlying a statute. (VW Aktingesellschaft v. Federal Maritime Commission,1968)*

But by 1984, the Supreme Court held *"first the Court determines if Congress has a (stated) intent on the point in issue, if so that intent governs, no matter what the agency says. However if Congress did not have such a specific intent, **the agency's interpretation is binding** on the* *courts, so long as the agency stays within the outer limits of possible interpretations of the law."* (*Chevron USA v. Natural Resource Defense Council,* 1984)

Do not blame the courts. The transcripts from administrative law court proceedings that find their way up to the appellate court are in a complete state of evidentiary disarray; it is impossible to make much sense of the record. There is no meaningful way to judge the quality of the evidence. The whole experience in administrative law "courts" is such a charade, so bereft of due process, that the appeals court has been deprived of the tools for meaningful review. There is little choice for the appeals court to do more than apply a rubber stamp to sanctify a political decision, to dress it up as having a basis at law. But in reality the ALJ is no more a judge than a political puppet. One is far more likely to get due process from a municipal justice who frequently has no judicial training other than watching TV dramas like *Law and Order.*

It is a sad thing when a client notices that whenever the attorney for the administrative body is speaking, the judge is listening and writing things down. When the private attorney is talking, the ALJ is completely ignoring the proceedings or is mildly angry or hostile or critical of the proceedings. Often the client concludes and comments that they feel the decision by the ALJ was reached well before the evidence was presented in court.

Many tribunals do not publish their decisions. Fewer index their decisions. The decisions are for the parties and their attorneys alone. It is virtually impossible to show and argue precedent. There is no decision to cite in future cases. There is no record of decisions *that can show a pattern of abuse of discretion* and lack of due process. Usually nothing is published, unless it is something a newspaper chooses to print, and most newspapers are not accurate reporters of court proceedings. The reports fall far short of competent case reporting, where facts are reported, issues are outlined, decisions and the basis for decisions are reported, dissent is recorded, together with the rationale for the dissent. The reasons for a decision can be completely arbitrary. The reasons for decisions can be completely vacuous. With no published decisions, all this is neatly swept under the carpet.

## Regulatory "Work Product" in Courts of Law

Occasionally an administrative and regulatory "*work product*" finds its way into the real courts. There are generally two narrow pathways: appeal of a decision, as above, where the affirmation is a foregone conclusion, or indirect ways, say perhaps a constitutional appeal based on an abuse of civil rights, or by trying to cite administrative law as binding on the state court. Here the courts need not apply the standards of review of administrative laws. Below are two examples of what real judges have to say when they get a chance to comment:

Superior Court Judge Mark Rindner noted the incompetence of the FDA in a decision in *Alaska v. Eli Lilly*, reached on March 28, 2008. This was a case where the state of Alaska sued Eli Lilly to recoup medical expenses incurred from treating side effects caused by the drug Zyprexa, manufactured by Eli Lilly. Defense counsel argued that drug use was to be regulated by the FDA and not the state and that therefore the FDA regulatory ruling by those infallible, uncorrupted, ever knowing FDA officials, should trump the jurisdiction of the state court. After nearly three weeks of testimony Judge Rinder stated that "*evidence presented by the state had established that the **FDA isn't capable of policing this matter***." He was referring to claims that prescription drugs used according to guidelines may actually cause new health problems. He was convinced that in leaving the decision in the hands of the FDA, problems "***might go unaddressed***."

Evidence of the EPA'S agenda-driven willingness to fraudulently manipulate evidence and science, and abuse its authority, was noted by Federal Judge William L. Osteen, in *Flue-Cured Tobacco Corp et al v. U.S. Environmental Protection Agency* (1998). He found that the EPA "*cherry-picked*" the data and "excluded studies that "demonstrated no association between ETS (environmental tobacco smoke) and cancer." He also stated that the "***EPA committed to a conclusion before research had begun . . . adjusted established procedure and scientif-***

*ic norms to validate the agencies public conclusion, and aggressively utilized the act's authority to disseminate findings to establish a de facto regulatory scheme intended to restrict Plaintiff's products, and influence public opinion, failed to disclose important findings and reasoning, left significant questions without answer, left substantial holes in the administrative record, produced limited evidence, then claimed the weight of the agencies research demonstrates ETS causes cancer."*

The pettiness often found in regulation is evidenced by this statement of the FDA's Division of Drug Advertising and Communications. Branch Chief Nancy Strove ruled that *"having a woman talk about the risks of using an injectable impotence treatment does not fully convey the dangers associated with the therapy."* (*Regulation*, Vol. 21, p. 4) Strove has decided that a drug advertisement can cause people to make *"these kinds of decisions [high priced medications over generic medications, demands for drugs they do not need] without a learned intermediary,"* and *"is problematic."* This line of reasoning gets hit in courts.

Federal Judge Royce Lamberth held that *"to endeavor to support a restriction of free speech by alleging that the recipient needs to be protected from speech for his or her own protection . . . is practically an engraved invitation to have the restriction struck."*

"If there is one fixed principle in the commercial speech area, it is that a state's paternalistic assumption that people will use truthful non-misleading commercial information unwisely cannot justify a decision to support [the restriction]." (*44 Liquor Mart Inc. v. Rhode Island,* 1996)

## Bureau of Indian Affairs

The Bureau of Indian Affairs (BIA) should be the first federal agency to go. It started in 1824 as part of the department of the Army, and in about 1870 became involved in education, now characterized as cultural destruction. A program then started making specific grants, allocating 40 to 160 acres to individual Indians. Generally, the Indians were judged by the BIA to be not educated or sophisticated enough to take care of these lands. Consequently, most of the lands are managed in trust for the Indians by the BIA. Income for grazing, farming, timber and mineral and oil rights is collected and disbursed to the beneficiaries. There are thought to be 500,000 landowners in these programs. The owners are not told who is leasing their land; they are not consulted about leases or rents; there is no accounting as to minerals and oil removed from the lands; and there is no audit system in place to verify what is removed. In 1994, the BIA admitted to Congress that they could not account for $2.4 billion they had received up to that time. There is chronic suspicion the assets are undervalued. Attempts by beneficiaries to obtain accounting of and proceeds from their lands produce no results.

Proceedings in a lawsuit by the beneficiary Indians, against the Trustee (BIA) were suspended, because BIA documents were not forthcoming. In a scathing decision, Federal Judge Royce Lamberth found Interior Secretary Bruce Babbitt and Secretary of the Treasury Robert Rubin in contempt of court, and fined the two some $600,000. He found that *"they could not be trusted" and that they were engaging in "a shocking pattern of deception of the court,"* stating, *"Never have I seen a more egregious misconduct by the Federal Government. Only in this litigation could 8,000 cubic feet of records slip through the cracks."* (*Cobell v. Kempthorne,* 2006)

On July 11, 2006, Judge Lamberth was removed from the Indian Trust Fund case by the U.S. District Court of Appeals. Subsequently a special master was appointed for the case. He cited both past presidents Bush for withholding information. Presidents Bush and Clinton were both cited for contempt of court by Judge James Robertson. Nothing is settled. The central issue is the rents and mining/drilling revenues amounting to some $5 billion per year, which the government has been misappropriating for over 100 years.

Equally corrupt is the vast Indian gaming business, in which the annual revenue was reported (unaudited) to be $13.7 billion. Independent Nation status makes auditing impossible. Management contracts held by non-Native Americans are reputed to charge up to

40 percent of gross receipts for the first seven years of service. This is outrageous. Internal cash control is unreliable.

"Gaming" revenue mismanagement may dwarf those losses suffered for rental of land and mineral extraction. So long as politicos have anything to do with the management of Indian assets, bribery and conniving will continue. All the while, many reservation-dwelling Native Americans live in abject poverty, at or below Third World standards.

Should the government ever become responsible for their breaches of trust, the damages could reach an additional trillion dollars, not yet figured into the Indian trust fund damages. Can anyone suggest a way to correct this system? Big oil money will certainly corrupt any way politicos will "care" for the assets of the Native Americans. Unless they actively manage their own assets, the plunder is certain to continue. Is it not time to give them the reins, while there are still some horses in the corral?

We now see and understand that our prediction of two sets of laws, two sets of courts, two sets of judges is in fact fulfilled. We see there is no right to jury trial. We see that aside from the internal revenue code, there is little impetus to publish or index decisions; hence there is nothing to cite to the administrative law judge.

How can regulators be so arrogant? They are empowered by the president. As agents of the executive, they feel above the law. He even anoints some of them to be czars. How can regulators be so irrational in their thoughts and analyses? They do not do it on their own. They are taught policy and political "science" and social "science" at prestigious universities. And they are inspired by wonks.

## Inside View: Persons of the Regulatory Universe

Administrative agencies have a myriad of titles: they call themselves agencies, administrations, activities, bureaus, centers, committees, departments, laboratories, offices, institutes, programs, or simply a name description such as the U.S. Mint.

Persons within agencies are **appointed administrators** and **civil servants.** These are the regulators, inspectors, enforcement officers and administrative law judges. Their duty is to make behavior conform to standards. Usually historical objectives or historical standards are the basis on which to regulate behavior. Citizens are to conform to an historic, stated "norm" such as a stated price per gallon or pound of goods; miles per hour; times at which an act may not be performed.

They also have assumed the power to move society forward by creating new standards. They feel empowered by doctrines of modern political thought described in the Office of Management and Budget guidelines such as:

> Regulation should be based on the analysis of the **costs and benefits** of all the available alternatives and that agency should select that regulatory approach that **maximizes the net benefit to society**.

This is truly an impossible mission. It requires impossible economic measures and projections. It requires telling the future. The linkages between these terms are fanciful to nonexistent, but the **wonks** are happy to undertake these tasks. Where scientific proof is impossible they are happy to fill in with imagination. And they are proud to call this social science. But science is quite different.

**Science** has a methodology underlying a proof. In science, a fact or relationship is:

- Detected or discovered
- Described
- Defined as to properties
- Defined as to boundaries or limitations
- Measured, especially at extremes; properties are examined and studied for inverse consequences and counterintuitive properties under conditions of strain or stress at extremis
- Proven: multiple tests produce uniform predictable results.

- Verified: the hypothesis is checked by multiple disinterested, independent studies. They show conclusions are reproducible.
- Published.

## The Wacky World of Wonkdom

Welcome to the wacky world of wonkdom, where we find **policy wonks**, policy analysts and policy evaluators. These are forward-projecting persons, armed with agendas and rather odd ideas about the world, how it works, and how they feel it should work. Unfortunately they hold in their sway the legislators and the administrative code-drafting persons.

A wonk is a liberally educated person, usually raised in a feel-good environment, totally lacking in the concept of searching for a job, earning a living by labor, business, accounting, profitability, breakeven points, budgets, business failure and human nature. Wonks have been taught that it is proper to substitute imagination and fantasy for critical thinking and scientific proof. The result is a tenuous grasp of reality. For the most part, they dwell in and about Washington D.C.

Telling the future is always hard. But these wonks, dressed in dark robes, with peaked cone-like caps adorned with stars and crescent moons and armed with Ouija boards, are clueless and unconcerned about difficulties. They have been empowered by phrases such as *benefits to society* and *failures of the private market.*

Philosophers and pseudo-scientists all, they boldly plunge forward. Reality and unintended and unforeseen consequences will always appear and upset the applecart. But in the ivory towers of academia reality is trivial and unnoticed.

When dressed in more normal attire, they are easy to identify by the sounds they make called **econobabble**. Here is an example from the *Letters to the Editor* section in the magazine *Regulation: The Cato Review of Business and Government* (Vol. 20, Fall 1997, p. 2 and following). Two groups of wonks are in strong disagreement. Read carefully. In his letter, Professor Kerry Smith has just called one group unscientific. A group of 13 wonks responds by saying, "*Smith concludes* *from those observations that our 'analysis seems to combine bad economics and bad ecological science'"* and goes on to say that Smith's highly negative conclusions are, however, insupportable and deserve rebuttal. First they concede, "The short answer is (1) *although the WTP (willingness to pay) is admittedly flawed, and incomplete...*" Then they concede: "*Unfortunately economic science has not yet sufficiently evolved to solve all those problems at the micro scale, let alone at the global scale. . .*"

It seems that the gifted 13 have just conceded Professor Smith's point that the conclusions are not supported by science, which is measurable, predictable, and reproducible. Some of their points of disagreement are the causes of inefficient prices, inefficient auctions, linear aggregations, nonlinear ecological systems, incomplete markets and nonexistent markets. None of this **wonk babble** is clearly definable, measurable or even agreed upon among themselves. Which, of course, leads to loopy reasoning and inevitably strange conclusions.

One policy wonk insists, "[A] *future(s) market increases efficiency.*" Futures markets are invariably rigged, and the Chicago Board of Trade (CBOT), now MERC, is a classic example. The ease and efficiency with which prices are manipulated is carefully documented on pages 125-128 of *Rats in the Grain*, the well written, riveting and insightful history of Archer Daniels Midland's price fixing in Chicago. The only efficiency created is the ease with which speculators can engage in monopolistic and fraudulent trading practices. Policy wonks dwell in a universe unlike those of us living in the real world.

Policy wonks are united in their **universal disgust for profits**. Theirs is a constant search for an **"incentive"** which they can manipulate and regulate to drive the real world economy according to their fantasy inspired goals, along routes of their choosing. Their reasoning goes something like this, in the words of assistant Professor Catherine D. Wolfram:

"Reformers continue to debate how to structure a competitive market for [electrical] generation services."

"Incentives to make efficient investments, could therefore lead to substantial savings."

They somehow expect the real world to buy into this incentive plan, which never seems to work out. But the wonk is undeterred and learns nothing from each frustrating encounter with reality.

Wonks are completely unaware that the private sector supplies all goods, intellectual property and any reasonably priced services. Wonks are an extravagant and worthless cog in government. They produce no goods or services. They produce inefficiency, employment for administrative lawyers and lobbyists in legions, and they waste time and money. They cannot comprehend that government activity is the most extravagant way to do anything. A term like *cost of goods sold* draws a total blank look. They are clueless as to the meaning of the word budget or that it should somehow relate to income. They are willing to spend hours, months, years contemplating a new incentive to replace the profit motive. They want a new form of incentive they can regulate. They are unaware that the government way is always the slowest way to do anything. They themselves are never judged on productivity. What they do cannot be measured. It cannot be understood. It cannot be scientifically verified. Indeed they are clueless as to the discipline of science. To them research is to be agenda-driven. Data is to be harvested selectively, in support of a preconceived hypothesis. Skewed data is the norm. Data that does not support the desired conclusion should be suppressed. It simply wouldn't do to change the hypothesis.

Unsurprisingly, policy wonks and regulators wish to appear scientific. Unfortunately their attempts to calculate and predict the future always seem to go awry. They are light-years away from a sound scientific basis for their work. They cannot even agree on definitions of what they seek to study. They have no methodology for removing subjective variables from studies. Administrators and wonks have no objective standards in their universe. They have no agreed upon standards for measurements. They have no program of verification of findings by independent testing, substituting subjective intuition freely for proofs of economic tests. They use unreliable data, poor definitions of vital terminology, unscientific collection of data, small, and hence, unreliable databases, out of date data, misunderstood data, data of costs often skewed by regulated business. They formulate biased data interpretation. The effectiveness and benefits of proposed regulations are usually unrealistically optimistic. They have a poor understanding of how the real economic world works and a poor understanding of how the real world adapts to and evades regulatory intentions.

Clueless as to the parameters of real science and real proof, wonks happily apply "junk science" to "worthless data" which becomes the basis for most policy.

It is no surprise that they do not agree between themselves on what they are doing or how to do it. More econobabble:

"A policy maker can construct the environment and the rules of exchange that create incentives and thus affect behavior" (*Regulation*, Vol. 20 #4, p. 5)

"The point is that the linkage does not exist for non market final goods or services such as the worlds ecosystems services since they are not priced or (are) inadequately priced in the current markets…" (*ibid.*, p. 2)

These are concepts that are difficult to define and understand. The relationships between these terms are fanciful to nonexistent, but the wonks are happy to call it science or social science.

Unsurprisingly, the efforts of policy wonks and regulators to appear scientific and/or as knowledgeable economists are frustrated by the real world. They face:

- Unforeseen costs
- Unforeseeable costs
- Unknown risks (a percentage of likelihood of an occurrence happening)
- Unknown hazards (specific untoward results)
- Unknown unknowns

- Scope of future innovation
- Scope of future inventions
- Economic impact of innovations and inventions such as:
    Cell phones' impact on pay phones
    E-mail effect on post office mail
    GPS effects on lighthouses
    GPS effects on map sales
    Computer map/route planners on AAA
    Skype on long distance phone charges
    Internet on newspaper's classified advertising
    Internet on newspaper circulation
    Internet on "yellow page" phone books
    Micro generation of electricity on high voltage
        transmission
    UPS and Fed Ex on the post office
    DVDs on movie theaters
    ipods on record sales
    Personal computers on mainframe computers
    Digital cameras on film cameras
- Unreliable data
- Poor definitions of vital terminology
- Unscientific collection of data
- Small database
- Obsolete data
- Misunderstood data
- Data of costs often skewed by regulated business
- Biased data interpretation
- Projected benefits usually unrealistic-too optimistic
- Projected expenses to business unrealistically low
- Projected costs to society usually too low, or simply ignored
- Benefits to economy, being impossible to quantify, are unrealistic
- Effectiveness of proposed regulation usually unrealistic
- Dynamic market conditions as to cost
- Dynamic market conditions as to benefits

- Poor understanding of real world
- Poor understanding of how real economic world works
- Poor understanding of how real world adapts to and evades regulatory intentions

Hence their assumptions and conclusions are impossible to audit or verify. The costs are too complex to calculate. In addition, the following costs and expenses are never considered:

- The risk that the Federal Government will be called in to pay losses, real or feigned, of a program gone wrong is never factored in "costs to society"
- Political interference with regulations skews benefits to society
- Expense of litigation never factored into costs
- Expense of administration rarely factored into formula
- Expense of damage to political system not figured into formula
- It is never considered that some people are simply criminals and won't follow the laws
- Jurisdictional limits
- There are no meaningful checks or balances on their powers or inclinations
- There is no meaningful accountability for wrong policy or law

Policy wonks are blissfully unaware of reality. To wonks, bent on building the best of all possible worlds, money is no object. Budgets do not exist and reality is a relative state. They feel that studying historical precedents is a waste of time — what's the point in looking backwards? What could possibly be learned from that? These are the lifeguards of tomorrow, unaware of history, economics, laws, constitutional limitations. They have no experience in the business world: budgets, time tables or the idea that profit is generated only when sale price exceeds cost of goods sold.

Is it any wonder regulations never work out for the general welfare? Agendas of the executive, dictated by campaign contributions are hardly devices to lead to the general welfare. Yet the wonks, detached from the reality of world and market forces, respond to nothing else. It is easy to see why regulation doesn't work.

**Conclusion:** the science underlying "policy" is not very scientific or reliable. It is subject to unintended results and should not carry much weight for legislative considerations. In addition, the whole administrative machinery is a very expensive apparatus to run. It is completely ruinous to the free marketplace. It simply invites payola and corruption of government. It generates needless duties and tasks for businesses which is destructive to our international competition. These are luxuries we cannot afford in our modern world.

## Case Study: The "Deregulation" of California Electricity

What can we gain from an in-depth look at regulation? This example is not of federal administration. It is that of the State of California, but the parallels to federal regulations are instructive.

In 1998, California supposedly deregulated its electric power market. Their regulators came up with a scheme to assure Californians of getting low-priced electricity. The regulators **froze** the retail prices to consumers until 2002. This ensured that consumers would do nothing to reduce their demand for electricity by conservation. At the same time, electric retailers were prohibited from entering into long-term contracts for the purchase of electricity generated out of state. In this way, electric retailers could not argue for higher prices based upon increased future electric costs. But this also meant retailers could not protect themselves from spikes in wholesale prices. New electric energy that was generated outside California had to be bought at "spot price," or **spot,** on the daily market.

Because electricity is critical, it is highly desirable that it is always available. Since electricity cannot be stored in a bottle for later use, one way to ensure availability is to have more generators than are strictly necessary. Energy managers assume say, a 95 percent production level for this assurance. But in practice, generators can run dependably about 99 percent of the time. This means there is one percent down time for repairs. The spread between 99 percent and 95 percent is surplus generating capacity. Generators are usually run as much of the time as possible. Thus, *surplus* capacity generation is produced at quite a low cost, as the generator, buildings, grid and employees are already paid for. Fuel and a bit of employee time is all the cost associated with surplus electricity.

This surplus energy blended together from many generators is statistically a pretty dependable supply of electricity. Since it cannot be stored, it is sold on the free market, for whatever the generating company can get at spot price. Traditionally spot is far below normal market price. During this price freeze California purchased up to 30 percent of its energy needs at these steep discounts from as far east as Texas.

Out-of-state electric generation companies had little incentive to build new plants for a market of which they could not be assured. Within the state of California, NIMBY ("not in my back yard") attitudes assured no new plants were built there. It takes many years to build a new electric generator plant; indeed, just getting permits takes years. Low prices set by controls meant that alternative methods of generation such as solar, wind, and ocean wave, were not explored or exploited. California became addicted to cheap electricity. It had attracted high-energy-use companies, computer and chip manufacturers, and loved cheap air conditioning. There was never a thought given to conservation.

Remember that California utilities were barred from entering into long-term contracts (which would protect them from price spikes) and retail prices were set for years. Some would notice this is not then a free market. But not the politicians, who soon found that market forces are stronger than regulatory forces. (And these market forces do not pay attention to regulators' dreams and wishes.) California regulators found, to their surprise, that spot prices do not always stay low. In 2000, when summer demand for electricity outstripped supplies, the spot price shot up as much as 1300 percent over 1996 spot prices. Remember that the electric retail sellers were not permitted to raise prices.

Regulators smiled at the discomfort of the nasty electric companies who had been making what regulators thought were horrid profits. As much as 30 percent of daily electricity use was now being purchased at "spot." The out of state power generator's profits were increased up to 700 percent. Regulators may have smiled briefly, as the **local** power sellers were deprived of profits and were soon insolvent. But the real persons being punished were the people in or near retirement, who had invested in "safe" utility company stocks that had suddenly become worthless. Those smiles vanished, when the regulators found that "oldsters" are very organized and politically connected voters.

Regulators and utility managers were unable to comprehend that regulation in the best of times simply doesn't work, and can never replace the free market; and in the worst of times produces economic disaster of unimaginable proportions. Their stupidity was pointed out in multiple news publications circa February 2001:

"The simple fact is that a handful of people that were really smart figured out how to make a ton of money selling the same product in essentially the same market conditions as before at 10 times the price." (Michael Kahn of the California Electricity Oversight Board, *New York Times*, February 11, 2001)

"We hired the very best systems reliability operators, the people who knew how to keep the lights on.... in terms of matching wits with some M.B.A. who's got a Ph.D. in chaos theory, who's working with the derivative of whatever, the answer is no way, we can't do something like that." (Kellan Fluckiger, COO California Independent System Operator, *New York Times*, February 11, 2001)

"Did they break the law? They didn't have to." (Steve Klein, superintendent of Tacoma Power, *New York Times*, February 11, 2001)

"They knew we were desperate, we didn't have any leverage to do deals." (Jim McIntosh of Pacific Gas and Electric, *New York Times*, February 11, 2001)

This was no surprise, for he reported to his superiors five years before that *"a group of out of state energy generation companies had a group of MBA types who were figuring how to make money in the California (electric) market."* He concluded then, *"these guys are going to eat our lunch."*

"It was like buying insurance when your house was already on fire — you'll pay anything for it." (Robert Mc Cullough, a former California utility executive, *New York Times*, February 11, 2001)

Governor Gray Davis tried to right the situation by bullying; on January 8, 2001, he declared, *"Never again can we allow out-of-state profiteers to hold California hostage."* (*The Economist*, January 20, 2001) (Where was his jurisdiction or power over out-of-state businessmen?) He threatened to seize electric company assets and run them himself, if necessary. (This was a total delusion about his competency. "Beware of politicians with more confidence than they deserve.")

*The Economist* magazine (January 20, 2001) got it right when it said, *"What on earth has gone wrong? The short answer is botched deregulation. The peculiarly bad way in which California's deregulation was organized freed prices for wholesale electricity while putting a freeze on retail rates."*

The Federal Energy Regulatory Commission conducted a hearing and found *"no evidence the companies put their generators out of commission to drive up prices."* Through a spokesman, Governor Davis called the audit a *"see no evil, hear no evil type of audit"* (*New York Times*, February 11, 2001); but then the whitewash is what politicos instinctively do. Predictably, none of his ranting produced any results. The problem was not solved and he was defeated in his next election.

Perhaps the most saddening display of bias, prejudice and down-right stupidity was displayed in the continuation of the front page article in the Sunday *New York Times*, February 11, 2001, following this headline: "**New system of power made California prey to profit driven sellers beyond controls**."

Here is a major newspaper encouraging the belief that **regulation,** the cause of most economic problems, and doubtless the cause of this crisis, somehow deserves the public trust and confidence, and can somehow to be the solution to the problem it has created. Look at the implications contained in the article:

- That profit making is somehow bad, sort of un-American.
- That profiteering was involved, when the evidence was that electric use was steadily and dramatically increased, while the generation supply stayed constant.
- That price-fixing regulations will somehow make prices less expensive or more stable over the long-term. When in history has it ever done that?
- That prices of electricity in the California utility market can or should be controlled by regulation.
- That California's regulators **should** have the power to dictate the price at which those neighboring states sell electricity to California.
- That the California regulators, by setting unrealistically low electricity prices, might somehow cause consumers to use less electricity or keep electric usage within the surplus
- That the California regulators, by setting unrealistically low electricity prices, will somehow cause out of state producers to want to build new generation plants and generate and sell electricity to California at economic loss to themselves and their shareholders.
- That California's regulatory power should be greater than the economic law that price follows supply and demand. Clearly market forces are far more powerful than political regulators.

Shame on the *New York Times!*

California decided that the solution was now to buy electricity with long-term contracts — lots of electricity, for very long terms. This was the worst time to negotiate long-term contracts, for the price of western electricity was at an historic high.

Because California does not have the power to print money, and because the federal government was in no mood to give them a $10-billion bailout, the state decided to offer a $10-billion bond issue. It had to appeal to those citizens with savings. The same group of investors they had just shafted out of $12 billion they had invested in California electric utility companies.

The state's credit rating was at an all-time low. No investor was in a mood to be subjected to the will of politicians' whims again. California had to promise to pay huge premiums to raise $10 billion for the purchase of the electric futures. What a great legacy for the next governor to deal with. It left the state near bankruptcy.

**From this we learn that regulation of a free market does not solve problems, but that regulation has the amazing power to make small problems huge problems**

*The Economist*, on January 20, 2001, concluded: *"It would be sheer folly to let the state's incompetent and bungling politicians and regulators run the utilities as a reward for having run them into the ground in the first place."*

A little knowledge is a dangerous thing. Political sorts have shown they have very little knowledge of economics. They should not aspire to being in the cockpit of the marketplace. And the hacks they appoint as regulators are proving to be equally unqualified:

"I'm not an economist, so I'm flying by the seat of my pants, but it seems to me that orthodox economics got us into this mess in the first place." (Carl Woods, Public Utility Commissioner, California, to a regulator, *The Economist*, January 20, 2001)

Here is a woodsman who is so lost he doesn't know what forest he is in: political or economic. He doesn't even recognize a free market or lack of one. How do these people get so stupid? They couldn't do it by themselves. It's the universities.

## Academic Reflections on Administrative Regulation

Here are more words of wisdom from an assistant professor at an expensive eastern university, Catherine D. Wolfram of Harvard.

> "Restructuring [regulation] has been designed to foster competition and to create incentives in [electrical] generation assets." (*Regulation*, Vol. 22 #4, p. 49)

There is no need to "*foster competition.*" You are not raising children. Simply allow profits and competition will be there. Competition comes from the free market, and is only found in a free market.

Regulation is not needed for competition. Competition is a natural consequence of a free market. Competition occurs only in a free market, that is, an unregulated market. Regulation stifles competition, every time. Regulation is the anathema of competition. It strangles the free market, the home of competition. Regulation cannot improve on competition, ever!

> **Competition is a natural consequence of a free market. Competition occurs only in a free market.**

> "Some of the most costly decisions made under regulation or state ownership have involved investments in generation plants that turned out to be inefficient or uneconomical." (*Regulation*, Vol. 22 #4, p. 49)

It seems the professor is on the verge of enlightenment. She has discovered that government regulation is sometimes "inefficient or uneconomical." Indeed, is this not a bold-faced admission that regulation or state ownership is inefficient or uneconomical? With politicos at the helm, making decisions motivated by campaign contributions, and having no capital of their own at risk, who but a never-never land regulator would be surprised by that? She is getting close to something. The light is about to go on. Is she about to discard the notion of regulation? No. Her brain clicks off. Perhaps too much expensive eastern education takes over her powers of observation and recognition: Watch what she does.

"Incentives to make efficient investments, therefore could lead to substantial savings." (*ibid.*)

The professor now wants to create **incentives for efficient investment**. The marketplace already has that. It is called the "profit motive." And profits are kept in check by competition. But regulating the market degrades competition. There is no room in a free market for ham handed, thick skulled regulators. Instead of dumping all notions of regulation and her disgust of profit, the eastern education kicks in and she concludes:

"Economists have identified two basic characteristics of efficient markets: production should take place at the lowest possible cost and prices should be equal to the marginal cost of production." (*ibid.*)

When she says prices should not exceed the marginal cost of production she seems not to want to cover profits or the cost of building and dismantling a generation plant. In other words she proposes to take "profits" out of the price structure. She would disallow profits. There is no explanation why this element is to be removed from her notion of a functional economy. It seems regulators just hate profits. It is as if the word turns off whatever rational part of the brain they may have left after schooling.

If not profits, what does she think that businessmen compete for? Gold stars or a "thank you" wall plaque? Regulation, like price caps, is only a strong disincentive to the construction of future generation plants or developing alternative energy sources.

> Profit is what businessmen compete for in a free market.

She is right that economists have identified two "*basic characteristics of efficient markets.*" It is just that she doesn't know what those two elements are. They are **supply** and **demand**. She could have asked her parrot. One must wonder how she got her job, how she keeps her job. Having missed the turn in the road, she continues:

> "Though the idea of competitive unregulated (electricity) generation is one of the cornerstones of electricity reform programs, reformers continue to debate how to structure a competitive market for (electrical) generation services." (*ibid.*)

Notice she gets the idea that a (competitive) <u>unregulated</u> market is important ("a cornerstone"). But again her brain goes dead: she and her pals continue to ponder how to **regulate** a free market. They seek "*how to restructure a competitive market.*" The free market is one that is free from the structure of regulation. It is a market free from regulatory actions. This professor and her pals are simply not needed. They are not desirable. They are in the way. They are an extravagance and the cause of inefficiency and catastrophic market anomalies. They are the reason California nearly went bust.

Next, note that she has used the word reform. Regulators want to reformulate what is happening in the market. They want to change the form of the market. They want to change how the market works. They have the audacity to presume they can change the expression of the democratic will of the citizens — the free market. They think they can reprogram how people think about all things in the market. They think they can detach price from supply and demand. They think they can anticipate the future — desires, preferences, supplies and so on.

No one can structure a free market.
No one can regulate a free market.
No one can structure a competitive market.
Just get regulators out of the way and the free market
will occur.

One must wonder how many years this debate has been going on. One must wonder who pays these folks to debate this subject. And one can surmise that the debate must be chaired by philosophers. How did these people get their jobs? Are all government people like this or just regulators? How far will this disease spread? You make a market competitive by removing the impediment of regulation, not by engaging in Ptolemaic debates. We are paying taxes to support this kind of philosophical foolishness? These words were not generated by an unattended word processor left on cruise control. This is from an assistant professor at Harvard University. Her name is Catherine D. Wolfram. (Wolfram is another word for tungsten. Tungsten an element known for its extreme density.) The truly fearsome thing is that she is an assistant professor at an elite university, molding impressionable young minds, with a tyrannical position to pass or fail students who do not adopt these completely unrealistic notions of the world. She is tenured into a position to wreak havoc on young minds for years to come. It looks like we will get no help from the institutions of higher learning.

Ronald Reagan said, "*The trouble with our liberal friends is not that they're ignorant, it's just they know so much that just isn't so.*"

The sad thing about regulators is that they just can't conceive that they are pointless, useless, counterproductive, an extravagance, so unnecessary. All are a waste of time and resources; they are consumers. The vast bulk of them produce nothing that our society needs.

## Monstrosity of the Regulatory Beast

Our government has created self-generating agencies of pointless complexity, as evidenced by 472 standing federal agencies and hundreds of state agencies. We have at least 16 agencies controlling food quality (how did all of them miss the peanut poisoning scandal?). They have created over 91,000 pages of administrative code found in *The Federal Register.* There are nearly 400,000 federal employees in these agencies. They are planners, policy makers, regulators, political scientists, economists and attorneys. They are eager to regulate problems, real, and imagined, probable and possible. Yet we have bank failures, food poisoning, savings and loan scandals, Bernie Madoff and others doing Ponzi schemes. Clearly the administrative branch has encroached on the legislative branch. Congress is aware of the transgression, but is seemingly powerless. How did all of this come to pass? Where should lines of separation between the legislative and the executive be drawn? What do these agencies really accomplish? How much of this is needed?

## Congressional Awareness that There is a Problem

Clearly, federal administrative bodies have made a mess out of administration. Recall that the Cato Institute believes it costs the U.S economy 400 billion dollars per year in needless expense for regulation compliance. (*Regulation,* Vol. 20 #4, p. 17) The time lost because of pointless delay frequently is measured in years. Congress is vaguely aware of the problem but is clueless about what to do. Should they confront the president and take back their legislative powers? Should they disband agencies, all or in part? Should they start reading and deleting, line by line, the code that suffocates the people who create wealth and prosperity in our country? As evidence of the complete stupidity of the Congress, look what they have done: they have created five new acts to regulate efficiency in the existing agencies. These are:

(1) Office of Information and Regulatory Affairs (OIRA), established by President Clinton within the Office of Management and Budget (OMB), for "solid guidance for developing new regulations and revising existing ones."
(2) Regulatory Flexibility Act of 1993 (RFA)
(3) Unfounded Mandate Reform Act of 1995 (UMRA)

(4) Congressional Review Act of 1996 (CRA)

(5) Small Business Regulatory Reform Act of 1996 (SBREFA)

All were created to perform the duty of Economic Analysis (EA): "*provide detailed guidelines for estimating cost benefits, and benefits of a range of regulatory options and include sound guidance for treating risk and uncertainty, discounting future benefits and costs, and analyzing opportunities and costs, and market transactions.*" All are dedicated to defining indefinite and unreliable goals, measuring the immeasurable and wasting huge amounts of time and money, while other unencumbered international competitors to our businesses plunge ahead in the race for individual profitability and their national prosperity. This is quite much to ask of government employees; quite much to ask of the politically impaired and politically thwarted agency types.

Politicians say they believe in democracy. The most democratic thing in the world is a politically unencumbered free market. This is the job of the free market. Let the free market happen.

Administrators themselves know way down deep inside they have created a mess of our economy, but are fearful to admit their own worthlessness, lest they be out lucrative jobs. They want the nice feeling that they are needed, that they are helpful. The truth is they know they produce only worthless administrative "red tape." Regulators simply make problems more expensive problems every time. You can't beat the free market. With agencies there are policy flaws and inconsistencies. Legally there is denial of due process at every turn in the road. An agency is nothing but a political animal in the economic arena, an arena that flourishes in democratic freedom, the more the better. When everyone is voting daily with the same ballot, the dollar, businessmen know how to respond. They know how to allocate resources. They know which ventures are likely to be the desirable ones. Price structure reflects the desire of the public.

Congress just doesn't get it. Or do they realize if there is a free market, they will have no privileges to sell? How shocking is that?

> If Congress were to allow a free market to exist, they would have nothing to sell.

The misplaced confidence politicians have, that they can somehow do it better, that somehow they know better than the public, is really quite absurd. Add to that the distortion of slightly limited campaign contributions and an unworkable situation becomes worse. A new agency is not going to solve the inherent problems of administrative agencies. Layers of new administrative agencies can't do it either. The solution to the problem may lie within the Constitution, which has proven to be the framework of the most powerful government the world has ever known. Perhaps the Founding Fathers knew best. The politicos just don't get it. Administrations are the problem. Creating more will not fix it.

## Agency Reaction to Congressional Attempts to Limit Agencies

In spite of the above five acts of congress, those creating agencies to limit agencies, the policy wonks have decided that instead of reduced administration and regulation it is best for society to increase regulation. **Administrators and regulators have decided to expand their own jurisdiction.** Because of the fear we have not done enough to regulate our society, or the economy, we now have the "**precautionary principle**" which expands the scope of regulations by lowering the threshold of proof needed to empower regulators to act. Instead of even a loose and unscientific "cost-benefit calculation," the new standard, stated in general terms, is:

> If an activity raises the threat of harm to the environment or human health, precautionary measures should be taken by regulators, even though science has not established a cause and effect relationship.

Regulators have unilaterally decided we need more regulations, not less. All progress is backwards. It is clear that limiting administration cannot be left to politicos or administrators.

## Limits to Proper Presidential Power and Activity

What then is the proper role of the president? What limitations are there on his administrators? Returning to the words of the Founding Fathers:

"Against a gradual concentration of several powers in the same department consists in giving . . . necessary constitutional means . . . to resist encroachments of the others." (F 51 pp 4)

"Gradual preeminence in government finally transforming it into tyrannical aristocracy." (*ibid.*)

Or Montesquieu:

"When the legislative and executive powers are united in the same person, . . . there can be no liberty." (Montesquieu, *The Spirit of the Laws*)

"The executive power . . . ought to have a share in the legislature, [but only] the power of rejecting. . . . If the Prince (executive) were to have a part in the legislature by the power of resolving, liberty would be lost." (*ibid.*)

"Again, there is no liberty if the judiciary power be not separated from the legislative and the executive." (*ibid.*)

". . .the most glorious attribute of sovereignty, namely, that of granting pardon, for it would be quite ridiculous of him to make and unmake his decision; surely he would not choose to contradict himself." (*ibid.*)

The realm of the executive is the execution and implementation of existing laws. His role is not to anticipate or to look ahead, but to make the government he has been given to run smoothly. He has taken the oath of office, which provides he will follow and protect our Constitution. If he does not live within those strictures, has he not broken that oath?

A president's lawful powers do not include the powers to expand existing law or create new laws. Hence any "visions," agendas, policies, programs, missions, mandates, initiatives, ideas, or ideals must be viewed with suspicion and alarm. These tenets are simply license to assume legislative functions.

The valid functions of the agents of a president are also limited in the same ways. Those agents wear many names and titles: cabinet members, ministers, judges, administrators, regulators, civil servants. For all of them it is illegal to assume or expand the powers of the presidency. And any attempt of the president to delegate expanded powers would also be an illegal delegation of powers.

"No one can transfer to another more power than he has in himself." (Locke, *Second Treatise on Government*)

The valid or proper functions of these agents are simply to measure, quantify, qualify, compile, discover, investigate, identify, and regulate according to set norms. Their world is strictly the objective. Their world does not morph into the future, or into anticipation of what the future may bring.

## Limits of Regulatory Power:
## The Objective/Subjective Divide

Certain **objective** things can and should be regulated: weights, measures, speeds, weight limitations on highways, full measure in packaged goods, drug and chemical purity, water purity, freedom of food products from adulteration or dangerous substances, minimum reserves a bank must carry; perhaps air traffic and air traffic control (minimum distance between airplanes in flight). These are all scientifically measurable, and verifiable; hence standards are easy to define.

Beyond that point, we cross over into **subjective** behavior and things become more complex. The definition of standards of behavior becomes blurry. What should a reasonable doctor do when confronted with test results for a male, age sixty, with a family history of high blood pressure and cardiac problems? What would a reasonable surgeon do in an abdominal surgery when confronted with an unexpected and suspicious lump, time is short, because the patient is a "bleeder"? How to determine an appropriate medication when dealing with variables like family history, blood sugar issues and abnormal blood chemistry? In such examples we have reached the limit of regulator's ability to create guidelines and to make judgment on behavior. **Objective criteria are the outer limitation of the power of effective regulation.** Subjective behavior is simply beyond the device of regulation.

Administration has the same theoretical limitation as regulation. They are simply two names for the same animal. Administration can handle prohibited acts and acts where there is a clear black and white objective standard. When they get into enforcement of acts of **behavioral judgment**, where black-letter rules and regulations become smudged by the complexity of *reasonable choices,* administrators are in trouble. It is when we pass from **objective** (things measured or ascertainable with scientific certainty) to **subjective** (those based on feelings, hopes and beliefs) that both administrators and their regulators flounder.

The next dynamic that makes codification and regulation impossible is that progress changes standards. Codification and regulation are always behind those changes. The dynamic of creativity and innovation would be suppressed by plodding regulators. The administrator is often hopelessly lost and painfully struggling to appear competent.

Finally, judgment based upon standards is so dependent on personal beliefs, preconceived notions, even prejudices, that the judgment of a single person is not reliable. Decisions made by a committee depend upon the composition of that group. Impartiality depends upon how that group is selected. Enforcement must be done on a case-by-case basis, with plenty of discovery about the facts for each variable, before a just judgment can be rendered. Once we get to subjective standards, both the administrator and the regulator are in trouble.

The objective/subjective divide is, then, the **practical limitation** to administration and regulation. In its most expansive definition, that limitation falls somewhere between objective standards for actions of persons in common everyday experiences, such as driving an automobile, and pure subjective standards, as for professional conduct. Such codification and judgment of acts, beyond the experience of the common man, generally needs special treatment.

To leave them in the hands of political appointees has been shown not to work. To leave professions to police themselves has not worked either. Look at the present state of regulation of the financial industry. What to do?

## The Big Problem Created by Regulation

The big problem is that people rely on administrative regulation to work, and when it turns subjective it is flawed; it cannot work. Regulatory failure caused and made more severe the recession/depression of 2008-2009. Public reliance on regulations that could not possibly work led to banks thought to be "too big to fail." Crooks were left at the helm of these banks and billions of dollars were pumped into these banks, mostly to support unconscionable salaries and bonuses for the crooks. Many suggest that the biggest of the crooks were those placed in charge of the regulatory systems that caused the whole debacle in the first place. They were given billions of dollars of income tax forgiveness to assume these roles.

These were doubly rewarded, because to assume roles in government they had to divest themselves of investments, to assure impartiality of judgment. The old device of "*blind trusts*" has been replaced. All financial interests must be sold. The doctrine that has replaced the blind trust is the old idea of *involuntary conversion*. Because sale of these assets, stocks, bonds, stock or bond options, deferred compensation packages, and the like were made necessary by government's call to public service, all gain from these sales is completely free from income taxation. Imagine the benefits from multimillion dollar salaries and hundreds of millions in deferred compensation. This means their compensation can be many times the government paycheck. Why do newspapers not point out this loophole?

The big problem is this: people rely on agencies to work, to perform. Agencies cannot control subjective behaviors. Agencies have shown they do not solve problems, instead they allow problems to accelerate and grow. The corrections are more disastrous. Small people get hurt, the politically connected get richer.

## Conclusions Regarding Administration

Regulation is expensive, terribly expensive; the machinery makes it so. It is burdensome, often needlessly, to productive business and other governments alike. The next problem is it simply doesn't work for complex behaviors. It is no substitute for competition, yet is the government's only answer to competition. It is constantly thwarted by politicians granting privileges to the favored few. For all the expense, it produces no goods or services. Regulation beyond the objective, the scientifically verifiable, is not in the general welfare.

Because of the insights we gain from looking at our economy and our political machinery (econopolitics) from the point of view of grants of privilege, we now discover that most of the federal government's administration is in place simply to create, distribute and administer privileges to campaign contributors. To do so the executives have created a second set of laws, courts and judges to benefit the privileged. There is no jury, lest the public get wise. There is virtually no right of appeal, because due process is not a consideration. The only basis is who is willing to pay the most money.

The existence of such a dual court system destroys the validity of the legal process, for the job of courts is to dispense justice: a "species of equality." It validates the corruption of the political process by allowing, indeed rewarding, those who bribe. And it skews the democratic voice of the people, the free market. We would be better off if the vast bulk of federal administrators and their minions were off the federal payroll, weeding organic gardens if they can find no other productive endeavors. We need to reinstate a true court system in which juries keep our businesses honest.

The limitations of the regulatory tool of administration make it obvious that on its best day it is an insufficient device to control business enterprise. Regulators are constantly behind the curve, businessmen are always light-years ahead and the taxpayers are left with bigger and bigger bills. The only hope is to dismantle many of the layers of privileges, prohibit the formation of new privileges, remove limitations of liability that shelter business enterprise and increase the scope of jury review by dismantling the administrative law and court system.

Simply stated, administrative regulation doesn't work; example after example shows it makes goods and services more expensive, and in the realm of subjective behavior it simply has the effect of making economic problems bigger and bigger. Administrative regulation, in the subjective realm, cannot work. It is an insufficient engine to regulate subjective behavior. Finally, it won't work because political intervention from every direction by politicians selling privileges will distort the best intentions. The intentions of politicos, regulators and administrators, motivated by grants of economic privileges, invariably collide. This is because of the law of unintended consequences.

# The Judiciary

## The Fundamental Duty of Courts

L et us begin with the primary duty of the supreme and lesser courts. Aristotle had it right when he said:

"No government can stand which is not founded upon justice." (Aristotle, *Politics*)

"Justice is universally regarded as a species of equality." (*ibid.*)

"Equals ought to receive an equal share." (*ibid.*)

"What is justice if not a species of equality, the right to be treated equally?" (*ibid.*)

"Should not equals be treated equally?" (*ibid.*)

"Equality consists of the same treatment of similar persons." (*ibid.*)

**First,** the most important function of the court is to dispense justice: it is the basis of sound and enduring government. The president and Congress make this difficult, for they have been shown to be in the business of legislating and administering privileges. Citizens come to court demanding their rights and the privileged appear demanding their prerogatives of privileges. Equality is not possible. In the words of Orwell, some animals have become "more equal than others."

**Second** is the duty of courts to harmonize the mishmash of poorly drafted legislation and codes. Contrary to the direction of the Constitution, these were written by anyone but congresspersons, do not arise from representatives, are not reviewed by sagacious impartial senators and are not studied by an unbiased president. Too often they are drafted by attorneys for lobbyists and special interest groups. The court has, then, a virtually impossible duty to harmonize these laws.

**Third** is the duty of the court to present to citizens and businesses decisions that are predictable and cohesive. Citizens and businesses alike require this for guiding their actions and business plans. A stable society, the liberty of citizens and prosperity for businesses, hence society at large, demand this.

## Doctrines of Laws That Are Out of Touch with Reality

To this end, our Supreme Court has developed various **doctrines of law** that are the basis for such predictability and stability. The following doctrines are out of touch with the reality of the modern world and its econopolitics:

- *Res judicata* and *stare decisis*
- Corporate citizenship
- Money equals free speech or freedom of expression
- Corporate sovereignty (tyranny)
- Delegation of legislative functions
- Administrative due process
- Eminent domain
- *Caveat emptor*

### RES JUDICATA AND STARE DECISIS

**Res judicata** means the matter or dispute between the parties is tried and settled, and cannot be tried again. **Stare decisis** means stand by the decision, or adhere to the decision, do not disturb what is already settled. These doctrines save the court from deciding issues that have already been tried. But when reviewing Supreme Court decisions regarding corporate citizenship, we saw that the court does change its mind.

In the case of *Bank of the United States v. Deveaux* (1807), the Supreme Court unanimously decided that corporations were "*certainly not citizens.*" Next it decided that corporations were "quasi citizens"; next they became full citizens, then by 1907 with the Tillman Act their ability to contribute money directly to candidates in federal elections was lost, and they became less than full citizens again. So much for *res judicata* — clearly the Supreme Court can overrule itself.

## CORPORATE CITIZENSHIP

The preceding paragraph shows the rise and fall of the legal status of corporations as citizens. They have again become mere "quasi citizens" by federal laws banning their contribution of hard money to federal election candidates. The Supreme Court need not recognize corporations as full citizens to have subject matter jurisdiction over them. Quasi citizenship is quite enough. But the power they have attained even as quasi citizens is much in ascendancy, and needs to be revalued. First let us trace how they became virtual sovereign entities.

## MONEY EQUALS FREE SPEECH OR FREEDOM OF EXPRESSION

When corporations became citizens, they soon demanded freedom of speech or freedom of expression. They demanded unlimited right to express themselves with monetary contributions for political candidates. This occurred because corporations are inanimate and thus cannot speak. They must employ advocates to speak for them. These advocates must be paid money. Soon money was flowing from corporations to lobbyists to politicians: *quid pro quo*. So it is that money has become expression.

Recall the history of Marcus Alonzo Hanna, in Chapter 6. Congress was first to catch on with the Tillman Act (1907), saying corporations could make no cash contributions to federal elections. (However, the prohibition didn't cover state elections.) In the following years, the Supreme Court consistently ruled against most legislative attempts to limit campaign contributions with the broadest interpretation of free speech imaginable, declaring these limits unconstitutional.

Massive campaign corporate contributions led to the Senate hearings of 2001, and the McCain-Feingold Act (2002) and the distinction between "*hard money* campaign contributions" paid directly to candidates (illegal for corporations, and limited by amount to citizens) and "*soft money* campaign contributions," money paid by corporations to political action groups or for issue advertising (legal) without limitation so long as one particular candidate was not identified. However, Congress left in a loophole: there was no meaningful and timely accounting for soft money. The U.S. Senate found:

"Soft money loopholes led to a meltdown of the campaign finance system."

When the case of *Mc Connell v. Federal Election Commission* got to the Supreme Court, it found:

"The history of campaign financing regulation proves that political parties are *extraordinarily flexible* in adapting to new restrictions on their fundraising abilities."

Most limitations on cash contributions to candidates were upheld by the Court. Corporations could still spend unlimited amounts to make "issue ads" so long as a particular party was not identified or clearly implied. But cash contributions to individual candidates were out. Most readers overlook the idea that in *McConnell* the Supreme Court threw the traditional, strict interpretations of freedom of speech and freedom of expression right out the window. Most legislation regulating hard money was not stricken by the court. Is this a new day at the Supreme Court?

Unfortunately, in *United Citizens v. Federal Election Commission* (2010), the Supreme Court expanded the right of corporations to make soft money contributions to identified candidates. But Justice Stevens points out in the dissent that

"The conceit that corporations must be treated identically to natural persons in the political sphere is not only inaccurate, but inadequate to justify the Courts disposition of this case. Our lawmakers have a compelling constitutional basis, if not a democratic duty, to take measures designed to guard against the potentially deleterious effects."

So corporations are still lesser or quasi citizens, as they are unable to make hard money contributions.

A big problem still remains: soft money is contributed without limits to parties, who are conduits to individual candidates, and parties are free to bribe members of the opposite party by cash, compromise or favors. Coupled with the fact that there is little meaningful accounting for the $6.1 billion spent last year for lobbying, it is hardly surprising that money equates to freedom of expression.

As long as Congress is allowed to pass laws of privilege and economic favor, the rot in politics will continue. The solution is a prohibition on Congress's assumed right to grant laws of economic privilege. Striking laws of economic favor and privilege will quickly address the problem head on. Nothing else will.

## CORPORATE SOVEREIGNTY (TYRANNY)

By 1876, corporate sovereignty arose when the Supreme Court tried to solve the diversity of citizenship issue in lawsuits against corporations. Recall that attorneys sued the corporation and its officers and directors personally. The court held that because corporations protected officers and directors from personal liability in most cases, it was therefore improper to sue officers or directors personally. One could sue only the corporation, which preserved diversity of citizenship in most cases. At this point corporations had been granted full citizenship. They had gone from *"certainly not citizens"* to full citizens. But the Supreme Court simply created more and bigger problems.

By granting citizenship to corporations and strong insulation from personal liability to officers and directors, the court had created **corporate sovereignty,** the notion that corporate business is only the business of the corporation. The courts held that corporations should be governed only by the board of directors, who answer to the shareholders only. If the shareholders do not like what is happening within the corporation, they can change the board of directors.

Corporate tyranny is based upon the idea that the board of directors is elected by the shareholders, and thus can cause the corporation to be run in the interest of the shareholders. The devices by which the directors are selected would make folly of any notion of democracy in corporate governance. *Incumbents* have at their disposal the list of names and addresses of those holding voting shares, as well as unlimited free publishing and data processing and postage for solicitation of proxies. This is a huge advantage. The proxies go out with beautiful glossy annual reports, speaking in an effusive manner of the wonders of present management, touting their business skills and often with a nice section noting their ecological concern. Challengers must fund the data processing, publishing and mailing of their proxy solicitations. They don't have access to corporate records or assets. It is difficult to acquire even a shareholder list of eligible voters.

Incumbents get to challenge nominations of new directors and disqualify anyone for frivolous reasons. Arbitrary dismissal from ballots is not uncommon. The final decision on nomination and election procedures usually lies with the board of directors. Courts are reluctant to invade and review such proceedings, creating corporate tyranny.

The methods of counting votes within the boardroom are varied but positively Byzantine; ballots may be disqualified for any imagined reason. Then consider d*emographics.* If half the shareholders vote, only 26 percent of the shares can control the selection of a corporate board of directors. Consider the idea of *voting shares.* A corporation can be organized so only certain of its shares have the power to elect the board

of directors. Control of the board of directors can be had with ownership of as little as two to five percent of the shares of stock. The general rule is that incumbency wins.

Most startling is the idea that if there is any wrongdoing by officers or directors, it gives rise to a cause of action (right to sue), which
is not the property of the shareholders, but a property right of the corporation. This means the decision to sue or ignore the transgression is
made by the board of directors, not the shareholders. The board may
decide it is not in the best interests of the corporation to pursue the
wrongdoing of an officer, for it may drive the share price down, which
may not be in the shareholder's interests. The board may decide it is
not in the corporate interest to even disclose the wrongdoing to the
shareholders, but rather bury it in a footnote in the annual report,
couched in the most arcane language. This doctrine shields the officers
and makes them quite brazen. It explains the staggering executive
compensation and fringe benefits that are so commonplace in corporate America. When times are bad, they take more compensation,
explaining they must work harder and smarter. In good times they feel
quite comfortable rewarding themselves for a hard job, well done. The
reality is that they are not doing a good, competitive job at all. They
are all too often simply squandering company resources on lobbyists
bribing politicians for new laws of privilege. Does this help us compete
in the world economy? Is any of this in the general welfare?

The boards quickly seized on the notion that action against officers was a right of the board exclusively. It has gotten to the point
where the board of directors can even disqualify candidates to the election of the board, because the candidate has the wrong ideals; perhaps
they are too "green." Appeals of such actions lie not in court, but in
the hands of the board of directors.

Under the doctrine which attorneys call **shareholder derivative
suits,** we find that the apparent rights of shareholders are usually
crushed by **corporate sovereignty.** Evidentiary rulings usually go the
way of corporations, shareholders have few rights or remedies and corporate officers are free to be tyrants — free from oversight by
courts.Predictably, officer and director compensation took off to

heights never before imagined. How is this in the general welfare of the nation? The solution will be addressed later in this chapter.

## DELEGATION OF LEGISLATIVE FUNCTIONS

The methodology of delegating legislative powers to the administrative agencies was discussed and analyzed and generally bludgeoned in Chapter 9. The whole idea that Congress can delegate its rule-making authority is simply foolishness. It is clearly a non-delegable duty. The Court's submissive implied ratification of this delegation to unqualified agents of the executive to write administrative code is outrageous. All products of the delegation of legislative function should be stricken. And exercise of any administrative power past the objective standard should be given no force of law. Such rulings are within the proper powers of the Supreme Court.

## ADMINISTRATIVE DUE PROCESS

It is time to confess that most administrative codes are a disgrace to fundamental due process by any measure. The business of courts is the administration of justice. There is no need for two sets of courts, two sets of judges, two sets of codes or laws. In administrative proceedings, the right to a jury trial is out the window. This is in derogation of the right to jury trials guaranteed to us by our Constitution and the Constitutions of every state. With no meaningful recording and indexing of decisions, there are no meaningful appeal rights. This is simply tyranny wearing its thinnest disguise. This duality only benefits those who seek and those who dispense privileges; agents and minions of the executive, be it state or federal. This duality exists simply to make the administration of justice (equality) impossible. Administrative "law" courts are offensive to the ideas of due process, fair play, equality before the bench. They administer no due process whatever. All these privileges create the aristocracies we are not to have in America. Stop the elaborate deception. Why do we need two sets of courts, laws and judges? The whole notion is simply a legal sophistry to facilitate the executive in his sale and delivery of privileges.

The Supreme Court should strike administrative courts and laws in their entirety. As to remaining administrative regulation, we must observe the objective/subjective divide. Subjective administration should be stricken. Doing so is within the proper powers of the Supreme Court.

## EMINENT DOMAIN

This has become another ill-conceived court doctrine. The link between prosperity and strong property values is unquestionable. While fighting urban blight is a noble cause, so long as politicians have the power to grant laws of economic favor and privilege, the best of intentions will be overwhelmed by unforeseen consequences. Businesses simply move on, as did Pfizer after *Kelso v. City of New London*, without delivering the promised benefits to the city. TIFs (grants of tax privileges) far outmatch the few jobs that are created. Foreign corporations like Honda and DaimlerChrysler are subsidized with local revenue.

Municipal officers use the power of eminent domain to intimidate citizens into relinquishing their property rights with a threat of condemnation, telling them, "You can't fight city hall." Local political hacks are free to take properties for less than they are worth and sell the condemned properties for a dollar. Then they make huge grants and loans to the purchasers (usually campaign contributors) who develop these properties, often into glamorous stores and the like. The established businesses must pay increased taxes to cover the expense of the program as well as compete against the new competitors they have been forced to create and subsidize. This much power in the hands of local political hacks under the influence of bribery is not in the general welfare. This power forces property owners into expensive litigation to try to remain in their homes. This is outrageous. This is tyranny, simply to create privileges to sell to campaign contributors. Where is the justice? Eminent domain administered by politicians receiving campaign contributions can never be in the general welfare.

## CAVEAT EMPTOR

This Latin phrase means "buyer beware." It is the rationale that courts usually turn to when someone appears in court asking for relief from a bad deal. The court usually rules that a deal is a deal and you live with the consequences of the agreement you made. The basis for such a ruling is that historically there is a general parity between parties, and courts cannot assume the burden to review each and every contractual dealing, especially after the fact. If contracts could not be relied upon until the parties to the contract held a trial, for each contract, "velocity" of business would stop, and the courts would be overwhelmed. On rare occasions, courts will grant relief from a contract; for example, in dealing with shyster home improvement contractors and little old ladies with no business experience who have been talked into outrageous home repair contracts for unconscionable amounts of money.

Turning to derivatives and other financial products, many of which are founded on an unenforceable "heads I win, tails you lose" proposition, we find a similar disparity in education, sophistication, business and legal acumen. For example, compare a municipal corporation buying these financial products for its pension plan to a seller such as Goldman Sachs; compare the sophistication of MBA types to simple folks investing their savings in the stock market in hopes of funding their retirement. Such disparities should cause a rethinking about finance on the part of the Supreme Court. Caveat Emptor has simply become a rubber stamp approval of frauds of every style imaginable. These must be recognized as a separate class of contract. Because the financial world affects everyone in so many ways, the general welfare demands facilitated jury review of financial products. It would be cheaper to have a few more courts and thousands fewer toothless administrators and regulators. The beauty of this idea is that the power to restore jury trials is within the proper exercise of the Supreme Court.

## How to Accomplish Financial Reform:
## The Power of a Jury

It is time for us to do as our Founding Fathers did: return to the classicists for guidance. We need go nowhere else but Aristotle:

"It is obviously necessary that all citizens alike shall take their turns of governing and being governed." (Aristotle, *Politics*)

Is he not suggesting a jury?

"A city can be virtuous only when the citizens who have a share in the government are virtuous" (*ibid.*)

Again, is this not a jury? Who else is better attuned to the general welfare? Recent developments show that regulators, administrators, even the secretary of the treasury do not have a clue. The $1.2 trillion dollar give away to the "bad banks" for those toxic mortgages has been trumped. On August 9, 2010, the *Wall Street Journal* announced that Geithner ordered printing an additional 500 billion dollars to buy back treasury bills from the bankers. Where is the virtue in that deal? Why favor those "citizens" again?

"Equality consists of the same treatment for similar persons." (*ibid.*)

To illustrate the impact of a jury on justice, consider the following case study: *Helmbrecht v. St. Paul Insurance Company.* There is no right to a jury trial in a divorce proceeding. They are deemed special proceedings and are handled by judges. As a result, massive injustices for women and children are quite routine. In Wisconsin, judges (usually male) had become quite brazen in their inequitable awards, for men and against women and children. One day in Wisconsin all of that changed, because of a jury. The case got before a jury because it was a legal malpractice case arising out of a divorce where the divorce judge awarded a woman with six children a mere ten percent of the marital estate. The statute said that she should have half, more or less depending upon circumstances. The judge did not explain the paltry award. In this legal malpractice trial again the new judge was anything but fair or impartial. Every defense attorney objection was sustained (over 50 in number). Every plaintiff objection was overruled. In an unprecedented act the trial judge allowed a sitting judge to testify on behalf of the defendant attorney and his insurance company.

Then the trial judge dismissed the court reporter, so jury instructions and closing arguments were not recorded. The court reporter was not present for jury instructions and the trial judge proceeded to tell the jury to find that there was no negligence, and if there was, it did not cause harm to the plaintiff and her children, and finally told the jury it should find no damages as a matter of law.

The jury ignored the judge's instructions and awarded one third of one million dollars to the family. After the jury was dismissed, the judge struck their findings, calling them a rogue jury. The state Supreme Court unanimously disagreed and reinstated the verdict, adding 25 percent to the verdict plus interest and costs. That jury, all women, and none with any special education, changed the way divorces were handled in Wisconsin. Such is the power of the jury system.

The whole administrative system is in place only for granting and administering privileges. The administrative law system is in place simply to grant and enforce laws of privilege. What could possible be wrong with replacing administrative law courts with a jury system? Who but politicians and the privileged would object?

A **modest proposal**: replace the bulk of the regulatory structure with a simpler, more direct, more effective system — a trial by jury. This system employs persons with known and proven skills, superior and far more advanced than anything possessed by the most gifted regulator. The system requires no new government structure, few employees, very little governmental space, and very slight government expense. The attorneys would be paid a percentage of recovery, and this only if they win and collect money.

The modest proposal employs the keenest sense of general weal ever formulated. It is beyond the taint of the moneyed interests. It is flexible. It is always up to date. It is focused on the most relevant issues, as they change, day by day, month by month, year by year. Both the attorneys and the jurors are always short term employees, on a case-by-case basis.

> The new system would employ only short-term employees and attract the keenest minds.

The new system operates openly, publicly, during daylight hours. It crafts remedies for any wrong. It metes out the most precise redress for wrongs and, where necessary, appropriate criminal punishment. It restores ill-gotten gains back to the rightful owners to the largest measure possible. It operates at no increased cost to society; in fact it generates billions of dollars of savings each year. It releases tens of thousands of regulators from drab, pointless jobs, freeing them to pursue productive employment, thus contributing to our national prosperity.

Let us employ that group that is most respected and feared by monopolistic businessmen, lobbyists, scofflaws, fraud motivated financiers and evaders of the tax laws in general. The proposed group is the most aggressive, brightest, best funded, indeed, self-funded group of persons to police these subjective acts. These "policemen" are not under the control of government purse strings. Let us fine-tune our laws and turn the plaintiff bar loose on corporations, financiers and investment bankers and their activities.

The proposal is to measure the conduct of the business sorts against the standard of care of *a reasonable person under like and similar circumstances.* The standard of care will need to emphasize that the reason for the corporate form of business is the shareholder or investor; not the management. The interests of the investor-owner come first, ahead of the massive and unconscionable bonuses that corporate chieftains take for granted. Placing the financial interests of the management ahead of the shareholder is a no-no. In the field of banking and sale of financial services, the standard of care is higher. It is one of a fiduciary. But the test is the same: compare the behavior of the defendant financier to a reasonable financier, under like and similar circumstances. But in no case is the standard of care the *behavior* of the average financier. It must be the reasonable financier acting in a trustee capacity. The defendant can rest assured that the jury, being carefully instructed by the judge will do the right thing.

> Who could better know the general weal than a jury?
> Who is least likely to sell out the general welfare?

Politicos constantly say they want more public involvement in the political process. Perhaps they have in mind cash contributions without any accountability. But what could be better than jury involvement helping set the reasonable standard of care for our financial operators? We will not have to rely on dimwitted administrators, puppets of the executive and his agendas. The proposed system is removed from political intervention prompted by campaign contributions. In this way we can bring new meaning to *self-regulation*. We will do it ourselves. We will have a meaningful input on the way business and finance is regulated.

> Aren't juries, after all, the American way?

Most of the legislation for these actions is in place. The power to decide the rights of an aggrieved person belongs to a jury of citizens. Ask businessmen who they would rather have in pursuit of them — a fire-breathing plaintiff attorney, or a pack of toothless regulators and some youthful federal prosecutor who can be deflected by the executive branch with campaign contributions.

We will need protection, indeed indemnification, for whistleblowers. Shouldn't the wrongdoers pay in full? Should the whistleblower be branded as such and blackballed from the business community? What less than a lifetime pension would be equitable for the whistle-blower, funded by the private assets of the corporate officer found guilty of wrongdoing?

This proposal has the immense advantage of not dealing with a written, and therefore dated, and often unrealistically limited, standard of care for the defendant. The standard of care (the act of a reasonable person, under like and similar circumstances) is presented on a case-by-case basis. It is established by the testimony of experts, pro and con, to inform the jury what a reasonable person is to do. Experts, prodded by attorneys, will display reasons for their opinions as to standards of care. These explanations and sharp questioning will usually give the jury sufficient up-to-date background as the just basis for its verdict. A seasoned trial judge is there to filter out unscientific or irrelevant evidence and evidence that is emotionally suggestive. The judge has the power to ignore the **verdict** and allow the party a new chance for trial. Appeals are to skilled judges and the basis for appeal is the quantum of probative evidence that supports the court's **judgment.** It is a system that has evolved over hundreds of years.

The loudest criticisms are from those who get caught doing wrong, who would prefer a decision meted out by politics or diplomacy or an administrative law judge (run, of course, by appointees of a susceptible executive) and shown to be practically immune from appeal to real courts. Scoundrels fear the jury system of review of their behaviors.

## PROCEDURE

The Shareholder Bill of Rights (Exhibit 1) would require that two members of the board of directors would be hourly employees of the corporation. Meaningful whistleblower protection with indemnification would supply motivation to disclose criminal practices, and the risk of job loss to whistle blowers who cannot present sufficient evidence to sustain proof of felony charges would discourage groundless or frivolous charges being brought.

Finance and banking is special and requires special treatment. Again it is Aristotle who gives us our best starting point for understanding the problems of the financial world:

"Some think a very modest amount of virtue is enough, (but) set no limit for their desire to wealth, property, power, reputation and the like." (Aristotle, *Politics*)

A liberalized discovery procedure in claims of banking financial wrongdoing would cause disclosure of corporate and personal tax returns of all in any way involved in the design or sales of financial products, business plans and projections, consultant reports, computer records, minutes of meetings, E mails, drafts of prospectuses and the like. In financial "products" cases claiming trade or proprietary secrets would not be available to thwart discovery. Because of their quasi-criminal nature, mere allegations of fraud would mean attorney client privileges would not be available to the financiers or bankers. A law could be drafted saying once a minimum quantum of evidence is proven in court, the burden of convincing the jury of fair play shifts to the defendant(s). This would mean the defendant would have to show there was valid consideration in the financial product, that the plaintiff had some reasonable chance for benefit from the product or derivative.

The chance for a peaceful solution for government's breach of civil contract is here in courts. These doctrines should be quickly aligned with the general welfare and the court should start thinking about issues such as: when municipalities go bankrupt due to reckless spending, are the unfunded pensions discharged in the governmental bankruptcy? And can voters threatened with the loss of their homes and estates, induce municipal bankruptcy, before all of the personal assets within the jurisdiction of the municipality have been seized and sold to cover such governmental spending? And can fiscally responsible states opt to leave the United States?

Thomas Jefferson said,

"I believe that banking institutions are more dangerous to our liberties than standing armies. If the American people ever allow private banks to control the issue of their currency, first by inflation and then by deflation the banks and corporations that will grow up around banks will deprive the people of all property until their children wake up homeless on the continent their fathers conquered."

# Chapter 11

# Taxation and Reform Thereof

N ow that we understand laws of economic privilege and the nature of the privilege/opportunity equilibrium (that grants of privilege to the few diminish the opportunities to the rest of society), tax reform becomes quite simple. Laws of economic favor and privilege must be removed from the tax codes; state and federal. Justice, or the fair treatment of citizens, demands nothing less. History teaches us that the formula for prosperity is nothing but the maximum opportunity extended to the maximum number of citizens. This is contrary to the notion of economic privilege. Think of the impact that eliminating these laws will have on bad government: our politicians will have nothing left to sell.

## Overview of U.S. Income Taxation

Why does the United States Tax Code, with comments and case law, contain some 5,600 pages of code, some 14,000 pages of regulation — and why, between 1987-2007, has it generated approximately 116,000 pages of revenue rulings? (This is one of the few agencies to publish its rulings.) Why is the code in constant flux? How can one single person understand and untangle the privileges that lurk therein? How does it relate to the billions of dollars spent every year on lobbying politicians? Who is being taxed and who skates through the system free of taxation? Unimaginable inequities abound, carefully hidden from public view and comprehension.

Much has been written about taxation; some of the best and clearest expression is from the magazine *The Economist: "The present system of taxation is an amazing soup of revenue gathering functions, and of political ideals, attempting to do too many things, doing none of it well."*

On January 13, 1996, the magazine analyzed the goal of America's tax system as follows:

"First, obviously they expect to raise enough revenue to pay for [government] activities. [Second,] not so obviously, they want to redistribute income from those with more, to those with less. Lastly, they want to give tax advantages to causes deemed worthy, or at least popular."

Unfortunately, at this point the editorial staff completely ignores the fourth goal — the secret or unstated goal — that is the source of all distortion and inequity and perversion in the economy and the political process. This is the goal to create economic privileges to sell to privileged persons to raise money to keep politicians' hold on office and increase their own net worth.

What is worse, *The Economist* covers up this fourth goal with policy drivel about the benefits of a neutral tax system (one that does not penalize certain economic activities). They say, "*One compelling objective of a tax policy, therefore, is to make taxes as neutral as possible: rather than punish some productive activities a lot, punish all a little.*"

It should be totally obvious that you can't have any sort of neutrality and at the same time make grants of tax privileges and tax favors. And to further assume that the political animals can create a neutral system by unlimited grants of privileges and favors, can only be the product of the **stupid-think** that is the foundation of modern higher education.

We now know that if politicians are left with the power to grant any amount of economic privileges in any form, neutrality is simply not possible. We have seen that the granting of privilege is not a slippery slope, in reality it is a cliff. The privileged will be the biggest, hence most successful purchasers of economic privilege.

The analysis continues, *"After half a century of experimenting, it is clear that these goals are simply too much for one tax system to deliver.* . . . *Indeed, the first objective alone is overwhelming.* . . . *By siphoning resources from the private sector, it puts a drag on people's wallets. Unfortunately it is also a necessary cost of government, and thus unavoidable."* The conclusion that taxes are a "drag" on the economy is critical. This is to say that taxation should be minimized, to maximize *prosperity.*

The analysis continues, *"If research and development is good, people ask, why should we tax it? The same logic extends easily to all sorts of other apparently worthy causes. Never mind the fact that, in market economies, almost any economic activity can sometimes be said to meet this test."*

## Theory of Income Redistribution

Unfortunately, at this point the analysis again gets shaky. Income redistribution receives no meaningful analysis or proposals, and the dynamics of human personalities are given no realistic acknowledgement. The demographics of any nation are that the wealthy are few and the impoverished are numerous and fecund. With our present tax system, poverty is encouraged, at the least, or subsidized. It is the concentration of privilege within the wealthy class or corporations that deprives the masses of meaningful employment opportunities.

## Motivational Dynamics and Impacts

Because of decades of grants of privilege, all too often there is simply no meaningful opportunity to work. When people do find jobs, imbedded tax burdens make take-home pay trivial, below subsistence level. Temporary help agencies must charge $13.50 per hour to pay out the minimum wage of $7.25. Landscapers must charge $58 per hour to pay their skilled help $15 to $20 per hour. The shop rate for heavy truck repair is $92 per hour ,of which the mechanics get about $22 per hour. Much of the increases are due to taxations of various forms.

With redistribution there is no mechanism to motivate the poor to work. Indeed supplying the basics and more increases their demands for more benefits without any productive effort. Charity fosters dependence and does not build self-esteem and positive motivation. Teaching self-sustainment needs to be like parenting. Government programs do not teach thrift, saving, deferred gratification, wise nutrition or money management, which even in the best of circumstances are not fail proof.

The fallacy of redistributing wealth to the less fortunate is that they do not learn to be productive. It is far better to redistribute opportunity. Give a man a fish and you feed him for a day. Teach him to fish and you feed him for a lifetime.

Ignored is the impact on the motivated and the frugal and the hard worker. Why work hard if after taxation there are no benefits to enjoy? Too often and too soon productive persons slow down before their prime simply because of the tax burden.

Perverse motivation: too often time and energy are wasted on avoiding taxation and doing unproductive things to minimize taxation, such Christmas tree farms that produce a glut of unneeded trees, race horse hobby farms and other farms that exist simply for tax avoidance.

*The Economist* article does note there are psychological and economic costs to the present tax system other than the money paid as taxation. Even bookkeeping and preparation and filing requirements are a burden and expense. This is probably intentional politics — keeping people too exhausted and frustrated to mount meaningful demands for reform.

The missing dynamic is that the formula for prosperity (the maximum opportunity for the greatest number of persons), is neither observed nor addressed, nor is there any act to implement such an idea. We should redistribute opportunity, not wealth. That means no more grants of privilege.

## Funding or Wealth Redistribution

As government generates no wealth, where does it get money for its activities, including redistribution? There are three sources: confiscation and taxation, inflation (printing of money), and borrowing.

*Inflation* is the most popular, because it is invisible and generally misunderstood. This means it is the easiest for government to deny. Because the government lost control of the money supply, it is harder for it to control inflation. And with banks creating ersatz money with fractional reserve requirements, or in the case of credit cards, no requirements, or in the case of investment banks, the derivatives, which the government feels the need to bail out, our currency is made worth less and less.

*Borrowing,* too, is immensely popular with governments. It seems limitless or limited only to the colors of printing on paper. It is hard to track and easy to deny. Unfortunately its appeal is limited by the perceived capacity of the government to repay, which in bad times can plummet catastrophically. And borrowing is hard to control. Also, inflation undercuts the desire of people to hold debt for the long-term or even at all.

*Taxation,* the power to confiscate, has limitations. Its burdens are incredibly uneven. Because the truly wealthy have 71,000 pages of privilege to diminish or avoid taxation entirely, the burden shifts to the upper middle and middle classes. Increased taxation cannot go on indefinitely. For the biggest limitation is: after you eat the seed corn, what do you plant for next year? Socialism is fine until the all the capital and assets are confiscated. Then what?

## Fallacies and Analytical Errors in *The Economist* Article

Consider the fallacy of the third noted policy: *"causes deemed worthy or at least popular."* Once we identify privileges and laws of economic favor we can quickly see that *"causes deemed worthy or popular"* are simply political license for grants of these very economic privileges, malignant tumors on our economy. Now that we have insight into the corrosive impacts of privilege, we see that the politicians judge the "worthiness" of such "causes" on the basis of campaign contributions. Judgments about quantification of grants of privilege, too, are made upon the basis of campaign bribery. These have been shown to be unreliable bases for judging the general welfare. Nothing good can come from this.

Further, the greatest shortcoming of the analysis in this article occurs in the sixth paragraph. The writers wander hopelessly off track and their clear thinking goes abruptly awry when they write: "*any advantage a tax break can achieve, a subsidy can accomplish just as easily.*" The legitimacy of grants of privileges sneaks into their reasoning. Because this is a British analysis, they overlook the illegality of laws of economic privilege. England still has a heritage of laws of conquest. Privileged economic classes are a way of life in England. Regrettably, the writers of the *Economist* miss the opportunity/privilege equilibrium: the grant of privileges to some has a cost to society by incrementally diminishing the opportunities to the rest of society. The writers also overlook the fact that maximum prosperity comes from delivering opportunity to the greatest number of citizens.

> The writers of *The Economist* are completely unenlightened as to the privilege/opportunity equilibrium and the definition of prosperity: maximum opportunity for the maximum number of citizens.

By the end of the sixth paragraph they do wander back to reality by noting that "*every year the entire sordid auction starts all over again, as the lobbyists descend on the government to guard their loopholes and pry open new ones.*"

Because we now recognize the formula for maximum national prosperity and the privilege/opportunity equilibrium, we are in a position to see failures, and at liberty to design a taxation system to fund our government activities, to restore our free market and to put integrity into politics. The principle is simply this: no more laws of economic privilege/favor. Strike those laws that we already have. Restore our free markets. Limit political action to the search for the general weal.

332

We can reduce our personal tax code to about 20 pages, and our business tax code to perhaps one hundred pages, and facilitate tax preparation and collection, saving billions of dollars in preparation fees alone. We could free thousands of accountants to audit the corporations that create phony business entries. Remember, corporations were created to pay taxes (in an indirect manner), not extract money from governments. With a fair tax code, we could collect taxes from corporations instead of exempting them from taxation, paying them cash subsidies and showering them with bailouts.

## General Observations about Tax Breaks

Tax breaks take many forms. Here are some popular ones.

**Deduction** from taxable income: the worth of the deduction depends on the tax bracket of your top dollar. It is worth from 20 to 60 cents per dollar. It can be lost to alternative minimum tax.

**Depreciation** depends again upon the tax bracket of your top tax dollar and it too is worth from 20 to 60 cents per dollar and can be wiped out by an alternative minimum tax.

**Subsidy** is direct cash payment to the beneficiary. This must be picked up and reported as income in the following year, so it has only a fraction of the value received.

**Bailout** seems to come in two forms, one to be repaid, the other not. Usually these find their way offshore and are not taxable in our present system of taxation.

**A tax credit,** if you owe taxes, is just like a check from the government for the full amount of the credit. Tax credits are invisible on the books of the government, hence impossible to quantify with any certainty. There are over 60 of them at present.

Most people believe that a *tax credit* is equivalent to a *tax deduction*. Nothing could be further from the truth. A tax deduction is worth only a fraction of a credit. For example, a mortgage interest deduction in the amount of $10,000 in a 28 percent federal income tax bracket is worth $2,800. But a tax credit of $10,000 is worth $10,000 regardless of the tax bracket. For most large corporations tax credits are worth about three times more than a deduction.

As another example, consider research and development (R&D) credits for the pharmacy industry. They are illogical. Why should they get credits for R&D? They should get only deductions for R&D. They mass-produce tiny pills for pennies and sell them for $1 to $50 each. What else is their business? Often the true research and development is done by small startup companies. Also, much research is being done abroad; why subsidize foreign activities and businesses with our tax dollars? Most of the time and money of the pharmaceutical companies is spent on mergers, consolidations, bribery of government persons and frivolous, indefinite extensions of patents based upon little more than change of pill color and name. Since they get such lavish tax treatment, why is it that one person gets pills from Canada for $60 per month and identical pills stateside cost $700 per month?

Next consider the example of ethanol credits. Ten cents of tax credit per gallon of ethanol is given to ethanol producers, those who set up and run the expensive distilleries. This has proven to be a very risky proposition as many of these new plants go bankrupt. Yet 51 cents of tax credit per gallon goes to the company that blends (simply dumps) the alcohol into the gasoline. The lion's share of the credits goes to the big five oil companies (huge campaign contributors) for the simple, inexpensive and risk free act of mixing ethanol into gasoline. But the big question is: why are we giving gasoline refiners a tax credit of approximately $70 billion per year for diluting gasoline with ethanol? The tax code is to raise money, not give it away to big corporations.

## Proposed New System of Taxation

A new system of taxation might go something like this:

### I. SOCIAL TAX

All residing within these United States, citizens and aliens alike, shall, from the first dollar of earnings, without upper limit, be taxed a 10 percent social tax. United States citizens shall be so taxed on income regardless of where in the world it is earned.

All campaign contributions found to be used for "personal purposes" shall be subject to the social tax and to penalty provisions described under tax evasion in the section following. Determination of the term "personal use" shall at all times be an issue for six-person juries. To leave the determination of this issue in the hands of administrators and their minions, appointed and controlled by politicians, would not be sound policy. Because of the "*avoid appearance of impropriety*" standard, the receipt and expenditure of all funds shall be relevant to such a trial. Impeachment (removal from office) remains exclusively a function of Senate review.

## II. PERSONAL INCOME TAX: FEDERAL

Federal taxation shall be of gross receipts; there shall be no deferred income to any other year. Income earned in one year and received in another year shall be imputed and taxed to the year it is earned.

Income taxation shall begin when the income for any year is above 2000 times the federal minimum wage.

The rate of federal income taxation shall be from 10 percent up to a maximum of 35 percent according to the following table:

|  | Social Security | Marginal Tax Rate | Tax in New Bracket | Total Taxation | Tax as % of Income |
|---|---|---|---|---|---|
| $1to 14,500 | $1450 | 0.00 | 0.00 | $1,450 | 10% |
| $50,000 | $5000 | 10% | $3,550 | $8,550 | 17% |
| $100,000 | $10000 | 15% | $7,500 | $22,100 | 22% |
| $150,000 | $15,000 | 20% | $10,000 | $37,500 | 25% |
| $200,000 | $20,000 | 25% | $12,500 | $59,600 | 30% |
| $250,000 | $25,000 | 30% | $15,000 | $84,600 | 34% |
| $300,000 | $30,000 | 35% | $17,500 | $106,600 | 35% |
| $350,000 | $35,000 | 40% | $20,000 | $131,000 | 37% |
| $400,000 | $40,000 | 45% | $22,500 | $156,000 | 39% |
| $450,000 | $45,000 | 50% | $25,000 | $186,000 | 41% |
| $500,000 | $50,000 | 55% | $27,500 | $218,500 | 44% |

Over $500,000, social and federal income tax to be 50%

Allow no income paid to any individual that *is net of income taxation*.

All fringe benefits will be taxed as income in the year "earned," based upon fair market value. The receipt of such benefits shall subject the return to an audit, and their value will be determined by a tax auditor, with the right to appeal to a six-person jury.

No deductions (heretofore itemized deductions) shall be allowed, except for inflation in the area of *capital gains*. They shall be recognized as follows: each taxpayer may claim the gain on the sale of a single item of property per year, to which they have continuously held title since its purchase. Such property may be taxed on the basis of inflation-corrected dollars. Taxation in such an event shall be on the basis of gain, or the sale price reduced by the purchase price. The basis (or amount exempt from taxation) may be adjusted or increased according to the following table of inflationary index:

| | | | | | |
|---|---|---|---|---|---|
| 2009 | 6 percent | 1999 | 66 percent | 1989 | 126 percent |
| 2008 | 12 percent | 1998 | 72 percent | 1988 | 132 percent |
| 2007 | 18 percent | 1997 | 78 percent | 1987 | 138 percent |
| 2006 | 24 percent | 1996 | 84 percent | 1986 | 144 percent |
| 2005 | 30 percent | 1995 | 90 percent | 1985 | 150 percent |
| 2004 | 36 percent | 1994 | 96 percent | 1984 | 156 percent |
| 2003 | 42 percent | 1993 | 102 percent | 1983 | 162 percent |
| 2002 | 48 percent | 1992 | 108 percent | 1982 | 168 percent |
| 2001 | 54 percent | 1991 | 114 percent | 1981 | 174 percent |
| 2000 | 60 percent | 1990 | 120 percent | 1980 | 180 percent |

**Gifts:** in the event of a gift, the gain will be considered one-half of the sale price. The aforesaid tax table then applies.

**Tax evasion:** penalties for tax evasion shall be a doubling of the social tax and, in addition, interest at the rate of 12 percent per annum, upon the amount of taxes due, which shall be adjusted for inflation. These sums shall not be the reduced in the event a tax settlement becomes necessary. Citizens may claim the right to a jury trial on all matters of taxation. The issue of tax evasion by any elected or appointed official, because of the "avoid appearance of impropriety" standard, must be resolved by a jury trial. Impeachment (removal from office) remains exclusively a function of Senate review.

To deter government acts of inflation, bullion shall be a standard of value. Because it is a standard of value, its value is constant, and hence there can be no income taxation on sale or use of bullion to pay debts, for any apparent increase in the price of bullion is by definition simply a measure of inflation. Such sale or use does not give rise to a taxable event.

## III. TAXATION OF BUSINESS ENTERPRISE

In business, the principle is not taxation of gross receipts; it is taxation on profit.

**Sole proprietorships** and **partnerships** are taxed at the same rates as personal income taxation.

**Taxation of corporations:** Corporations have become artful at the avoidance of paying their social dues, known as taxation. They are gluttonous users of infrastructures. They have become "veils" for economic abuses and exploitations of astounding and ever-expanding scope and magnitude. In the 2009 bailout, Goldman Sachs walked off with as much wealth as there were dollars in circulation. The impact of $700 trillion in derivatives is yet to be measured. Multinational corporations operating with corporate sovereignty are at liberty to keep multiple sets of books and numerous accounting schemes and bogus book entries to "move" internal transactions around the world to avoid taxation. Thus taxation of corporate activities begins with the recognition that corporations have evolved into several sorts:

- Professional domestic corporations such as the ubiquitous LLCs
- Larger domestic corporations
- International or multinational corporations
- National businesses, such as the Red Army of China, a special econopolitical sphere where the worker has virtually no voice. Here, traditional American or European accounting systems have no relevance because all is contrived by the government.

Some suppose that taxation of corporate activity is fruitless, since they simply pass the cost on to the consumer. The fallacy is that the same argument can be made for all who supply goods and services in the marketplace.

There is total injustice in making the small businesses pay social dues and in permitting tax avoidance to the larger corporations who have enjoyed years of privileges such as cash subsidies, tax credits and laws of favoritism to create economies of scale, and business relations with suppliers that the small business can never match. These advantages have made a free market impossible to establish.

Each corporation requires different taxation treatment because each has different characteristics and properties. The basic premise is that business should be taxed on profit, not gross receipts. With multinational corporations, the "venue" or situs of profitable acts is a nightmare to establish. Which country has the right to tax each action? And with what rate of taxation? With national businesses (like the Red Army of China) it is impossible. Additionally, there is the problem of collecting tax proceeds, once fairly established, from foreign entities.

Perhaps the best solution is to require a deposit of 28 percent of the fair market value (as determined by present retail value) of goods imported into our country to be placed in trust with our department of revenue. At year's end the funds can be adjusted for the price the goods actually sold for, and for taxation paid to other countries of origin, based upon the declarations of profitability each corporation has made to its shareholders. This method would clearly distinguish this taxation from a "tariff." It would also offer employment to the numerous CPAs that the income taxation reform would leave unemployed.

## Proposed Rates of Corporate Taxation

For **domestic corporations and LLPs** with less than ten officers, directors or professional employees, in aggregate, and with less than twenty-five full-time employees, and which are not engaged in finance or banking, the rate of income taxation shall be 3 percent of profits (for the privilege to partially limit personal liability).

For **domestic corporations** with over ten officers, directors or professional employees and with more than twenty-five full-time employees, a standard rate of income taxation shall be 28 percent of all business profits and 28 percent of all corporate officers' and directors' fringe benefits and deferred compensation. Officer and director compensation that is net of taxation shall be taxed at the corporate level of 35 percent.

**Stock options** to officers and directors are prohibited, and if discovered are taxed at 100 percent. Existing stock options are to be scrupulously audited, and if genuine, shall be taxed as ordinary income.

In **financial enterprises** where "products" are sold to the public in any form or manner, 15 percent is added to any applicable rate of taxation.

**Intellectual property** shall be taxed in the domicile of sale of goods or services.

**Monopolistic trade practices** will be taxed at 5 percent to 40 percent as herein described.

## Regulation of Monopoly by Taxation

A monopoly is presumed if a corporation has over 20 percent of the national market or over 30 percent of a local market. The condition must persist for two consecutive years for a tax penalty to be incurred. The penalty is taxation of one-half of one percent for each percent of market control over the aforesaid national and local standards for each year of such monopolistic practice.

For example: XYZ company has 60 percent of the national market for its widget, for three years running. For each of those years the 25 percent federal corporate tax in increased by 20 percent (60 percent - 20 percent, divided by two = 20 percent).

Exceptions to the regulation of monopoly might include fluctuation in the market or the economy; any taxpayer not engaged in monopolistic behavior gets the presumption of the fluctuation of the market or economy and can claim one year in any three years' relief, and receive an additional 15 percent of either market share without monopolistic income tax penalty. Also, patents would be excluded from taxation for 17 years from recognition by government.

Think of the impact this will have on bad government: our politicians will have nothing left to sell.

# Chapter 12

# Other Reforms

## Limits on State, County and Local Government

Spending by each state, county and big city government should be limited by an Executive Council, based upon the New Hampshire model. In its state constitution dated October 31, 1783, New Hampshire established a council *"to direct the affairs of the state, according to the laws of the land."* These duties are presently described as:

"to serve as watchdogs for the state treasury."

"to make certain that those appointed to the executive branch . . . are all responsible to the citizens of New Hampshire, and not to special interests."

"to approve both the expenditure and receipt of state and federal funds, budgetary transfers within departments, and contracts with a value of $5,000 or more."

"to ensure the executive branch of government is fiscally conservative, and beyond reproach. "

The council approach works; this is one of the few states without a state income tax.

Approximately forty states created their constitutions after New Hampshire. Why have none of them followed this bold lead?

In the national arena, this approach probably places unreasonable restraints upon the ability of our president to act with the expediency his office requires. We will have to make do with a prohibition on passing laws of economic privilege and economic favor.

## Where and Why to Cut Federal Spending

First, let us have no more bailouts. They cost us at least $1.2 trillion, or **half** the federal tax revenue for an average year. Why foster business dependency on bailouts? They will certainly come begging for more funds; it is easier than working for money.

Second, let's cut out all funding for cash subsidies. This will save about $82 billion in an average year. But far greater savings will come because it costs from $4 to $10 to administer each dollar of cash subsidies, expenses for office buildings, utilities, cars, and staff. These expenditures should be promptly stopped, as they have been shown to be *ultra vires* or beyond proper powers of Congress to grant. Those who administer these benefits should be dismissed from public service.

Doing this will decimate the lobbying industry, for what will politicians have to sell the lobbyists? It should have a cleansing effect on political behavior.

Those in subjective administration should be put out to pasture. They are expensive, counterproductive in that they destroy the free market, and make big problems into huge and more expensive problems. The objective/subjective behavior divide should be clearly defined in the minds of all: the public and government employees alike. Since history shows that the regulation of subjective behavior is beyond the ability of administration, government should get out of the business of regulating subjective behaviors. We can begin to cut back on the 400,000-plus federal administrative employees who generally produce no goods or services. Let's start by disbanding the USDA and creating a free market in agriculture.

All administrative law courts should be closed within a short, fixed period of time, perhaps six months. Administrative law judges should go home. Their functions should be replaced by real courts with juries. The executive should be out of the business of selling and managing privileges for business interests. Corporations must come under more scrutiny by juries. Laws for much of this scrutiny are already in place. The Shareholder's Bill of Rights (Exhibit 1) should be promptly passed by Congress. Corporate sovereignty is not in the public good. It must be rethought and accountability of the board of directors must be expanded with more exposure to personal liability. The statute of limitations should be expanded to two years past discovery of acts.

Finally, compensation and fringe benefits of government employees should not exceed that of similar persons in the private sector. Why should federal employees be paid more? Have they been shown to work harder? Have they been shown to work longer? Have they been proven to be more effective than those employed in the private sector? Why should their salaries and benefits exceed those paid in the private sector? Perhaps compensation should be set by six-person juries especially empanelled. Let us get our government back on track. The private sector, which is the source of all production, and most revenue, undergoes downsizing and contractions all the time. Pension plans are periodically looted, ravaged by corporate raiders, diminished by economic slowdowns or depression — largely due to government inaction, administrative stupidity, and soul-selling by legislators and the executive. Why shouldn't the public sector face a 75 percent downsizing and downgrade in pay like the rest of us?

# Conclusion

A very important politician once asked me, "What is your problem? How can I help you?" He was embracing, warm and sincere. I explained I was studying political science and pondering if it were possible to govern without grants of privileges. He was perplexed, obviously pondering the question as I explained my privilege/opportunity/equilibrium theory, and said I had concluded grants of privilege were both *ultra vires* and against the public policy of prosperity that demanded the broadest opportunity to the greatest number of persons. He never answered my original question.

We have seen that simple, apparently innocuous **grants of privilege** have created amazing and monstrous consequences in our econopolitics:

(1) Money has drifted from government control into the hands of investment bankers and no longer serves the general welfare; it has lost the ability to store value.

(2) Accrued savings and investment accounts no longer increase in real value but are diminished by inflation and taxation.

(3) Through corrupt presidential policies, future investment opportunities have been contorted by administrative codes and their enforcement. Even acts of the secretary of the Treasury

benefit only investment bankers, financiers, and investment counselors. The average citizen is encouraged to gamble his savings, but is assured to lose. The real opportunities rest only in the hands of the ultra-rich.

(4) Even the best traditional investment, your home, is losing real value due to inflation and horrendous increases in annual real estate taxation. These increased taxes presage pending real estate devaluation. When persons can no longer afford to pay their real estate taxes, more properties become distressed and go on the market. This accelerates market forces that dictate that all real estate will dramatically drop in value. A rout may ensue.

Thomas Jefferson's quote bears repeating:

"I believe that banking institutions are more dangerous to our liberties than standing armies. If the American people ever allow private banks to control the issue of their currency, first by inflation and then by deflation the banks and corporations that will grow up around banks will deprive the people of all property until their children wake up homeless on the continent their fathers conquered."

With $1.2 trillion recently placed in the hands of a few investment bankers and TARP assets being used to redeem the treasury bills they now hold, these investment bankers may be the only bidders at the coming fire sale.

What is there to learn from the past history of democracy? The first thing is that the widespread distribution of opportunity is the key to prosperity. The example of Athens shows us how, in a remarkably short time, a single city state grew from illiteracy to a world power because of democracy. The first law of econopolitics then is that democracy (the absence of tyranny) gives citizens rights of opportunity that lead to **prosperity**.

What caused the demise of Athens? It was nothing but human nature, which is quite selfish. It is natural to want some special advantage or recognition or privilege over others. It is natural that we focus on privileges for ourselves, our families, our neighborhoods, our states. We all want privilege. But the second law of econopolitics is: grants of privileges undermine and destroy the prosperity of a nation.

It is because of our democratic heritage that is possible for us to reform our republican representatives. It is possible for us to exist in peace and prosperity in a changing world.

The stuff that made our country great was not administration, regulation, and czars. It was not welfare, a regulated or politically contrived economy, or transfers of wealth. It was not confiscatory taxation of income and property. It was not a strong centralized government. These simply diminish opportunities and hence prosperity.

Prosperity is predicated on a sound money supply and sound monetary policy. It is the opportunity to embrace personal risk: to succeed and to fail, to win big or lose big, the chance to increase our estates and holdings or to lose all in foolish adventures. All of this occurs in a free market. Subsidies, laws of economic privilege, and government programs of every nature, especially bailouts, were not part of the program that made America great. Grants of privilege, if not recognized and expunged, will lead to our fall.

The path to greatness lies in the direction of widely distributing opportunity. That path is obstructed by privileges on top of privileges. Can we reform our politicos and wean them from grants of privileges? The future of our children and our nation depends on nothing other than this.

Our only hope is to **recognize** the problem and **state** the problem so clearly that citizens of all backgrounds and political persuasions recognize and agree that we have accurately stated it. We must cause a consensus so deeply accepted by most citizens that the coming storm of political rhetoric, spin, and the like does not dissuade our citizens away from the general welfare.

Next, we must **formulate and agree on a course of action.** This, too, must be impervious to the distractions and attacks of the established interest groups, the "issue advertising," the disinformation of the media, and the political panic-mongering that politicians will mount as we near our goal of political change.

Finally, we must **act in concert regardless of prior political convictions** so politicians cannot deflect, dissuade, or splinter our focus or our purpose.

Our Constitution and our heritage give us the right, the perspective, and the legal power to do all of this. We must conquer our apathy, frustration, and feelings of impotence. We must resolve to throw everyone holding elected office out of office at the first opportunity. We must change the rules by which politicians play ball, lest the new faces be promptly corrupted. **To do this, we must recognize privileges and laws of economic favor in their every disguise and root them out of politics.**

It is my hope this book has unmasked the danger of economic privilege and helped to reveal its various forms. The suggestions herein will help in formulating the new rules for reforming our government. Only through a return to the ultimate democracy of a free market will we regain the economic power that is necessary for a safe United States of America.

# Bibliography

## Books

Aristotle. *Politics: A Treatise on Government,* vol. VII. Trans. Benjamin Jowlett, 1893. New York: Encyclopedia Britannica, 1952.

Aristotle. *Politics: A Treatise on Government,* vol. VII. Trans. J.E.C. Welldon, 1883. New York: Columbia University Press, 1960.

Augustine of Hippo. *The City of God.* Trans. Marcus Dods. New York: The Modern Library, a division of Random House, Inc., 1950.

Drucker, Peter F. *Innovation and Entrepreneurship.* New York: Harper Business Press, 1993.

Fugger, Jacob. *Articles of Association,* third ed. New York: Columbia University Press, 1960.

Lieber, James. *Rats in the Grain: The Dirty Tricks and Trials of Archer Daniels Midland.* New York: Four Walls Eight Windows Press, 2000.

Locke, John. *A Letter Concerning Toleration.* Trans. William Popple. New York: Encyclopedia Britannica, 1952.

————. *Second Treatise on Government*, third ed. New York: Columbia University Press, 1960.

Mill, John Stuart. *Considerations on Representative Government*. New York: Encyclopedia Britannica, 1952.

Montesquieu, Charles de. *The Spirit of the Laws*. Trans. Thomas Nugent. New York: Encyclopedia Britannica, 1952.

Rousseau, Jean-Jacques, *The Social Contract*. Trans. G.D.H. Cole. New York: Encyclopedia Britannica, 1952.

Machiavelli, Niccolò. *The Prince,* third ed. Trans. Luigi Ricci, 1903. New York: Columbia University Press, 1960.

Hamilton, Alexander, John Jay and James Madison. *The Federalist Papers*. New York: Penguin Books, 1961.

Zepezauer, Mark. *Take the Rich Off Welfare*. Boston: South End Press, 2004.

## Court Cases

*44 Liquor Mart Inc. v. Rhode Island* 440 F Supp 437 (1996)

*Alaska v. Eli Lilly* 3AN-06-05630 CI (2008)

*Bank of the United States v. Deveaux,* 5 Cranch 6 (1807)

*Buckley v. Valeo* 424 US 1 (1976)

*Chevron USA v. Natural Resource Defense Council* 467 U.S. 387 (1984)

*Citizens United v. FEC* 558 U.S.

*Cobell v. Kempthorne* 455 F 3rd 317 (2006)

*Cuno v. DaimlerChrysler* at 154 Fed Supp 1196 (1991)

*Cuno v. DaimlerChrysler* at 154 F. Supp 1196 (2001)

*Cuno v. DaimlerChrysler* 386 F3d 738 (2003)

*Cuno v. DaimlerChrysler* 547 U.S. 332 (2006)

*Federal Election Commission v. National Political Action Committee*
470 U.S. 480 (1985)

*Flue-Cured Tobacco Corp et al v. U.S. Environmental Protection Agency*
4 F.Supp435 (1998)

*Helmbrecht v. St. Paul Insurance Company* 122 NW 2nd 94 (1985)

*Hood & Sons v. DuMond* 336 U.S. 525 (1949)

*Hughes v. Alexandria Scrap Corp.* 426 U.S. 793 (1975)

*Kelso v. City of New London* 545 U.S. 461 (2005)

*McConnell v. Federal Election Commission* 124 S. Ct. 619 (2003)

*Northern Securities Company v. United States* 193 U.S. 197 (1904)

*United Citizens v. Federal Election Commission*

*United States v. Butler* 297 U.S. 1 (1936)

*United States v. E. C. Knight Company* 156 U.S. 1 (1895)

*VW Aktingesellschaft v. Federal Maritime Commission* 390 U.S. 267,
273 (1968)

*Zubulake v. UBS Warburg*

# Exhibit 1: Shareholder Bill of Rights

## PREAMBLE

Because corporate governance has been dominated by astounding executive compensation, shadowy stock options, spectacular "golden parachutes" for leaving, even after dismal performance, and the court doctrine of corporate sovereignty, the deck of cards is stacked against persons who would challenge such activities. Compare the task and expense of assembling shareholder lists, organizing a campaign against incumbents, printing and disseminating a meaningful and effective proxy solicitation, and validating and organizing proxies to withstand legal challenge at board meetings to the task of management. The incumbents have the list of shareholders and can simply include a proxy with the high gloss, very polished annual report already sent to shareholders. What little expense there is is borne by the corporation in question, not by the individual incumbent. As a result, management stays in office, whether its performance is good, bad, or indifferent. Because of high pay for directors and their often interlocking crony network, obscene pay packets are extracted from corporate coffers. Since the corporation is often left to pay the income tax bill, the actual expense may be double the outrageous sums of money the public sees in print. The cumulative effect of the pay packets and the millions in stock options granted to directors and managers tends to mortgage the financial future of corporations. The extent of this burden can only be estimated in a general way. For these reasons and more, is it not time for a change? A proposed shareholder's bill of rights might look like this:

## Proposed Shareholder's Rights Statute

All corporations selling common stocks in the U.S.A, listed upon the New York Stock Exchange or the NASDAQ, as of January 1, 2011, shall have a board of directors, at least 50 percent of whom are shareholders, and two of these shareholders shall be chosen at random from that company's employees working for wages, who:

- have a net worth of less than $250,000,
- are over age 25,
- are less than three degrees of kindred from any past or present officers, directors, or persons doing over $50,000 per year of business with the corporation,
- and have never been employed by any business that has done over $50,000 per year of business with the corporation.

The two shareholders selected at random shall be from the complete list of employee shareholders, with such selections to be performed and announced at the annual shareholder meeting.

All directors on the board shall have an equal vote on all issues.

Compensation and insurance for all directors shall be identical, and shall include a per diem of at least $500 together with first class airfare to and from their residence, and first class hotel accommodations for the duration of the meeting.

Compensation direct and indirect of all officers and directors, shall be approved by a two-thirds vote of shareholders.

## OFFICER OR DIRECTOR MALFEASANCE OF OFFICE

A cause or right of action shall arise from either a felonious (crime punishable by one year or more in jail) or fraudulent misuse, misallocation or misappropriation of corporate assets, or any personal use of corporate assets that are in excess of $250,000 in a single transaction, or in the aggregation of a series of such transactions within any five-year period. The cause of action shall be a property right of the corporation, and shall lie against the aforesaid corporate officers and/or directors, and the civil prosecution of such cause of action shall lie in the hands of the executive council.

Mere allegations of officers or directors intentionally violating this statute shall cause the corporate secretary to immediately freeze all stock options for all officers or directors under investigation until the end of inquiry or prosecution of these violations. In addition to damages caused to the corporation each director or officer found guilty of fraud, misuse, misallocation, or misappropriation of corpora rate assets or concealment of such behaviors shall be exposed to:

(1) Forfeiture of all outstanding stock options held by each officer or director guilty of any felony against the corporate interests.

(2) Personal liability for full reimbursement to the corporation of all salaries, bonuses, fringe benefits and other compensation paid the officer for each year of violation.

(3) Reimbursement to the corporation for gain on all stock options exercised for each year in question.

(4) Damages as defined immediately hereinafter.

Because this is a crime against the economy of the United States and actual damages against corporate officers and directors may be difficult to prove, once civil liability for fraud upon the corporation is established, the executive council (plaintiff) may elect as a measure of damages, against officers or directors, twice the actual attorney fees and double actual costs of any action to enforce this statute. The court shall presume upon affidavit of the attorney so stating: that the billable hours of attorneys, but not paralegals, and the itemized costs, are reasonable and necessary.

Or plaintiff may elect damages to be the reimbursement of one-half of salaries, bonuses, stock options and fringe benefits of all officers proven to have acted feloniously or fraudulently, together with attorney fees as allowed by the court. Knowledge of concealing or covering up such claim must be actual (not imputed) and proven beyond a reasonable doubt.

It is the intent of Congress that each officer and employee acting in violation of this statute shall be personally punished and Congress is aware that the plaintiffs may receive multiple measures of damages under this statute. Costs and damages awarded under this statute are in violation of public policy, and are therefore not covered by any insurance or indemnification agreement.

## EXECUTIVE COUNCIL

Any director at any time may upon posting a certified letter to the corporate secretary cause an **executive council** to be convened. The executive council shall be headed by the **director** writing said letter. He or she may name two additional directors to the council. They shall remain permanent directors so long as the council is in session. The council shall remain in session until the director of the executive council shall dissolve the executive council, or until a majority of shareholders shall dismiss the director.

Any director shall have the right to inspect, or cause to have inspected, any books, records, writings, and computer files of the corporation, its subsidiaries or any corporation, sole proprietorship or partnership in which the corporation is an investor, or in which any officer or director of the corporation has any business interest. All attorneys past or present paid for with corporate assets shall answer to said executive council, and shall not be able to claim attorney client privilege on behalf of any officer or director. Funds for such investigation and any legal or accounting or auditing consultations shall be authorized and paid freely by the corporation without limits, upon written demand by any director.

Any director shall have the right to question and demand answers of any officer or director, without limitation, except the Fifth Amendment. All such questions answered by the Fifth Amendment shall be promptly reported to the SEC and the U.S. Attorney's office and at least two newspapers with circulation above 300,000 paid subscribers, and a website established by the director.

The executive council shall have the power, and indeed has the duty to shareholders, to bring and prosecute actions against officers, directors and employees for civil damages to the corporation. Such prosecution shall be by outside attorneys for wrongdoings discovered by the investigation of the executive council.

## WHISTLEBLOWER PROVISION

In addition to the aforesaid claim for corporate damages, there may arise a whistleblower cause of action.

Who may be a whistleblower:

A whistleblower many be an employee, co-worker, independent contractor or business competitor, but not any of the following: attorneys, physicians, religious counselors, those elected to public office, those in government service, excepting any branch of the military.

Duty or performance giving rise to a claim of benefit:

A whistleblower, to receive benefits, must give or produce legally admissible evidence capable of a felony conviction, (beyond a reasonable doubt) or civil fraud (clear and convincing) of either multiple fraudulent business activities or practices, or a single business transaction of over $250,000, leading to loss of shareholder equity. Direct diminution of share price need not be shown. Establishment of personal offshore accounts and deposits thereto may qualify as a practice giving rise to a claim under this section.

Benefit to be paid a qualified whistleblower:

A whistleblower shall be entitled to an indemnification annuity comprised of 125 percent of his/her salary to a projected age of 70, together with reasonable annual increases or raises and any fringe benefits presently being paid, together with reasonable cost of living adjustments for the term of benefits. This will be funded with an annuity from the insurance company of the whistle blower's choice. This annuity shall be paid for by the personal assets of the officers and directors committing these acts of malus or in the event of insolvency, finally by the corporation.


## PROCEDURES AND DEFENSES FOR BOTH CAUSES OF ACTION

Existence of a valid cause of action and culpability for damages and the extent of damages proven shall in all cases be issues for juries which cannot be waived by any procedure.

**Felony allegation or conviction** of the whistleblower shall not bar this recovery. Evidence of whistleblower income tax evasion is not admissible for impeachment purposes.

**Election of remedies** between the income tax bounty and the whistleblower remedy may be made after any trials or other disposition of the case. In the event of trial, the whistle blower may elect to have the same judge reconvene the same jury to determine all relevant issues for the whistleblower. In the event the whistleblower has or is receiving an income tax bounty, an election of remedies must be made, for there shall be no double recovery.

**Confidentiality**, or nondisclosure agreements, are against public policy and hence are not enforceable as a prohibition against discovery or admissibility.

**Plea bargain**: evidence of a reduced charge shall not be admissible to show or infer diminished culpability of officers and directors.

**Sales tax evasion:** the motive of a buyer to reduce the price paid for goods and services may lead to fabrication of evidence against seller counterparty testimony and shall not be available in such cases.

# Exhibit 2: Plunder of Kravits Kohlberg & Roberts

# Investment History

Following is a list of all investments made by KKR since its founding in 1976 along with the total value of each transaction. Please note that the total transaction value refers to the entire amount of acquisition financing. However, where KKR is a strategic minority investor in a company, or where it invested additional equity in an existing portfolio company (unrelated to ¿ add-on acquisition), total transaction value then represents actual equity dollars.

| Year of Investment | Company - Total Transaction Value |
|---|---|
| 1977 | A.J. Industries, Inc.- $26 million<br>L.B. Foster Company - $94 million<br>U.S. Natural Resources, Inc. - $23 million |
| 1979 | Houdaille Industries, Inc. - $380 million<br>Sargent Industries, Inc. - $39 million<br>F-B Truck Line Company - $13 million |
| 1980 | Eaton Leonard Corporation - $14 million |
| 1981 | The Rotor Tool Company - $26 million<br>The Marley Company - $330 million<br>Lily-Tulip, Inc. - $160 million<br>PT Components, Inc. - $135 million<br>Norris Industries, Inc. - $440 million<br>Fred Meyer Inc. - $530 million |
| 1983 | Pacific Realty Trust - $55 million<br>Dillingham Corporation - $500 million<br>Golden West Television - $300 million |
| 1984 | Amstar Corporation - $520 million<br>Wometco Companies - $1.0 billion<br>Malone & Hyde, Inc. - $700 million<br>Cole National Corporation - $330 million<br>Pace Industries, Inc. - $1.6 billion |

**1985**    Motel 6, Inc. - $945 million
M & T Inc. - $110 million
Union Texas Petroleum Holdings, Inc. - $1.76 billion
Storer Communications, Inc. - $2.4 billion

**1986**    Beatrice Company - $8.7 billion
Safeway Inc. - $4.8 billion

**1987**    Owens-Illinois, Inc. - $4.68 billion
Walter Industries, Inc. - $3.26 billion
Seaman Furniture Company, Inc. - $390 million

**1988**    The Stop & Shop Companies, Inc. - $1.53 billion
Duracell International, Inc. - $2.06 billion
First Interstate Bancorp - $234 million

**1989**    RJR Nabisco - $31.3 billion
PRIMEDIA Inc. (formerly K-III Communications) - $320 million

**1991**    PRIMEDIA: Field Publications - $160 million
PRIMEDIA: Magazines - $650 million
Fleet Financial Group/Bank of New England - $283 million
Granum Holdings, L.P. - $16 million

**1992**    KC Cable Associates, L.P. - $140 million
American Re Corporation - $1.5 billion
Flagstar Companies, Inc. - $1.9 billion
Granum: Orlando and Boston stations - $21 million

**1993**    KSL Recreation Corporation - $536 million
World Color Press, Inc.:The Alden Press Company - $145 million
Granum: Boston station - $25 million
World Color Press: George Rice & Son - $90 million

**1994**    PRIMEDIA: Channel One - $270 million
Borden, Inc. - $4.3 billion (RJR Nabisco equity)

**1995**   World Color Press: The Lanman Companies, Northeast Graphics, and Wessel
Company - $160 million
Canadian General Insurance Group - $160 million
Neway Anchorlok International, Inc. - $100 million
Walter Industries - $59 million
Granum: Radio Stations - $180 million
RELTEC Corporation - $500 million
Bruno's Inc. - $1.22 billion
Merit Behavioral Care Corporation - $370 million

**1996**   Newsquest plc - $340 million
Spalding Holdings Corporation - $1.0 billion
Newsquest: Westminster Press - $489 million
RELTEC: Rainford plc - $134 million

**1997**   KinderCare Learning Centers, Inc. - $609 million
Amphenol Corporation - $1.4 billion
Randalls Food Markets, Inc. - $728 million
Act III Cinemas - $703 million
Alea Group Holdings AG - $211 million
Spalding - $83 million

**1998**   Accuride Corporation - $485 million
The Boyds Collection, Ltd. - $729 million
Regal Cinemas, Inc. - $1.57 billion
Bristol West Insurance Group - $209 million
PRIMEDIA: Cowles Enthusiast Media - $200 million
MedCath Corporation - $450 million
Spalding/Evenflo Companies, Inc. - $523 million
Willis Group - $1.7 billion
KSL Recreation: Grand Wailea Resort Hotel & Spa - $375 million

**1999**   TI Group plc - $157 million
Nexstar Financial Corporation - $132 million
Zhone Technologies, Inc. - $500 million
Alliance Imaging, Inc. - $981 million
Birch Telecom, Inc. - $145 million
Wincor Nixdorf Holding GmbH & Co. - $710 million (€679 million)

**2000**    Evenflo (acquisition of Spalding stake) - $24 million
Shoppers Drug Mart - $1.83 billion (C$2.7 billion)
Intermedia Communications Inc.- $200 million
Birch Telecom - $50 million
Ardent Communication - $100 million
DPL Inc.- $550 million
Wassall plc/Zumtobel AG - $1.2 billion (€1.2 billion)
Tenovis Germany GmbH - $331 million (€343 million)
DSSI Group - $17 million
NewSouth Communications - $170 million
LNG Holdings SA (formerly FirstMark Communications SA) - $601 million
(€629 million)
Alea Group - $150 million
Broadnet Mediascape - $47 million (€51 million)
Centric Software, Inc.- $30 million
Rockwood Specialties Inc. - $1.2 billion

**2001**    Alea Group - $347 million
PRIMEDIA: emap - $588 million
NewSouth Communications - $85 million
Birch Telecom - $106 million
DSSI Group - $7 million
Ardent Communications- $20 million

**2002**    Demag Holding SÀRL - $1.5 billion (€1.5 billion)
Yellow Pages Group Co. - $2 billion (C$3.1 billion)
Legrand SA - €4.6 billion (€4.6 billion)
PRIMEDIA - $72 million
Broadnet Mediascape - $4.0 million (€4.1 million)
Evenflo - $146 million
Zumtobel - $105 million (€104 million)

**2003**    International Transmission Co. - $650 million
NewSouth Communications - $63 million
MTU Aero Engines GmbH - $1.3 billion (€1.1 billion)
Rockwood Specialties - $974 million
KSL Holdings (La Costa) - $169 million
KSL Holdings (Hotel Del Coronado) - $424 million

**2004**        Jazz Pharmaceuticals - $250 million
                Sealy Corporation - $1.6 billion
                Royal Vendex KBB - $3.1 billion (€2.5 billion)
                Rockwood (Dynamit Nobel) - $2.9 billion (€2.5 billion)
                PanAmSat Corporation - $4.3 billion
                A.T.U. Auto-Teile-Unger Holding AG - $1.8 billion (€1.5 billion)
                Visant Corporation - $2.3 billion
                Texas Genco - $3.7 billion

**2005**        Duales System Deutschland AG - $393 million (€295 million)
                Masonite International - $2.2 billion (C$2.7 billion)
                Toys "R" Us, Inc. - $7.6 billion
                SunGard Data Systems - $11.8 billion
                Avago Technologies, Inc. - $2.8 billion
                SBS Broadcasting S.A. - $2.1 billion (€2.1 billion)
                Accellent Inc. - $1.3 billion
                Selenia SpA - $1.0 billion (€865 million)

**2006**        Capmark (GMAC Commercial Holding Corp.) - $10 billion
**( to date)**  TDC A/S - $15.4 billion (€12.8 billion, DKK 95 billion)
                AVR - $1.7 billion (€1.4 billion)

# Index

### X

### Z